Educating by Design

Creating Campus Learning Environments That Work

C. Carney Strange
James H. Banning

Consulting Editor
Ursula Delworth

JOSSEY-BASS
A Wiley Company
San Francisco

Published by Jossey-Bass
A Wiley Imprint
989 Market Street, San Francisco, CA 94103-1741   www.josseybass.com

Jossey-Bass books and products are available through most bookstores. To contact Jossey-Bass
directly call our Customer Care Department within the U.S. at (800) 956-7739, outside the U.S.
at (317) 572-3986 or fax (317) 572-4002.

Jossey-Bass also publishes its books in a variety of electronic formats. Some content that appears
in print may not be available in electronic books.

Credits appear on page 252.

Library of Congress Cataloging-in-Publication Data

Strange, Charles Carney.
   Educating by design : creating campus learning environments
that work / C. Carney Strange, James H. Banning. — 1st ed.
      p.   cm. — (The Jossey-Bass higher and adult education
series)
   Includes bibliographical references (p.   ) and index.
   ISBN 0-7879-1046-5
   1. College environment — United States. 2. Campus
planning — United States. 3. College students — United
State — Attitudes. I. Banning, James H. II. Title. III. Series.
   LB2324 .S77 2000
   378.1'98—dc21   00-008938

Printed in the United States of America
FIRST EDITION
HB Printing   10 9 8

The Jossey-Bass
Higher and Adult Education Series

Contents

List of Exhibits and Figures

Preface

I n American culture, "heading off to college," whether by flying across country or driving across town, is an event that marks for many a significant change in life. For traditional age students, college attendance coincides with the transition from late adolescence to young adulthood (Chickering & Reisser, 1993). For many adult students, the choice to pursue higher education often marks a change in career interests or relationships (Aslanian & Brickell, 1980; Cross, 1981) requiring further training or the exploration of new goals and personal networks. Regardless, this experience is an immensely powerful one, and the institution selected becomes an important place to establish new relationships, test aspects of autonomy and identity, explore values, sample the wealth of human culture and knowledge, and pursue vocational interests and goals.

Not all college experiences are successful though, as retention studies often indicate. Anywhere from 30 to 60 percent of the students who enter college, depending on the type of institution, decide to leave before completing a degree or program certificate. At times this decision to drop out of school is highly appropriate, given the developmental status and needs of some students. At other times the decision to leave a particular institution may result from its failure to offer a sufficiently supportive educational environment or one congruent with its stated purposes and goals.

Student behavior, whether in the form of leaving or persisting at a college or university, must be examined in terms of characteristics of the person and characteristics of the environment (Lewin, 1936). What distinguishes a college or university that is successful in attracting, challenging, and retaining students? What are the patterns and design characteristics of supportive educational settings? Are certain environmental characteristics essential for all students? Are some designs appropriate for only certain students? These are concerns of profound significance for any institution proposing or affirming the centrality of student learning, growth, and development, as they occur in the classroom, residence hall, student organization meeting, at the service learning site, or on the intramural field.

The capacity of any postsecondary institution to carry out its educational mission depends, in part, on how well its principal environmental features are understood and shaped accordingly. This volume focuses on the status of the literature on human environments and its implications for the policies and practices of higher education. Educators in the classroom, beyond the classroom, and in various administrative posts will find here a comprehensive framework of ideas for structuring their work and ultimately improving the learning outcomes of the students they serve. From physical plant operators and maintenance personnel to faculty members, academic administrators, and student affairs staff, all participants in any particular college or university setting can benefit from a broader understanding of how the campus environment, in all its dimensions and features, serves to shape and influence the behavior of those who pursue its opportunities. The purpose of this volume is to assemble and orient the many disparate pieces in the literature that address the definition, description, and outcomes of campus environments, with the expectation that staff, administrators, and faculty who read this will return to their work with greater purpose, intention, and effect with regard to the design and understanding of the environments they create and function within.

This volume is organized in two parts. Part One: Types and Impacts of Campus Environments offers an overview of models and concepts of human environments, focusing on their manifestations in the college and university setting and their implications for the design of educational facilities, systems, and practices. Chapter One examines the physical dimensions of human environments, including campus architectural features, layout, and spatial arrangements, with emphasis on understanding how such features influence students' behavior and experiences of campus life. Chapter Two explicates the dynamics of campus environments as reflections of the collective characteristics of individuals who inhabit them. Through the lens of human aggregate theory this chapter incorporates a review of models that share in common an emphasis on understanding how people create dominant characteristic features of an environment. Chapter Three discusses campus environments in terms of the organizational structures they create in response to, and in support of, the specific goals they pursue. This chapter draws from the sociology of complex organizations and other related frameworks as they inform decisions about how various campus units are organized to achieve certain ends. Chapter Four explores the nature of campus environments as socially constructed reflections of those who inhabit them. Included in this review are models of campus environmental press, social climate, and campus culture. Collectively, these four chapters establish a broad foundation for understanding and assessing the key components of any human environment— physical dimensions, people, organizational structures, and collective social constructions—as well as environments created more specifically in the service of higher education.

Part Two: Creating Environments That Foster Educational Success focuses on the conditions thought to be important for the design of effective educational environments. Moos (1986a) raises an essential question in that respect: "What are the criteria by which an environment can be judged as favorable?" (p. 4). We propose that educational environments are most powerful when they offer students three fundamental conditions: a sense of security and inclusion, mechanisms for involvement, and an experience of community. Accordingly, Chapter Five discusses how environments can contribute to or detract from a sense of inclusion and safety on campus, with a focus on campus design features, the importance of territoriality and defensible space, the effects of dominant groupings, organizational size, and campus culture. Chapter Six characterizes and discusses features of campus environments that encourage student involvement and participation in learning, both within and beyond the classroom, emphasizing the importance of human scale design, differentiated aggregate groupings, a dynamic organizational structure, and a supportive cultural milieu. Chapter Seven follows with an overview of the nature and characteristics of human communities, with implications for the design of educational environments, particularly in regard to their capacity for including, securing, involving, and ascribing to participants the status of full membership in a setting. Chapter Eight considers the nature and dynamics of computer-mediated forms of human environments, focusing on the design and potential of virtual communities, as currently understood, in the inclusion, security, and involvement of students. Finally, in Chapter Nine, we pull together the various strands of environmental theory and design to suggest strategic initiatives institutions might consider to attract, satisfy, and engage students more successfully in the achievement of their educational goals.

This volume is meant to be neither an exhaustive nor definitive critical review of extant research on the effects of campus environments. The literature is too unwieldy and disparate to submit to such a synthesis. Rather, we have attempted to offer a select sampling of concepts and models organized around a distinctive framework and reflective of themes critical to the successful functioning of higher education institutions today. We trust that we have unearthed a rich harvest of ideas for educational researchers and practitioners who will further evaluate their validity and their application. We hope these ideas will help to construct an institutional agenda to stimulate changes in policies and practices that might improve campus environments as places of learning. Institutional resources should focus on questions of whether or not current practices are effective, as they relate to the ideas presented here, and if they are not, changes should be considered.

We complete this preface with the belief that, if postsecondary educators had had access to many of these concepts about effective educational environments, especially over the past fifty years, a number of features taken for granted today on many campuses (such as high-rise residence halls and large theater-style lecture halls) might never have been proposed in the first place, assuming that student learning is the primary goal. We also believe that within the next fifty years many of the features of the higher education systems and facilities we take for granted today must be transformed or risk disappearing altogether. Students deserve nothing less than an educational environment that is affirming, energizing, challenging, and productive. The concepts contained in this book can be helpful in rising to such a challenge.

August 2000   C. CARNEY STRANGE
                                               JAMES H. BANNING

In memory of
Dr. Martin B. Strange, MD
(1907–1949)
and to
Mary Pat Strange
whose stories, legacy, and loving care have shaped
the learning environment of my own life
for these many years.

CCS

To Sue

JHB

Acknowledgments

I like circles. Circles include, circles enclose, and circles go 'round. They come in friends, they come in songs, and they sometimes point to who's right and who's wrong. This book has been about circles—my family circle, my circle of friends and professional colleagues, and a circle of editors and careful reviewers who have helped me move this project to print.

First, from my family circle, are Dorothyann, Julia, Martin, and Clare. I thank each of them for accepting and understanding the other circles in my life. As husband and dad I am especially grateful for their adjustments of need and expectation, at moments inconvenient, allowing me the time and energy to complete this work.

From my circle of friends and professional colleagues there are many unnamed individuals who took the time to stop and ask "How's the book coming?" I am thankful in particular for those disbelieving souls who greeted me at annual conferences with, "You haven't finished that book yet?!" or who insisted, "We need that book! When will it be out?" All of them have been instrumental in motivating me to get over the hump and to put on paper what had been floating around in my brain all too long. Many thanks.

I must also acknowledge the circle of those who have read, reviewed, and offered suggestions for improving earlier iterations of these ideas. At times, this book has been about going around in circles, but I was hardly ever alone. I include among those who have joined me in this chase a cadre of former graduate assistants whose academic legwork contributed much to this project—David Hannah, Debra Dehn, Mike Gillilan, Lorraine Alston, Jeff Philpott, John Lowery, and Renee Bornes.

Finally, with the completion of this book, I have indeed come full circle. As a graduate student at the University of Iowa from 1974 to 1978, I enrolled in a seminar taught by the late Dr. Ursula Delworth where I first learned of campus ecology and the work of my coauthor James Banning. It has been a slow distillation of questions and thought about the power of campus environments since then, but I am thankful that it came together on Ursula's watch. She was a tremendously supportive consulting editor whose gentle and encouraging reminders were all that I needed to accomplish the next task.

I thank all of you.

C. CARNEY STRANGE
Bowling Green, Ohio
August 2000

The Authors

C. CARNEY STRANGE is professor of higher education and student affairs in the Higher Education Administration and College Student Personnel graduate programs at Bowling Green State University, Bowling Green, Ohio. He teaches courses on college student development, the impact of educational environments, spirituality and higher education, and methods of qualitative research.

Dr. Strange received his B.A. degree in French (1969) from St. Meinrad College, Indiana, his M.A. degree in college student personnel (1976) from the University of Iowa, and his Ph.D. degree in student development in postsecondary education from the University of Iowa (1978). Dr. Strange has been an active teacher-scholar for twenty-two years, authoring publications on college student development, campus environments, and multicultural pedagogy. He serves or has served on the editorial boards of the *Journal of College Student Development*, the *National Association of Student Personnel Administrators Journal*, and the *CASE International Journal of Educational Advancement*. In 1978 he was the recipient of the Ralph F. Birdie Memorial Research Award from the American Personnel and Guidance Association. He was selected by the American College Personnel Association for an Annuit Coeptis Senior Professional Award in 1996 and was recognized as an ACPA 75th Anniversary Diamond Honoree in 1999.

JAMES H. BANNING is professor of education and teaches environmental psychology for the Department of Psychology at Colorado State University, Fort Collins, Colorado. He received his B.A degree in psychology (1960) from William Jewell College, Missouri and his Ph.D. degree in psychology (1965) from the University of Colorado.

Dr. Banning has served as director of the Counseling Center, University of Colorado; program director, Western Interstate Commission for Higher Education; vice chancellor for student affairs, University of Missouri—Columbia; and vice president for student affairs, Colorado State University. He played a pioneering role in the campus ecology movement and has authored monographs, numerous book chapters, and journal articles on the ecological relationships among students and their campus environments.

Part I

Types and Impacts
of Campus Environments

A number of critical perspectives have informed educators about the relationship between students and their institutions of higher learning. According to what Banning and Kaiser (1974) identified as an "unenlightened perspective" (p. 371), one approach "is built on the premise that not all young people belong in college and that therefore it can be expected that a lot of students won't be able to make it. It follows, therefore, that student failure is evidence of the efficacy of our higher education system" (p. 371). The appropriate role for educators holding this perspective is to ease students out of the institution through counseling them toward other opportunities. A second perspective focuses on the concept of adjustment. Accordingly, "if there are students who can't make it, they should be provided with counseling and other services in order that they might change and be better able to benefit from the educational environment" (p. 371). In other words, the institution's role is to help students solve their adjustment concerns. A third perspective is characterized as a developmental approach. This perspective assumes that "college students are in a transition or growth period and that there are certain tasks they must perform in order to reach maturity . . . they need to grow up some before they can really benefit from the educational environment" (p. 371). The institution's role in this case is to be appropriately supportive as students reach a point of readiness to benefit from their educational experiences.

Although an element of truth is contained in each perspective, according to Banning and Kaiser (1974), "none speaks sharply to the issues of institutions changing, institutions adjusting, or institutions growing up, or more importantly, to the relationship between students and their environment" (p. 371). In response to the limitations of these approaches is the ecological perspective, incorporating "the influence of environments on persons and persons on environments" (p. 371). Implicit in this perspective is the assumption that institutions themselves bear responsibility for the design and creation of campus environments, arranged appropriately for meeting educational purposes.

In a comprehensive review of environmental correlates and determinants of human behavior, Moos (1986) concluded that the "arrangement of environments is perhaps the most powerful technique we have for influencing human behavior. From one point of view, every institution in our society sets up conditions that it hopes will maximize certain types of behavior and certain directions of personal growth" (p. 4). Colleges and universities establish conditions to attract, satisfy, and retain students for purposes of challenging them to develop qualities of the educated person, including a capacity for complex critical reasoning, communication, leadership, a sense of identity and purpose, an appreciation for differences, and a commitment to lifelong learning. Such goals are the traditional purview of educators, and as Dewey (1933) suggests, they are better served by specificity rather than serendipity: "We never educate directly, but indirectly by means of the environment. Whether we permit chance environments to do the work, or whether we design environments for the purpose makes a great difference" (p. 22). To be more fruitful in our efforts, we concur with Dewey in the assumption that educational settings designed with an understanding of the dynamics and impact of human environments in mind will go further in achieving these ends.

As we approach this topic of the design of effective campus environments, we are persuaded by Moos' (1986) distinction between an ideal and an optimum environment.

> There are no clearly defined criteria for an ideal environment that can meet everyone's requirements. But we are much more likely to achieve an optimum environment when critical decisions about constructing and changing the environment are in the hands of people who live and function in it. These decisions are currently in our hands, and to make them wisely we urgently need more reliable information about human environments and their impacts on human beings. [p. 4]

Thus Part One (Chapters One through Four) of this volume gives an overview of what we believe to be the best information we have on the nature of human environments and their impact on human beings in an educational context.

In recent decades considerable information on the impact of human environments has emerged in the literature on college students and their experience of higher education (Evans, Forney, & Guido-DiBrito, 1998; Pascarella & Terenzini, 1991). However, what seems missing is an "integrated perspective regarding the human environment" for purposes of creating "conditions to maximize certain intended effects" (Moos, 1986, p. 4). Toward that end our review and synthesis of these materials begins by identifying some of the assumptions and understandings that have shaped our work.

Like Moos (1986), we too are guided by the tenets of a social ecological approach, with its emphasis on a "multidisciplinary study of the impacts of physical and social environments on human beings" (p. 28). This approach attempts "to understand the impact of the environment from the perspective of the individual" and "to synthesize the study of the physical and social environments." It "emphasizes individual adaptation, adjustment, and coping," "maintains a practical applied orientation," and "has an explicit value orientation," that is, it is humanistic and "dedicated to increasing individual freedom of choice in selecting environments" (p. 31). These tenets, we conclude, are consistent with and supportive of the role of educators as they seek to understand and create environments that will maximize learning.

As educators acquire a more sophisticated understanding of human environments, they will be better positioned to eliminate those features of institutions that are needlessly stressful or inhibiting, and ultimately, to create those features that will challenge students toward active learning, growth, and development. Whether we want them to or not, or whether we understand them or not, educational environments do exert an impact on students. Our preference is to approach the design of these environments with eyes wide open and intentions clearly informed. This goal will require grounding in a range of behavioral science concepts and models that inform such questions, the purpose we now turn to in this volume.

These first four chapters outline and illustrate core constructs related to the description and understanding of human environments. Although we often become insensitive or perhaps even immune to the components and effects of our environment, the experience of a typical day for faculty, administrators, and students alike on any campus will reveal the scope of its effects. The sidewalk that encourages us to walk around a building rather than across the rain-soaked muddy pathway to an office, classroom, or residence room; the characteristic styles, conversations, and actions of colleagues, students, and staff; the expectations, patterns, and procedures we follow (or ignore) in the execution of our responsibilities and assignments; and finally, the distinctive values and impressions we seem to intuit from the very air we breathe in the setting that help us understand and communicate to others "what it's like to be here." These are all exemplars of the components of human environments that serve to prod, bend, and shape behaviors. Understanding what to look for and how to name the components of the environment are the first steps in this overview.

Key components of all human environments include:

- Physical condition, design, and layout

- Characteristics of the people who inhabit them

- Organizational structures related to their purposes and goals

- Inhabitants' collective perceptions or constructions of the context and culture of the setting

Each of the four chapters in this part begins with a case scenario reflective of the various environmental features explicated in the chapter. In Chapter One, "Physical Environments: The Role of Design and Space," the most obvious features of any campus environment—its physical characteristics and designs—are addressed. Basic layout and spaces (Griffith, 1994), accessibility and cleanliness, interior color schemes, and even the weather on the day of a campus visit, for example, all shape initial attitudes in subtle yet powerful ways (Stern, 1986; Sturner, 1973; Thelin & Yankovich, 1987). Components of the campus physical environment, both natural and synthetic, serve functional and symbolic ends. They define spaces for various activities, functions, and events; and they send out nonverbal messages containing a range of possibilities. Collectively, campus physical environments contribute to four compelling needs: community, territory, landscape, and wayfinding (Miller & Banning, 1992).

Chapter Two, "Aggregate Environments: The Impact of Human Characteristics," recognizes that information about the collective characteristics of environmental inhabitants, whether demographic (such as gender, age, or ethnic composition) or psychosocial (personality types or learning styles), is indicative of the dominant features of an environment. A profile of these collective human characteristics reflects the pattern, strength, and character of an environment, according to degrees of differentiation (type homogeneity among inhabitants) and consistency (type similarity) (Holland, 1973).

Highly differentiated and consistent environments (that is, those dominated primarily by one type) are readily distinguished and clearly focused to those within them, as well as to those outside them. Such aggregates actively reinforce their own characteristics over time and exert a powerful influence on the degree to which people are attracted to, satisfied within, and retained by them. Thus, campuses of a particular cultural, ethnic, or age-based group, for example, are more likely to attract, satisfy, and retain individuals who share traits in common with the dominant group. This perspective also suggests that the quality of any student's experience is a function of his or her congruence, or degree of "fit," with the aggregate. Those who share similarities are predicted to be most attracted to that environment, and those who bear little resemblance are least likely to be reinforced for preferred behaviors, values, attitudes, and expectations, in which case they are more likely to become dissatisfied and leave that environment.

Chapter Three, "Organizational Environments: How Institutional Goals Are Achieved," begins with the observation that all environments maintain some degree of organization (formally or otherwise) in order to meet certain goals, explicit or implied. On a typical college campus most faculty, staff, and students spend a good deal of time, from day to day, in purposeful environments, such as residence halls, classrooms, department offices, recreation centers, services, and programs. To the extent that these environments are designed to achieve certain ends, "getting organized to get things done" is a natural conclusion to a number of decisions that must be made with respect to their purposes. Who is in charge? How will decisions about distributing resources be made? By what rules, if any, will the organization function? What must be accomplished and how quickly? How will participants be rewarded for their accomplishments? Answers to these questions generate various structures that, in turn, define the organizational dimensions of an environment. Thus, concentrating decision-making power within one or a select few individuals, for example, may define an environment that is highly centralized, in turn, creating milieus of varying flexibility or dynamism. These characteristic milieus then influence certain central performances of the environment, such as degrees of innovation, efficiency, production, and morale experienced in the setting.

To complete Part One, Chapter Four, "Constructed Environments: Different Views Through Different Eyes," focuses on models highlighting the subjective views, experiences, and constructions of participants in an environment. Consensual perceptions, in the form of environmental presses, social climates, and meanings attributed to various cultural artifacts, exert a directional influence on inhabitants' behaviors. Thus, whether individuals are attracted to a particular environment, or satisfied and stable within that environment, is a function of how they perceive, evaluate, and construct the environment. In effect, their perceptions are the reality of that environment for them.

These four sets of environmental components—physical, human aggregate, organizational, and constructed—comprise the various sources of influence on human behavior. Recognizing them, as well as their dynamics, is an important first step in understanding how they may be shaped to achieve educational purposes.

1

Physical Environments
The Role of Design and Space

Scenario: The Campus Visit

The Carter family—Joe, Dorothy, and son Eric—picked up their rental car after landing at Mountain International Airport and started on the forty-mile trip to Mid-Rocky University (MRU). The occasion for their visit was twofold: to attend Dorothy's niece's graduation later in the day and to visit the admissions office for a campus tour as Eric is thinking about attending MRU.

They found the interstate to MRU without a problem. As they approached the community of Redville, the home of MRU, they began to look for signs directing them to the university campus. The first sign indicated that the next three exits would lead to the university stadium. While discussing the question of whether the university stadium exit would be the same as the university exit, they missed the first exit. The first exit went by so quickly, that when the second exit came up they decided to take it. At the top of the exit ramp the sign indicated that the stadium was to the left. After going several miles without any additional signage, they discovered that they were in an area that resembled a university. On further inspection at the next stoplight, they noticed a faint Mid-Rocky University sign embedded in a concrete pillar. They also saw a directional sign with the word *Visitor* on it. They appeared to be in luck and faithfully followed the next three visitor signs assuming that they would lead to the admissions office, a welcome or information center, or at least to a visitors' parking lot. But after obeying four directional signs they found themselves at a dead-end in front of the university's power plant.

After asking a few people for additional directions, they backtracked and eventually found a visitors' parking lot. After examining MRU's you-are-here map (located in a faculty parking lot), they discovered the admissions office was at least nearby. After being confused by the sign outside the admissions building, they finally entered to find the admission office located on the second floor of the building. At the top of the two flights of steps they were not at all sure they had found the correct admissions office because the signage seemed to suggest that it was admissions for the university's graduate school. They were correct, however, and so they acquired the needed information about MRU, a college catalogue, and the admissions application material.

Next on the Carter's agenda was a quick self-guided campus tour. They wandered through several buildings just to get a feel for the campus. They noted that the buildings, while showing some age, were well kept and that there was very little litter around the grounds or inside the buildings. Dorothy, a professor herself at a large land-grant university on the East Coast, peeked into several classrooms. She found what she had become all too familiar with—large classrooms with the seats bolted down in rows with an elevated lectern some distance from the first row of students. In the Education building she did notice a carpeted classroom with moveable chairs, tables, and several pieces of visual aid equipment. This was what she was hoping to find, since MRU was marketing itself as "a learning university with a college feel." Finding only one such classroom, she remained a bit skeptical about the marketing slogan.

After a quick tour of the academic buildings, the Carters asked for directions to the student union. Finding the student union was relatively simple; it was in the center of campus and almost every sidewalk eventually led to the plaza in front of the building. The student union was busy with activity but looked well maintained with little trash or signs of abuse. In fact, it was obvious that a renovation project had just been completed. The decor was oak and mauve, and most of the "institutional" stainless steel and plastic had been removed. From a table in a quiet corner of the food court, a pleasant lagoon could be seen with geese swimming near the shore. Just west of the lagoon was a nice rolling landscape with a few pines and old elm trees marking the area in a rather stately manner.

On the way out of the building, Eric asked a passing student how far it was to walk to the stadium. The student responded with a polite laugh and indicated that the stadium was five or six miles from campus and there was no direct walking route. It now seemed to the Carters that it was a bit of luck on their part that they did not try to find the university by following highway signs to the stadium.

After checking into the local motel and grabbing a fast bite to eat, it was time to find the field house for the graduation ceremonies. The ceremonies went smoothly despite what seemed to be an unusual amount of rowdiness. But Dorothy and Joe just passed it off, lamenting the need to reintroduce civility as subject matter for university and college curricula. By evening's end, they had accomplished their goals. Their niece was pleased that they were able to attend her graduation, and the campus visit, though frustrating at times, did expose Eric to Mid-Rocky University.

The Carter family's experiences in this scenario are common to all who visit, study, or work on a college or university campus. This scenario also illustrates just how complex and important the physical design and spaces of these institutions and their environs are in terms of how individuals interact with them. Two questions are implicated in this case and form the framework for discussion in this chapter: What is the general nature of the physical environment's influence on human behavior? and How do the physical dimensions of any campus environment specifically impact the behavior of participants?

The Physical Environment Influence

From the view of prospective college students, the physical features are often among the most important factors in creating a critical first impression of an institution (Sturner, 1973; Thelin & Yankovich, 1987). The basic layout of the campus, open spaces and shaded lawns (Griffith, 1994), the accessibility and cleanliness of parking lots, interior color schemes, the shape and design of a residence hall or classroom building, a library or gallery, an impressive fitness center, and even the weather on the day of a campus visit all shape initial attitudes in subtle ways (Stern, 1986). In a firsthand study of campus life on twenty-nine different college campuses, Boyer (1987) observed:

> Little wonder that when we asked students what influenced them most during their visit to a campus, about half mentioned "the friendliness of students we met." But it was the buildings, the trees, the walkways, and the well-kept lawns that overwhelmingly won out. The appearance of the campus is, by far, the most influential characteristic during campus visits, and we gained the distinct impression that when it comes to recruiting students, the director of buildings and grounds may be more important than the academic dean. [p. 17]

It is clear that the campus physical environment is an important feature that influences students' attraction to and satisfaction with a particular institution. What then is the nature of that influence, and how does the campus physical environment shape specific behavior?

Most introductions to the topic of how physical environments influence behavior begin by noting Winston Churchill's observation that "we shape our buildings and then they shape us." While the observation is a simplistic one, it does fit many of our everyday experiences with building designs and spaces. Once the shape of the traffic flow within a campus building is fixed by doors and hallways, walking behavior within the building is pretty well determined. But we know it has not been entirely determined. Despite many design efforts to direct pedestrian flow through campus or through buildings, it is also a common experience to see someone going the "wrong" way.

In the literature, the influence of the physical environment on behavior has been conceptualized in three distinct positions (Bell, Fisher, Baum, & Greene, 1990; Porteus, 1977). First is the position of architectural determinism, which suggests that there is a rather direct link between the built environment and behavior within it. Often referred to as "environmentalism," this philosophy suggests that behavior to a large extent is determined in a direct, causal, and mechanistic manner by the physical environment (Ellen, 1982). People move in a certain direction, sit at one end of a room, and exit a building in a predictable pattern presumably because the physical structure and design allows few other options.

Architectural determinism, however, is too simplistic and does not do justice to the complexities within an environment. For example, the series of "welcome to campus" signs in the introductory vignette did not really welcome the Carter family but instead communicated a "not welcome" message due to their poor design and placement. This position also does not easily account for the influence of people on the physical environment, as when people on campus often rearrange, change, or remove physical structures like bicycle racks, benches, and picnic tables to meet their own needs rather than allowing these features to determine their behavior.

In reaction to the shortcomings of architectural determinism, a second position, environmental or architectural possibilism has emerged (Ellen, 1982). Possibilism views the physical environment as a source of opportunities that may set limits on, but not restrict, behavior. The causal attribution of architectural determinism is replaced by a view of the environment as an influence of "passive limiting agency" (Wissler, 1929, p. 339). Again, there are many commonsense examples within any campus environment to support such a position. If the campus does not have a football stadium available, the development of a traditional intercollegiate football program will be difficult. Or, if the stadium is several miles away from the campus, its location may limit the extent of student support. Likewise, the presence of a large convocation hall on campus enhances the opportunity for large campus constituent groups to meet.

The assumptions of environmental passivity associated with possibilism, however, have also been questioned. For example, an attractively designed campus restaurant is much more than just an opportunity; it is an attraction that appears to draw patrons. The facility does not cause people to come, but yet it appears to be more than just there. If campus walkways eventually lead to the student union, as was the experience of the Carters in the opening scenario, then their design and layout increase the probability that campus visitors will find the union during a tour. In turn, the probability of the student union being used is increased by its location and the design of campus walkways. These physical features do not determine use, but they appear to do more than just make use of the student union possible. This observation leads to a third way of viewing the nature of the influence of the physical environment on behavior, that is, environmental probabilism.

This third position, architectural or environmental probabilism, emerged to capture the probabilistic relationship between physical environments and behavior. As noted above, it assumes that certain behaviors have probabilistic links to the built environment. For example, an attractive, warm, and welcoming entrance to a campus building will increase the probability of it being entered more so than if it is cold and unwelcoming. The welcoming entrance does not cause entry, but the probability of entry can be increased with proper design. An admissions office hidden on the second floor of a building, away from typical traffic flow, has less probability of being found and used than one located at the main entrance on the ground floor.

Although features of the physical environment lend themselves theoretically to all possibilities, the layout, location, and arrangement of space and facilities render some behaviors much more likely, and thus more probable, than others.

All three positions (determinism, possibilism, and probabilism) offer insight into the relationship between the campus physical environment and the behavior of those within. However, viewing the relationship in terms of possibilities and probabilities appears to be more in tune with everyday experiences on campus. These positions also support the intuitive notion that the campus physical environment, with its designs and spaces, can influence and make a difference in the lives of students, faculty, and visitors to the campus.

How the Physical Environment Communicates Nonverbally

The complexity surrounding campus physical environments and the influence of their designs and spaces becomes clearer when the nature of that influence and how the features of various campus environments impact specific behaviors are considered. Whether natural or synthetic, the physical aspects of any campus environment offer many possibilities for human response, rendering some behaviors more probable than others. It is the nature of this influence to be both functional and symbolic. An admissions office located on a second floor is functional in that its design is capable of allowing the duties and activities of the admissions office to be carried out, but the location also sends out messages or symbolizes various possibilities. For example, the symbolic message of a second-floor location may communicate that the institution does not give serious consideration to the users of the service nor their needs for accessibility and convenience. Or the message may be that the institution does not see this function as an important aspect of its mission. Perhaps the second-floor location also indicates that the university is without the necessary funds to relocate the office. The symbolic view of campus environments suggests that they can potentially convey all of these messages, depending of course on the meaning people ascribe to them.

It is this link between the functional and symbolic aspects of campus physical environments that leads to an understanding of how campus physical environments impact behavior. Rapaport (1982) suggested that the important link between function and symbol in the physical environment is nonverbal communication. He noted, "Since environments apparently provide cues for behavior, but do not do it verbally, it follows that they must represent a form of non-verbal behavior" (p. 50). Nonverbal communication incorporates "those messages expressed by other than linguistic means" (Adler & Towne, 1987, p. 188). Cues from the physical environment naturally fall into this category. Rapaport (1982) states: "environments are more than just inhibiting, facilitating, or even catalytic; they not only remind, they also predict and describe" (p.77). The environment "thus communicates, through a whole set of cues, the most appropri-ate choices to be made: the cues are meant to elicit appropriate emo-tions, interpretations, behaviors, and transactions by setting up the appropriate situations and contexts" (Rapaport, pp. 80–81).

The functional aspects of campus physical environments are designed and built, but the function of designing and building cre-ates nonverbal messages that users of the campus environment then read. For example, if the campus decides to make a curb wheelchair accessible by molding some asphalt to the curb, instead of installing proper curb cuts, such an adaptation might be technically func-tional, but it may also encode messages of "not caring enough to do it correctly," "not valuing the user," or just "responding minimally to needs of the physically challenged." When the student in a wheelchair rolls up to the makeshift curb, the decoded message may reveal that "the institution doesn't care about me; I am not valued." On the other hand, if the curb cut is correctly designed and con-structed, the encoded and decoded messages may strike a different tone, conveying a sense that "the institution cared enough to do it correctly." Consequently the person concludes: "I feel valued" and "You care about me." Again, both adaptations are functional, but they are quite different in their symbolic messages. The functionality of the campus physical environment not only affords and constrains certain activities, but it also communicates important nonverbal, symbolic messages.

The research supporting the nonverbal communications link between the physical environment and behavior is well established. For example, it has been shown that the attractiveness of a room influences positive affect and the energy level of those working in the room (Maslow & Mintz, 1956). Low lighting, soft music, and comfortable seats encourage people to spend more time in a restaurant or bar (Sommer, 1978); the artifacts on the walls of a student room can reflect messages about the student's adjustment to the university (Hansen & Altman, 1976).

Mehrabian's (1981) work adds another important element to the conceptual link between the physical environment and nonverbal communication, pointing out that nonverbal messages are often seen as more truthful than verbal or written messages. The nonverbal messages of the physical environment may sometimes contradict those given verbally. For example, the visitors' signs in the opening scenario, although intended to say "Welcome," in fact, communicated to the Carter family a nonverbal "Not Welcome!" message. While the campus president may speak about the open posture of the campus and welcome ethnic minorities, the presence of defamatory graffiti on buildings may suggest just the opposite. Double messages have strong impact, and when a person on campus perceives an inconsistency between the verbal and nonverbal, or between the language and the nonlanguage message, the nonverbal often becomes most believable (Eckman, 1985). For example, Dorothy Carter, in the opening scenario, had a difficult time believing the slogan "a learning university with a college feel" due to the restrictive physical designs of the classrooms she observed.

To paraphrase Anderson's (1971) quote attributed to Sir Kenneth Clark: "If one had to say which was telling the truth about the school, a speech by the principal or the actual school building, classrooms, and material he or she was responsible for providing, one should believe the building" (p. 291). Mehrabian and Wiener (1967), Mehrabian (1981), and Birdwhistell (1970) all suggest that the emotional impact of communication is primarily carried by the nonverbal component of communications. If a picture is worth a thousand words, viewing the campus physical environment not only leads to a more truthful picture but perhaps to a far more complete one as well.

Impact of Campus Physical Environments on Behavior

Several important concepts increase the understanding of how campus physical environments' nonverbal communication impacts campus behavior:

- Campus physical environments as behavior settings and the role of proxemics

- The role of physical artifacts in campus physical environmental communications

- Behavioral traces as communication

Campus Physical Environments as Behavior Settings

Behavior settings (Barker, 1968) are the social and physical situations in which human behavior occurs (Wicker, 1984). The college campus is a classic behavior setting, composed of essentially two parts: the human or social aspects of the setting and the nonhuman component or physical aspects. For example, on the college campus, as students, faculty, and staff interact, they do so within a physical environment including many nonhuman components such as pathways, parking lots, activity fields, statuary, artwork, and buildings, presenting a myriad of designs that vary in size, color, and arrangement. It is the transactional (or mutually influential) relationship between the human and nonhuman elements in the behavior setting that shapes behavior. The essence of this behavior setting impact was captured by Barker and Wright (1951) when they concluded from their observations that the behaviors of children could be predicted more accurately from knowing the situation (behavior setting) the children were in than from knowing individual characteristics of the children (Wicker, 1984). The behavior setting can function like a nonverbal mnemonic device (Rapaport, 1982) where encoded messages in the physical component of the behavioral setting serve to remind participants what behaviors are expected. For example, an athletic field house is a behavior setting. The seating, props, cheerleaders, and decor are all cues that loud and rowdy sports event behaviors are not only appropriate but expected in such a place. The rowdiness the Carter family observed during MRU's commencement ceremony might prompt consideration of a redesign of the behavior setting or a change to an alternative venue.

At more than a few campuses, the Carters' concern about rowdiness in the opening scenario is also shared by faculty and administrators. Many of the institutions experiencing rowdiness during graduation exercises often hold their ceremonies in an athletic field house. Students are sometimes seated in the same arrangement as when they attend a basketball game and are most often grouped into departments and colleges, which encourages a team identity. The cues related to sporting events are usually visible, including basketball backboards, hoops, scoreboards, and time clocks. In many cases the banners of previous victories and accomplishments are hanging from the rafters as well. With such reminders from the behavior setting, sporting behaviors, rather than commencement behaviors, are cued. It is the encoded messages of the behavior setting that remind students that yelling, cheering, and rowdy behavior are presumed appropriate for that particular setting. Improvement in student decorum can usually be made by removing as many of the sporting cues as possible and replacing them with cues associated with convocation. For example, the use of plants and flowers, seating arrangements on the floor of the field house rather than in the bleachers, use of classical music, and use of light, carpet, and other textured surfaces to soften the atmosphere can also send different messages about the importance of such events. These cues do not determine the behavior, but they may increase the probability of a more desirable outcome, in this case, a reduction of rowdy behavior.

Another important aspect of the behavior setting is the sometimes supportive or sometimes antagonistic relationship between human and nonhuman components. Physical features can set broad limits on the phenomena that can occur in a setting, making some behaviors more or less likely than others—a concept labeled "intersystems congruence" (Michelson, 1970, p. 25). For example, in a classroom it would be difficult to form small group discussions to increase communication skills if all the chairs were bolted to the floor in straight rows. On the other hand, by having moveable chairs or cushions, the physical aspects of the classroom setting would be supportive of the desired behavior. When the physical and behavioral aspects of a setting are compatible, a synomorphic relationship is said to exist (Wicker, 1984). In other words, the physical structures and designs of the setting allow participants to do what they desire, while participants in turn take full advantage of the possibilities of the setting. Apparent between the human and nonhuman components is a mutuality of support. Common sense and experience suggest that when the physical environment of a campus, building, or classroom supports the desired behavior, better outcomes result. From the behavior setting point of view, campus designs and spaces do not merely create a functional space, mood, or atmosphere, they facilitate certain behaviors (Wicker, 1984).

Proxemics

Other concepts underscoring the importance of the nonverbal communications occurring within a behavior setting are found in the study of the social implications of use of physical space, or proxemics. Hall (1996) provided the pioneering work on how humans use space in their everyday life. Important to the understanding of proxemics is the concept of spatial zones, which refers to the distances people tend to establish between themselves and others when they engage in social interaction. Four distinct zones or distances have been described in the literature: intimate (0 to 1.5 feet), used for relationships like comforting; personal (1.5 to 4 feet), used for everyday conversations with friends; social (4 to 12 feet), used for impersonal and business-type conversations; and public (more than 12 feet), used for formal presentations to a group. The social and psychological aspects of physical space also communicate messages to the inhabitants of campus physical environments. If a student walks into a classroom and the teaching podium is 20 feet away from the first row of chairs, then a distinct message regarding the formal nature of the upcoming classroom experience is communicated very clearly. It was this same cue about the formality of the classroom in the opening scenario that raised questions in Dorothy Carter's mind about the promotion of a "college feel" to Mid-Rocky University. On the other hand, a simple couch located in a secluded space in the student union will signal the possibility for intimate social interaction.

Campus Physical Artifacts as Nonverbal Communication

Physical artifacts on campus include synthetic objects made and often placed on a campus for intended purposes, for example, to give directions, to inspire, to warn, or to accommodate. These artifacts often send strong nonverbal messages about campus culture and are found most often in one of four forms: signs and symbols; art work or posters; graffiti; and specific physical structures (Banning & Bartels, 1993).

The nature and pattern of campus physical artifacts structure the content of messages reflecting campus culture.

For example, the physical artifact of signage on a restroom door can give nonverbal messages. The restroom sign saying "Ladies" gives a different message than a similar sign saying "Women." An "Admissions Office" sign next to a "Graduate School" sign at the same entrance location gives a confusing message. The reader does not know whether there are two different offices or whether it is the entrance to the admissions function of the graduate school. Many campuses continue to display "Men Working" signs at work sites, despite the fact that women are involved in the project. This message of the invisibility of women would not be supported verbally by any university official but is supported nonverbally through the communicative power of a campus artifact.

Campus art is more than aesthetics. It too gives nonverbal social messages. Many of the older campus buildings often have murals that were painted by artists whose fame now makes the murals very valuable both historically and monetarily. But often these older murals have social messages that are no longer supported by the campus. For example, murals depicting slavery can be found on some campuses. Murals depicting Mexican Americans only as farm laborers and Anglos as scientists continue to cause controversy at the University of New Mexico (Banning & Luna, 1992). Campus artworks, particularly statuary, often portray women in passive positions (sitting) and men in more active positions (standing or in motion) (Banning & Luna, 1992).

The issue of campus graffiti is a common one. While the content of campus graffiti can be seen as a message from its author only, the total of all campus graffiti begins to communicate campus culture. The institutional response (leaving it or removing it with due speed or considerable delay) can send important nonverbal messages about the presumed values of the campus administration. Racist messages that have been visible for months on the side of an academic building may communicate a lack of concern for creating a safe and comfortable environment for all inhabitants.

Physical structures themselves can be seen as artifacts that communicate nonverbally. The previous illustration regarding the design and placement of a curb cut is one example. Another example is a two-story admissions building with no elevator. The absence of an elevator may communicate nonverbally, but yet very directly, a lack of concern for students in wheelchairs or students with children in strollers. Buildings that are hidden or have poorly lit spaces may suggest that concerns for the safety of users have not been addressed. These examples underscore the point that campus physical environments are not just related to function and ambiance, but they also serve to communicate, through various physical artifacts, important campus values and expectations.

Behavioral Traces as Communication

Students, faculty, staff, and visitors use campus environments in a variety of ways. It is impossible to observe all campus behaviors at the time they are occurring, but behaviors leave "traces" (Bechtel & Zeisel, 1987) that can be reconstructed to produce increased awareness of the person-environment interactions on campus. Such traces, much like artifacts, also send nonverbal communications to campus users.

Campus observers were not the first to infer behavior from traces; archaeology as a science is grounded in this methodology. As Bechtel and Zeisel (1987) stated: "Few give a thought . . . to the fact that the fossils of tomorrow are the garbage dumps of today" (p.32). Zeisel (1981) presented a number of ways to read traces that can be useful in gaining a more complete understanding of how people use campus environments. Zeisel's methods focus on by-products of use, adaptation of use, displays of self, and public messages.

By-products of behavior are produced by people interacting with the environment and can be defined further with reference to the concepts of erosion, leftovers, and missing traces (Bechtel & Zeisel, 1987). Examples of erosion on campus are the worn paths students make as they find the shortest distance from one campus building to the next. These by-products (paths) can be useful in locating new sidewalks. In fact, on some campuses, sidewalks to new buildings are not constructed until student paths emerge, suggesting patterns of movement that are likely to persist.

Leftovers are traces represented by objects not consumed during behavior, trash and litter being the most common forms. Leftovers can also become associated with particular campus groups. For example, on one campus a "sitting wall" is used as a favorite lunch spot by "Greek" students. The resulting leftovers of pop cans and fast food sacks produce a negative image problem for the fraternity and sorority system on campus.

Bechtel and Zeisel (1987) used the concept of missing traces to indicate a lack of use in areas where erosion and leftovers are expected but do not appear. Some spaces, by virtue of their design, see very little use by campus constituents. Documentation of such missing traces is often helpful in gaining support for their redesign to better serve campus needs. Missing traces also show up as the results of theft or vandalism. For example, a prominent campus clock missing its hands suggests theft or vandalism, perhaps raising among campus members a concern for their safety.

Zeisel (1981) employed the concept of "adaptation for use" to encompass situations in the environment where a change has been made because of failure of the first design to serve its original intention. Many of the traces of adaptation include movement of objects in ways that separate elements once connected and connect elements of the environment once separated. For example the chaining down of campus outdoor furniture suggests concern for theft. The internal corridors of residence halls often are adapted as playgrounds because areas for outdoor activities on campus may be lacking.

A larger scale adaptation for use would include renovations, expansions, and other changes or improvements. The addition of a new lighting system on campus is an environmental adaptation to an increase in campus crime. Changing an open space area to a parking lot could signify an adaptation to an increase in commuter student enrollment. Often the attempt by students to adapt a space for an unintended purpose is the first clue that a redesign or renovation effort may be needed.

Zeisel (1981) used the concept of "display of self" to illustrate how the physical environment can be used to convey messages about individual and group ownership. The positioning of Greek letters on fraternity and sorority houses is one clear example of this. Such displays become important to the process of individualizing and personalizing spaces. Huge signs are often found in residence hall windows marking a floor or wing. No one can enter the campus environment without taking note of the use of t-shirts to display messages of self and group, from Greek affiliations to academic majors, from attendance at rock concerts to where one spent spring break. Again, these traces not only increase understanding of the social environment on campus, but an entire social environment is communicated to others. Many academic buildings also illustrate how props are used symbolically as "displays of self": a world globe on top of an international studies building, an oil derrick on the roof of a petroleum engineering building, and cannons in front of an ROTC building. These symbols give public messages concerning the values and interests of campus units and organizations.

The last category of behavioral traces for Zeisel (1981) incorporates public messages. Included in this concept are official signs, unofficial signs, and illegitimate signs. Common problems with signs include their design, location, and degree of clarity. The experiences of the Carter family in their campus visit to MRU in the opening scenario is a familiar testament to the confusion ambiguous signs can create when not carefully constructed. These problems often lead to the posting of additional signs or a redundancy of messages (Rapaport, 1982), frequently a signal that the intended messages are not being communicated. In addition to the more formal signs, observers of the campus environment are quite familiar with campus graffiti, which can signal creativity, local issues, or give insight into prevailing attitudes on such complex issues as tolerance for diversity.

The concepts of behavior settings and proxemics, physical artifacts, and behavioral traces offer useful tools for the campus observer. Understanding their power as communication mechanisms can assist in the improvement of campus environments.

Improving the Overall Campus Image

An understanding of the impact of a college or university campus can be facilitated by a careful examination from the viewpoint of a pedestrian (Banning, 1993). As pedestrians (visitors, students, faculty, and staff) walk around campus they encounter nonverbal messages embedded in buildings, pathways, signs, and symbols. Through the decoding of these nonverbal messages, they learn important cultural messages conveyed by planners, designers, builders, and even the users of the pedestrian space. Such an informative pedestrian experience can be viewed from a perspective of safety, functionality, pleasure, and learning.

Pedestrian safety is a major concern in campus planning. In addition to auto-pedestrian and bicycle-pedestrian accidents, there is an increasing concern for safety on campus from various health hazards associated with vehicle emissions, air pollution, noise, and the risks of robberies and personal assaults. (More specific attention is given to the topic of safety in Chapter Five.)

The functional features of a pedestrian trip through campus can sensitize participants to issues of pedestrian access and convenience. Untermann (1984) noted that convenience depends on the directness, continuity, and availability of the walk. Pushkarev and Zupan (1975) addressed the functional issues of the pedestrian experience in depth, including concerns such as pedestrian space requirements, sidewalk widths and standards, and other important aspects of functional design. Most planning efforts that include concern for the pedestrian focus on the design and development of convenient walkways that are efficient and barrier free (Smith, 1987).

Pleasure is a third category (Untermann, 1984) of campus pedestrian experiences, including factors of protection, coherence, security, and interest. Good campus physical space planning efforts do not stop at providing physical safety and convenience alone, but they also attempt to enhance the pleasurable aspects of the walking experience through a variety of design features such as sitting walls, benches, flowers, and weather protective features.

The importance of safety, functionality, and pleasure for the pedestrian is without question, but a fourth category, cultural learning, also adds to the walking experience. The campus physical environment teaches and, through decoded nonverbal messages, a sense of curriculum emerges. While the pedestrian's learning environment or curriculum is not intentionally programmed by any faculty committee, the informal curriculum may be the nonintentional, nonverbal communication of basic cultural values. Those values communicated by the campus physical environment have a direct relationship to the challenge of making any campus a place for all persons. (See Chapter Five for a more detailed discussion of inclusive environments.)

Banning and Bartels (1993) have pointed out that many of the nonverbal messages can be seen as sending inadvertent multicultural messages. For example, campus posters that never include any race other than Caucasian would not send a message of belonging to other groups. Dark and bushy areas around major pathways might send messages of insecurity to some campus users. Likewise, many campuses have statuary and artwork that endorse outdated or limited roles for women (Banning, 1992). All campus environments could benefit from an assessment of potential messages being communicated about specific groups.

Developing Positive Physical Features

It is clear from many people's experiences that some places simply feel more comfortable or better than others. A review of related literature (Miller & Banning, 1992) suggests several common denominators in the design of campus spaces that engender positive responses from participants. From surveying the work of Alexander (1977), Jackson (1984), Whyte (1988), and Hiss (1990), Miller and Banning (1992) identified voices that require attention for the design and creation of positive campus physical environments: the call for community, the call for territory, the call for landscape, and the call for wayfinding.

A sense of community is important to the inhabitants of any environment. (See Chapter Seven for a more detailed discussion of communal environments.) How can campus designs bring about and enhance a sense of community? What physical features lead to a feeling of community? Possible responses include gathering places, sitting walls, and green spaces. The need for territory or a place to call one's own is equally important. Selection of favorite niches on campus, private places in the library, or a favorite chair in the classroom are all examples of students seeking territory in various ways. Campus landscapes are important, too, and they can be defined around issues of safety and opportunity. Kaplan and Kaplan (1978) discussed these two counteracting components (safety and opportunity) in terms of "legibility" and "mystery."

Legible environments are those with open and distinctive landmarks, a landscape through which one could wander and feel safe but not become lost. Mysterious landscapes are those that invite participants with the promise of new information, tapping a natural yearning to know "what's beyond the bend." How do campus landscapes negotiate the balance between legibility and mystery? In addition to these elements of safety and opportunity in campus landscapes, there also appears to be a preference for landscapes that offer water features (Ulrich, 1983). Boyer (1987) noted that the presence of water in photographs of college campuses actually attracts prospective students.

Beyond the development of community, territory, and landscapes, campuses also need to address issues of "wayfinding" (Lynch, 1960). Wayfinding, sometimes referred to as spatial orientation, involves using past experience and immediate cues from the physical environment to plan and carry out movement in the environment. For example, from the opening scenario, when the Carters came to Mid-Rocky University they had had previous experience in locating towns, universities, and buildings. While visiting the campus they used their past experiences and cues from the immediate environment (in the form of campus signs) to find their way to the admissions office. However, in this case, wayfinding was inhibited by erroneous campus signs. As people move through campus environments, wayfinding questions abound. Where is the student center? Where is the entrance to this building? Is there an elevator? Where are the campus signs? Is there a you-are-here map? Is the information clear? The physical environment can be designed through signs, symbols, walkways, paths, and special features to be user friendly to campus inhabitants. If wayfinding is not addressed, campus environments often result in confusion and frustration on the part of users. Recalling feelings of being lost in a new environment is all it takes to realize just how important it is for the campus physical environment to support easy wayfinding.

Arthur and Passini (1992) concluded from their work that wayfinding design impacts users of the environment emotionally and functionally. Users can develop a sense of "feeling lost" or "feeling stupid," which can lead to stress and anxiety (Hunt, 1984). Users can also develop ambiguous feelings about the setting, as if to say, "if they want me to visit the admissions office why do they make it so difficult?" In addition, Arthur and Passini (1992) point out that poor wayfinding cues have a functional impact "which is measurable in terms of efficiency and monetary value" (p. 11). As campuses attempt to make their environments more inviting and hospitable to all users, wayfinding must be given serious consideration.

Evaluation of campus physical environments for positive improvements would be incomplete without reference to the work of Dober (1992). Dober, through concepts of placemaking and placemarking, offers a comprehensive and useful analysis of campus design, the principal components of which are "buildings, landscapes, and circulation systems" (p. 4). Placemaking is Dober's concept for the structure of the overall campus design and includes the "positioning and arrangement of campus land uses and pedestrian and vehicular routes, the location of buildings and functional open spaces, . . . the definition of edges, and the interface between campus and environs" (p. 4). Through participation of campus constituents, placemaking yields an overall plan in the form of an "institutional metaphor," which guides what can or may be built. It is this institutional metaphor that represents the collective picture presented by the nonverbal communications of the total campus design. Placemarking, Dober's second concept, focuses on "certain physical attributes which give a campus a visual uniqueness appropriately its own" (p. 5), including landmarks, style, materials, and landscapes. The combination of these elements leads to a distinct sense of place on campus. As an activity, "placemaking resembles town planning, producing the larger picture of the future, while placemarking involves the specifics of campus architecture, landscape architecture, and site engineering" (Dober, pp. 229–231).

In summary, campus physical environments can be understood better and improved by greater sensitivity to their nonverbal communications, by increasing designs and spaces that give a sense of comfort and security, by giving closer attention to the campus' wayfinding features, and by increasing the focus on the placemaking and placemarking aspects of campus design.

Designing for Student Learning and Development

College and university environments are places with a special purpose: student learning. Student learning and development embrace complex goals, requiring the input and coordination of all aspects of campus environments, including their physical design and space. Banning and Cunard (1986) noted that, among the many methods employed to foster student learning and development, the use of the physical environment is perhaps the least understood and the most neglected. The physical environment, however, can contribute to college student learning and development in two important ways. First, the actual features of the physical environment can encourage or discourage the processes of learning and development. Second, the process of designing campus physical environments can also promote the acquisition of skills important to the process of learning and developing.

Physical features of a campus environment can hinder or promote learning. For example, the entrance to a college library can communicate a warm welcome or not, depending on its design. To not enter a library and not use its many resources would likely have a negative impact on the intellectual growth of students. So too might entering a library to discover that the wayfinding aspects of the building are so confusing that they contribute to unnecessary levels of frustration and stress. Under these conditions, students gain less information and knowledge. With a more inviting entrance design and less intimidating wayfinding, the probability of becoming engaged in intellectual activities is increased.

Once a student is encouraged to enter by the design of the campus building, then an array of influences is both possible and probable. For example, the proxemics associated with seating arrangements in a lounge area in a student center can either promote or inhibit social interaction. The physical artifact messages of support or nonsupport can take many forms, signaling a sense of belonging, a feeling of being welcomed, a sense of safety, and a sense of role, worth, and value (Banning & Bartels, 1993). Such messages enhance or detract from students' ability to cope with college stress. For example, consider the contrast between a poster in the campus union advertising an upcoming gay, lesbian, bisexual, and transgendered awareness week as compared to the unfortunate homophobic graffiti found in many campus restrooms. Consider also a student wheelchair user anticipating the excitement of an on-campus event but who cannot find an accessible entrance to the sponsoring facility. Processes of growth and development can be readily hindered by such undeserved stress.

In addition to the direct impact of symbols and designs, participant involvement in the processes of designing and building campus spaces might also contribute to significant learning opportunities. As noted in Banning and Cunard (1986), "students who participate meaningfully in a design or redesign effort become involved in complex analytical behavior, participate in leadership positions, engage in significant oral and written communications skills, and work within the give and take of group settings" (p. 3). Participation of all users in the design process increases the probability of eliminating negative and unintended nonverbal messages. In fact, the likelihood that a campus design will meet the needs of the community may be a direct function of the extent to which community members participate in the design process. It is clear that they can assist in illuminating these complex issues of function and meaning, the effects of behavior settings, proxemics, wayfinding, and the power of nonverbal communications in artifacts and traces.

2

Aggregate Environments
The Impact of Human Characteristics

Consider the following scene at Midwestern University, as a group of students discuss their adjustments to college life during a biweekly Freshman Seminar meeting. Led by a faculty moderator, an orientation staff member, and one senior class student, group members are focusing on various experiences they have had during their first month in school.

Scenario: They're Not Like Me

"So, how is everything going in your accounting program, Sarah?" asked the faculty moderator.

"Not so well, Dr. Cummings," she replied. "I'm not so sure that being in the accounting department and taking accounting courses is a good fit for me. I can do that stuff, but I don't really enjoy it all that much. I'm hoping to meet with my faculty advisor next week to talk about it. Maybe I should think about another major, but I'm not sure."

Phil, a declared theater arts major, was anxious to say how thrilled he was to become acquainted with so many other students who shared his interests. "I always felt out of place with most of my friends in high school. None of them were all that much involved. Here it seems like everybody wants to get in on the act. It's great!"

Mike, a transfer social work student from a small private college, had an experience similar to Phil's but for somewhat different reasons.

"I've already met a lot of different kinds of people at this university," Mike said, "and I have so many more choices. I don't feel like I have to be like everybody else anymore." He went on to say how all the students seemed so much alike at his previous school and how difficult it was to be different from them. "It seemed like I was always in a fishbowl, with everyone watching, and no place to get away."

"Hey man, I know what you mean," said Randall, an African American student who was seriously questioning whether he was going to stay for the remainder of the semester. In fact, two of his friends from high school had already left. Randall was doing fine in his classwork as a biology major, but it was becoming increasingly difficult for him, on a day-to-day basis, to feel like he belonged at the university. "When I walk down the sidewalk, in between classes, all I see are white faces. Nobody looks like someone I should know. It's weird." He continued by saying how he couldn't wait to get home the coming weekend to a place that looked and felt familiar once again.

Jill, an undecided student whose parents both graduated from Midwestern University, acknowledged how uneasy she felt during the first few weeks of school until she became involved in a sorority. "This school is really big, in comparison to my high school," Jill said, "and I wasn't really sure what it was going to be like to make friends here. But I'm really comfortable in my sorority now. The friends I met remind me a lot of some of my friends back home. We have a lot in common," she said enthusiastically.

"Well, it sounds like some of you have really found your spot, and some might be questioning whether this is the place for you," said Carolyn, an orientation staff member.

"You got that right!" responded Randall.

"What do you think might make the difference for all of you this semester?" asked Greg, the senior student in the group.

"I know I'll feel a lot better when I find a major I like," said Sarah.

"I think it probably has a lot to do with the people you hang out with, and the friends you make, too," said Phil.

"Yeah," concurred Jill, "somehow, being with friends who like the same things you do makes it a lot easier."

"As long as you have a chance to meet others, too, though," Mike reminded the group. "We can't all be alike!"

Although these incidents may truly reflect aspects that are unique to each student in the group, collectively their experiences share a common dynamic basic to understanding the human aggregate approach to environments presented in this chapter. That is, environments are transmitted through people, and the dominant features of a particular environment are partially a function of the collective characteristics of the individuals who inhabit it (Holland, 1973). For the students in this opening scenario, the experience of Midwestern University the first few weeks on campus was greatly influenced by the collective composition of people with whom they interacted in academic departments, student groups, and campus organizations. For Phil, Mike, and Jill, they found a source of congruence and satisfaction in their association with others, while for Sarah and Randall, disparities of interests or personal-cultural characteristics caused them to question whether they even belonged at Midwestern. Such are the dynamics of human aggregates explored in this chapter.

Environments as People

Moos (1986) noted that "the character of an environment is implicitly dependent on the typical characteristics of its members" (p. 286). These human characteristics influence the degree to which people are attracted to, satisfied within, and retained by those environments. Thus, academic departments, depending on the nature of their work as reflected in the collective characteristics of present members, will attract, satisfy, and retain students and faculty of certain types.

Sarah's concern in the opening scenario reflected the fact that she found few similarities with, and therefore little enjoyment from, the characteristics of faculty and students in the accounting department. In like manner, as implicated in Randall's assessment, campuses dominated by one cultural, ethnic, or age-based group are inherently challenging and, therefore, are less likely to attract, satisfy, or retain any individual or group that does not share traits in common with the dominant group. Similarly, but with different results, is the case with Jill who found that a student organization focusing on special interests and traditions (a sorority) enhanced her satisfaction by contributing to a sense of fit between her and the campus.

What these vignettes suggest is that any information about individuals in an environment collectively informs the aggregate features of an environment. From each of the theoretical perspectives reviewed in this chapter, information about the collective characteristics of environmental inhabitants, whether demographic (such as gender, age, or raciai-ethnic composition) or psychological (personality types, interests, and styles), is predictive of the dominant features of the environment. We now turn to a consideration of the principal human aggregate models found in the literature on college students and their campuses.

Students of a Feather

In recent decades, a number of researchers have examined the nature of environments attributed to various human aggregates on college and university campuses. Employing what Astin (1993) called a "taxonomic or typological language that implicitly sorts students into a variety of discrete categories or boxes" (p. 36), several models have emerged from this line of inquiry, including those of Clark and Trow (1966), Astin (1968, 1993), Holland (1966, 1973), Myers (1980), and Kolb (1983). Clark and Trow (1966) examined the nature of aggregates through a typology of student subcultures, each with a distinctive orientation toward their institution and the world of ideas. Astin (1968, 1993) explained the effects of campus aggregates through empirically derived student subtypes. Holland (1966, 1973) focused his work on collective differences in vocational interest types found among students. Myers (1980) described a typology of personalities organized within a framework of Jungian types. Kolb (1983) created a descriptive model of learning and adaptive styles particularly relevant for understanding the dynamics of human aggregates in the classroom. Each of these models is summarized below with relevant illustrations and examples grounded in the context of campus life.

Clark and Trow Subcultures

Among the first to observe that students share "certain broad patterns of student orientation toward college which tend to give meaning to the informed relations among students" (Walsh, 1973, p. 41), Clark and Trow (1966) described four subcultures on college campuses, which result from combinations of two dimensions assessing the extent to which students identify with ideas and identify with their institution. The interaction of these two dimensions suggests the distinctive character of each subculture: the Academic, the Nonconformist, the Collegiate, and the Vocational student (see Figure 2.1).

According to Clark and Trow (1966), the typical character of an institution is partially a function of the dominance of one or more of these subcultures and an understanding of each is important for discerning their collective influence on campus environments.

The Academic subculture, identifying as much with ideas as with the institution, is for the most part composed of serious students who work hard, achieve high grades, and participate in campus life. They "are seriously involved in their coursework; and they identify themselves with their college and faculty. They perceive their school as an institution that supports intellectual values and opportunities for learning" (Walsh, 1973, p. 42). Many of these students go on to graduate and professional schools, placing a premium

Figure 2.1. Orientations of Four Student Subcultures

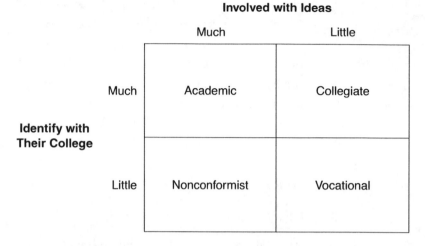

Source: Walsh, 1973, p. 42. Used by permission.

on the intellectual life of the institution, particularly its libraries, laboratories, and seminar rooms.

Sharing this involvement with ideas are the Nonconformists. Different from Academics, however, the Nonconformists maintain a "critical detachment from the college they attend and its faculty, and a generalized hostility to the administration. In sum, this subculture seems to value and reward individualistic styles, concern for personal identity and self-awareness, and, frequently, contempt for organized society" (Walsh, 1973, p. 42).

In contrast, the Collegiate subculture tends to be "loyal to their college but indifferent, if not resistant, to serious intellectual demands" (Walsh, 1973, pp. 42–43). They place at a premium campus social life, extracurricular activities, athletics, living group functions, and intimate friendships. Count on them to attend the homecoming parade and game but not the department discussion group.

Last is the Vocational subculture. These students care little about ideas or involvement in the institution. For Vocational students a college education is "off-the-job training leading to a diploma and a better job than they could otherwise obtain. Ideas, scholarship, social life, and extracurricular activities are not particularly valued" (Walsh, 1973, p. 43).

Although specific descriptions of these subcultures may be dated somewhat, their relevance for examining today's college students seems intact. Faculty and administrators readily recognize the serious student, the Academic, as one who places priority on studies and enjoys a good academic challenge. Student affairs administrators continue to rely on the leadership of the Collegiate student, who readily gets involved in campus opportunities. The Vocational student, who cuts a narrow path through the college experience, focusing only on those courses that are most marketable to a particular job, is still prevalent on most campuses. Even the Nonconformist is visible among students who, today, might be seen convening in small groups on the campus lawn dressed in the latest counterculture attire listening to alternative rock.

Furthermore, it is easy to imagine how the dominance of one or more of these subcultures on campus might shape institutional image and culture. Where would an Oberlin or Antioch College be without the presence of a dominant Nonconformist subculture? Could Williams College or Princeton survive in its present state without a strong Academic subculture? Could the rich traditions of residence life, campus activities, Greek letter organizations, and intercollegiate athletics survive at an Indiana University without a significant Collegiate subculture?

At the same time, the Vocational subculture among students today, both traditional and nontraditional age, brings a strong consumer ethic to campus, demanding nothing less than a practical and applicable education leading to a good-paying job. In the same respect, the experience of community and technical college educators becomes clear when one realizes the dominance of Vocational types and the absence of Collegiates at such institutions. While it may be easier for faculty to sequence courses in the curriculum, it is certainly more challenging for student affairs staff to develop a program of cocurricular activities without an extended presence of students on campus. These examples illustrate that the character of the campus culture, which supports or detracts from the institution's mission, is partially a function of the types of students enrolled who collectively create a human aggregate environment on campus. Both Phil and Jill, in the opening scenario, intuitively understood these differences as they each talked excitedly about being among students at Midwestern University who were involved, in Clark and Trow's scheme, as Collegiates.

Astin Types

Astin (1968) analyzed the collective activities of college students as an observable and measurable source for understanding the impact of a particular campus environment. According to this line of reasoning, the extent to which a campus environment influences intellectual or academic interests would be reflected in observable and quantifiable behaviors, such as the frequency of formal and informal discussions among students in and outside of the classroom and the number of faculty-student interactions. Differences in the strength of this influence, from one setting to the next, would be reflected in different frequencies and duration of such behaviors. Measurement of these environmental features involves self-reports of various individuals' activities and behaviors in the setting, and the collective effect of these activities constitutes the dominant feature of the environment. For example, at an institution, where 75 percent of the students report regular use of campus recreational facilities, the environment might be described as emphasizing physical fitness, social interaction, and out-of-class involvement. That profile would be quite different from an institution where only 10 percent of the students reported such behaviors.

Astin (1993) identified a typology of college students, empirically derived from self-reported student responses to the Cooperative Institutional Research Program's (CIRP) national freshman survey. This survey assesses student behaviors, attitudes, expectations, values, and self-concept. According to the data, seven student types demonstrated substantial concurrent and predictive validity. These are Scholars, Social Activists, Artists, Hedonists, Leaders, Status Strivers, and Uncommitted students. Each type can be differentiated from the others by characteristic behaviors, attitudes, expectations, values, and self-concept (see Exhibit 2.1).

In addition to these seven types, Astin (1993) also identified a sizable group he labeled No Type students, constituting about 40 percent of the students in his sample. These No Type students exhibited a very distinctive pattern, coming "from families with less education and lower incomes than any of the types" (p. 44), being less involved in leadership and extracurricular activities, and having lower degree aspirations and poorer academic records from high school. They are also "heavily concentrated in community colleges and underrepresented in public universities and all types of private institutions" (p. 44). Other patterns suggest that No Type students "show a lower degree of involvement in their undergraduate experience than any other student type, including the Uncommitted student" (p. 44).

Like Clark and Trow's subcultures, Astin's seven student types are also useful in describing the attributes of aggregates of students on campus. For instance, a predominance of Scholars would likely create an institutional emphasis on events and interests of an academic nature. In contrast, Social Activists and Artists would create by their dominance on campus an environmental influence toward social action and involvement. Last, the preponderance of No Type students in a community college makes more understandable the challenge of getting students involved in various campus-based activities and organizations in this kind of institution.

Holland Types

According to Holland (1973), "we can characterize people by their resemblance to each of six personality types: realistic, investigative, artistic, social, enterprising, and conventional" (p. 2). Thus,

Exhibit 2.1. CIRP Freshman Survey Typology of Students

Scholar High degree of academic and intellectual self-esteem, high expectations for academic success in college, aspirations for high-level academic degrees, and a significant disinclination toward careers in business and social work.

Social Activist Emphasis on participating in community action programs, helping others who are in difficulty, influencing social values, and influencing the political structure; propensity for discussion of political and social issues, participation in campus protests, attending racial and cultural workshops, and participating in volunteer work.

Artists From relatively well educated families, include a higher proportion of women (65 percent) than any other type; substantially more likely to major in fine arts, music, speech, theater, journalism, and English and to pursue careers in the arts (music, writing, theater), interior design, and architecture.

Hedonists Have poorer high school grades, report a greater frequency of poor study habits, and are more often bored in class; prefer careers that are professional or vocational in character (such as business, nursing, health technology, and secretarial studies); propensity for lower career aspirations; likely to spend more time partying while in college, less time attending religious services; more likely to participate in campus protests, spend a lot of time socializing with other students, and to get relatively poor grades.

Leaders Disproportionately concentrated in private colleges and universities, and underrepresented in the community colleges; excelled in speech and debate in high school, frequently studied with other students, and were far more likely to have been elected president of some student organization and to have won varsity letters in sports.

Status Strivers Committed to being successful in their own business, having administrative responsibility for the work of others, being very well-off financially, obtaining recognition from colleagues for contributions in their special field, and becoming an authority in their field; strongly materialistic values reflected in their inclination toward college majors and careers in accounting and business and toward partying, watching television, and joining fraternities or sororities.

Uncommitted Students More likely to be undecided about either their major or their career choice; associated with participation in study abroad programs, enrollment in foreign language courses, and hours spent discussing political or social issues.

Source: Astin, 1993, pp. 38–44.

individuals' interests, activities, and behaviors can be assumed to be a direct reflection of their personalities that, in turn, shape the development of interests and the degree of attraction to various experiences. In a description of each of these six types is found a characteristic set of preferences, activities, competencies, values, and interests (see Exhibit 2.2).

Extending his typology into a model of human environments, Holland (1973) concluded that information about the collective personalities in an environment is the key to understanding its dominant features. Assessment of various interests, activities, and behaviors represented among the participants of an environment, as is done in using the Environmental Assessment Technique (EAT) (Astin & Holland, 1961), for example, constitutes an adequate measure of that environment. Holland then builds a framework for understanding various human aggregates with reference to each of the vocational interest personality types. Thus, social environments encourage and reinforce those behaviors, attitudes, skills, and interests most compatible with characteristics of social personalities, enterprising environments reinforce enterprising characteristics, and so forth. The six templates of personality patterns described in Holland's typology become frames for understanding the collective features of human environments. Sarah, in the opening scenario, knew that something was amiss with her participation in the accounting program, but she lacked a formal understanding of how her interests seemed to vary significantly from those of the dominant conventional type in her department.

Myers-Briggs Personality Types

One of the more widely disseminated and influential models in the literature on personality differences has been the work, based on Jung's (1923/1971) theory of psychological type, of Isabel Myers and Katherine Briggs (Myers, 1980; Myers & McCaulley, 1985). Similar to other typologies, this model employs the assumption that

Exhibit 2.2. Holland Vocational-Interest Personality Types

Realistic Prefers activities that entail the explicit, ordered, or systematic manipulation of objects, tools, machines, animals; averse to educational or therapeutic activities; perceives self as having mechanical and athletic ability and lacking ability in human relations; values concrete things or tangible personal characteristics (money, power, status).

Investigative Prefers activities that entail the observational, symbolic, systematic, and creative investigation of physical, biological, and cultural phenomena in order to understand and control such phenomena; averse to persuasive, social, and repetitive activities; sees self as scholarly, intellectually self-confident, having mathematical and scientific ability but lacking in leadership ability.

Artistic Prefers ambiguous, free, unsystematized activities that entail the manipulation of physical, verbal, or human materials to create art forms or products; averse to explicit, systematic, and ordered activities; shows self to be complicated, disorderly, emotional, feminine, idealistic, imaginative, impractical, impulsive, independent, introspective, intuitive, nonconforming, and original.

Social Prefers activities that entail the manipulation of others to inform, train, develop, cure, or enlighten; averse to explicit, ordered, systematic activities involving materials, tools, or machines; perceives self as liking to help others, understanding of others, having teaching ability, and lacking mechanical and scientific skills.

Enterprising Prefers activities that entail the manipulation of others to attain organizational goals or economic gain; exhibits behavioral tendencies that lead to an acquisition of leadership, interpersonal, and persuasive competencies, and to a deficit in scientific competencies.

Conventional Prefers the explicit, ordered, systematic manipulation of data, such as keeping records, filing materials, reproducing materials, organizing written and numerical data according to a prescribed plan, operating business machines and data processing machines to attain organizational or economic goals.

Source: Holland, 1973, pp. 14–17.

"much seemingly random variation in behavior is actually quite orderly, being due to basic differences in the way individuals prefer to use their perception and judgment" (Myers & McCaulley, 1985, p. 1). According to the authors, "Perception involves all the ways of becoming aware of things, people, happenings, or ideas. Judgment involves all the ways of coming to conclusions about what has been perceived. . . . [People] differ correspondingly in their reactions, interests, values, motivations, and skills" (p. 1).

Through application of the Myers-Briggs Type Indicator (MBTI) (Myers & McCaulley, 1985), individual differences are described in terms of four dichotomous personality dimensions: extraversion (E) or introversion (I); sensing (S) or intuition (N); thinking (T) or feeling (F); and judgment (J) or perception (P). The extraversion-introversion (EI) dimension assesses whether an individual prefers to direct mental activities (that is, perceiving and judging) toward the external world of people and objects, as extraverts do, or toward the inner world of concepts and ideas, as do introverts.

The sensing-intuition (SN) dimension reflects "a person's preference between two opposite ways of perceiving; one may rely primarily upon the process of sensing (S), which reports observable facts or happenings through one or more of the five senses; or may rely more upon the less obvious process of intuition (N), which reports meanings, relationships, and/or possibilities that have been worked out beyond the reach of the conscious mind" (Myers & McCaulley, 1985. p. 2).

The thinking-feeling (TF) dimension "reflects a person's preference between two contrasting ways of judgment. A person may rely primarily on thinking (T) to decide impersonally on the basis of logical consequences, or a person may rely primarily on feeling (F) to decide primarily on the basis of personal or social values" (Myers & McCaulley, 1985, p. 2).

Last, the judging-perception (JP) dimension describes "the process a person uses primarily in dealing with the outer world, that is, with the extraverted part of life. A person who prefers judgment (J) has reported a preference for using a judgment process (either thinking or feeling) for dealing with the outer world. A person who prefers perception (P) has reported a preference for using a percep-tive process (either sensing or intuition) for dealing with the outer world" (Myers & McCaulley, 1985, p. 2).

The various combinations of these dimensions yield sixteen dif-ferent personality types (Exhibit 2.3), each with a unique set of pre-ferred attitudes, processes, and styles of dealing with the world. It is the persistent orientation on each dimension that takes on the qual-ities of a consistent personality style. The personality differences defined in this model have been shown to be useful in understanding peoples' occupational interests, interrelationships, and learning styles (Myers, 1980). Others have also applied the Myers-Briggs model extensively to campus issues of retention, the design of residential environments, student involvement, advising and counseling, career planning, and effective teaching (Provost & Anchors, 1987).

Kolb Learning Styles

Although a model for understanding the learning cycle, Kolb's (1983) theory of learning styles is helpful in examining the aggre-gate effects of academic environments, such as departments, majors, and classrooms. Kolb described two axes related to the learning process: a continuum from the concrete to the abstract intersected

Exhibit 2.3. Myers-Briggs Types

	Sensing Types		Intuitive Types	
Introverts	ISTJ	ISFJ	INFJ	INTJ
	ISTP	ISFP	INFP	INTP
Extraverts	ESTP	ESFP	ENFP	ENTP
	ESTP	ESFJ	ENFJ	ENTJ

by a continuum from the active to the passive. Some individuals prefer concrete experience as a learning mode while others prefer abstract conceptualization. Some prefer to actively experiment while others to passively observe. These preferences manifest themselves in predictable orientations toward learning, and they reflect differences in values and approaches to a variety of tasks.

In combination, these preferences yield four distinct learning styles: divergers, assimilators, convergers, and accommodators. Each style exhibits characteristic strengths and abilities (Exhibit 2.4).

Relationships between learning style differences and academic or professional career decisions yield interesting patterns. In fact,

---

Exhibit 2.4. Kolb Learning Styles

Divergers Emphasize concrete experience and reflective observation; interested in people and tend to be imaginative and feeling-oriented; associated with valuing skills, being sensitive to people's feelings and to values, listening with an open mind, gathering information, and imagining implications of ambiguous situations.

Assimilators Emphasize abstract conceptualization and reflective observation; more concerned with ideas and abstract concepts, with strengths in inductive reasoning and the ability to create theoretical models, and in assimilating disparate observations into an integral explanation; particularly skilled at organizing information, building conceptual models, testing theories and ideas, designing experiments, and analyzing quantitative data.

Convergers Emphasize abstract conceptualization and active experimentation; greatest strength lies in problem solving, decision making, and the practical application of ideas; prefer dealing with technical tasks and problems rather than social and interpersonal issues, creating new ways of thinking and doing, experimenting with new ideas, choosing the best solution to problems, setting goals, and making decisions.

Accommodators Emphasize concrete experience and active experimentation; enjoy doing things, carrying out plans and tasks, and getting involved in new experiences; tend to solve problems in an intuitive trial-and-error manner, relying heavily on other people for information rather than on their own analytic ability; at ease with people.

Source: Kolb, 1983, pp. 77–78.

learning orientations seem to be associated with educational specializations in college. "Undergraduate business majors tend to have accommodative learning styles; engineers on the average fall in the convergent quadrant; history, English, political science, and psychology majors all have divergent learning styles; mathematics, economics, sociology, and chemistry majors have assimilative learning styles; physics majors are very abstract, falling between the convergent and assimilative quadrants" (Kolb, 1983, p. 85).

The connection to various professional groups is also interesting. As Kolb (1983) observed, "The professions in general have an active as opposed to a reflective learning orientation. The social professions—education, nursing, social work, and agricultural extension—comprise people who are heavily or primarily accommodative in their learning style. Professions with a technical or scientific base—accounting, engineering, medicine, and, to a lesser degree, management—have people with primarily convergent learning styles" (pp. 88–89).

These patterned relationships suggest that the human environments characteristic of various academic specialties and professional fields, much like the vocational interest patterns identified by Holland (1973), select and reinforce certain learning orientations and styles over others.

A Synthesis of Concepts

Several key concepts emerge in common from these models of human environments. First, all of these theories are reductionistic in their approach to assessing human environments in that they all attribute environmental differences partially to the collective effects of individual members' personalities and styles. Thus, an environment dominated by a particular type is presumed to convey the characteristics of that type. For example, in the parlance of Holland's theory, an environment dominated by Social types (such as a residence hall floor of education majors) would stimulate people to engage in social activities, foster their social competencies, encourage them to see themselves as liking to help others, to be understanding of others, cooperative, and sociable, as well as to see the world in flexible ways (Holland, 1973). This Social environment would reward people for the display of social values, leading, in turn, to various "secondary effects," such as participants becoming "more susceptible to social, humanitarian, and religious influences;" "more attracted to social occupations and roles in which they can express themselves in social activities;" and "more apt to cope with others by being friendly, helpful, [and] cooperative" (Holland, pp. 31–32). Similarly, in the parlance of Myers-Briggs types, a human work environment dominated by judging and sensing types (such as a campus registrar or bursar's office) would place an emphasis on things being organized, systematic, and foreseeable (Myers, 1980). On the academic side, a classroom environment composed of Kolb's accommodators would place an emphasis on active and concrete forms of learning, just the opposite from the preferences for reflective and abstract learning assimilators would likely bring.

From each of these theoretical perspectives, information about the collective characteristics of environmental inhabitants, whether demographic (gender, age, or racial-ethnic composition) or psychological in nature (personality types, learning styles), are presumed to be predictive of the dominant features of the environment. Therefore, an assessment and amalgamation of the characteristics of inhabitants constitutes an assessment of environmental characteristics, which, in turn, can be understood in terms of their degrees of differentiation and consistency.

Environmental Differentiation and Consistency

The pattern, strength, and character of any human aggregate are a function of its degree of differentiation (that is, the degree of type homogeneity among inhabitants) and consistency (the similarity of type among inhabitants). According to Holland (1983), "the percentage difference between the most and least common personality [or demographic] types in a given environment equals the degree of differentiation of that environment" (p. 34). For example, a human environment composed of 75 percent Realistic types, 10 percent Investigative types, and 15 percent Conventional types would exhibit a higher degree of differentiation than an environment with 35 percent Realistic types, 30 percent Investigative types, and 35 percent Conventional types. Thus, a highly differentiated, or focused, environment is dominated by one single type (such as a Collegiate subculture), while an undifferentiated environment is more diffuse, being characterized by several different types (an even distribution of Social Activists, Leaders, Artists, Hedonists, and Status Strivers). Consequently, highly differentiated environments are readily distinguishable to those within them, as well as to those outside them, precisely because the dominance of a single type consistently encourages certain behaviors, values, attitudes, and expectations while discouraging those that are dissimilar. This is also the case with environments dominated by any given demographic profile (for example, women or African Americans). The effect appears to be that differentiated environments actively reinforce their own characteristics over time, while undifferentiated environments "stimulate a broad range of behavior and provide ambiguous guidance" (Holland, 1973, p. 34), being more flexible and open to a variety of inputs and influences. Until a particular type becomes dominant, a wider range of behaviors, values, attitudes, and expectations will be accommodated and encouraged, contributing further to the environment's variegated image. Thus, undifferentiated human environments are probably more difficult to understand and characterize because of their lack of clear focus.

The degree of consistency among types, that is, their similarity, also adds to the dynamics of human aggregates. For example, Holland (1983) presents his six personality-occupational interest types in a hexagonal arrangement that defines the degree of similarity between any two types (see Figure 2.2). Beginning at the top of the figure and moving clockwise, Realistic types are followed in order by

Figure 2.2. Relationship of Holland Interest Types

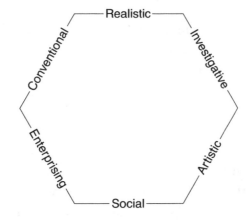

Investigative, Artistic, Social, Enterprising, and Conventional types. Types that are adjacent on the hexagon, for example, Social and Enterprising types, are presumed to share greater similarity than types that are opposite, such as Artistic and Conventional types.

In Clark and Trow's typology, students in the Academic subculture share common ground with Nonconformists in their involvement with ideas and are therefore more consistent on that dimension. However, students in the Vocational subculture are neither intellectually oriented nor inclined toward involvement with the institution and consequently are inconsistent with those in the Academic subculture. Astin's (1993) typology can also serve to illustrate this point; Status Strivers might be thought of as dissimilar to and inconsistent with Social Activists. In Myers-Briggs terminology, an ENTP type (extraverted, intuitive, thinking, and perceiving) can be said to have greater similarity with an ENFP type (extraverted, intuitive, feeling, perceiving), than with an ISFJ type (introverted, sensing, feeling, judging), because of their shared orientations toward extraversion, intuition, and perception. Finally, from Kolb's (1983) model, an assimilator's preferences include the same emphasis on abstract concepts found among convergers but are dissimilar with respect to their preference for reflective over active modes of learning.

Highly consistent environments contain individuals of similar types, and inconsistent environments are made up of individuals who are divergent types. Thus, according to Holland (1973), "consistent environments provide similar rewards and demands; inconsistent environments provide divergent rewards and demands" (p. 34). In summary, human environments most easily distinguished are those dominated by a single particular type (that is, they are highly differentiated) and the presence of other types who are most similar to the dominant type (that is, they are highly consistent). Both quantitative (differentiation) and qualitative (consistency) aspects are important distinctions for understanding the most likely dynamics of any particular human aggregate. An implicit goal in these conceptions is the achievement of person-environment congruence.

Person-Environment Congruence

Person-environment congruence refers to the degree of fit between persons and environments. A person is said to be congruent with an environment if his or her type is the same or nearly the same as the dominant type within that environment. Thus, an Artistic type experiences person-environment congruence within a theater arts department, and a Social-Enterprising type is congruent with a social fraternity comprised mainly of business majors. Dissimilarity with the environment's dominant characteristic (such as a Conventional type in an artistically dominated environment) results in incongruence and discomfort.

The degree of person-environment congruence is predictive of an individual's attraction to and satisfaction or stability within an environment. Individuals who share much in common with an environment are presumed to be most attracted to that environment. Once inside, the person is likely to be encouraged for exactly those behaviors, values, attitudes, and expectations that attracted him or her to that environment in the first place, thus reinforcing person-environment similarities. Consequently, the likelihood of remaining in that environment is quite high. Conversely, since people are presumed to prefer and be satisfied with a state of congruence rather than incongruence, a person is not likely to be attracted to an environment that bears little resemblance to his or her characteristics. If placed inside an incompatible environment, there is less chance of being reinforced for preferred behaviors, values, attitudes, and expectations, and the likelihood of leaving that environment is increased significantly. Congruent person-environment combinations allow individuals to exercise their strengths, "but of equal importance, [they also allow them] to avoid the activities [they] dislike, the demands for competencies [they] lack, the tasks and self-images [they] do not value, and the situations in which [their] personality traits are not encouraged" (Holland, 1973, p. 38). Thus, perhaps the most important question to be addressed, much like Sarah's inquiry in the opening scenario to this chapter, is whether or not a person seems to fit within any particular environment. Evidence of a high degree of person-environment congruence is usually apparent in higher satisfaction, a desire to persist, and ultimately greater retention (Smart, Feldman, & Ethington, 2000).

Since person-environment congruence is hypothesized to contribute to satisfaction and stability through selective reinforcement, by implication, lack of congruence must lead to dissatisfaction and instability, a condition that is likely to be resolved in one of three ways: by seeking a new and congruent environment; by remaking the present environment; or by adapting behavior to the dominant characteristics of the present environment. The option an individual is likely to exercise depends on the degrees of differentiation and consistency characterizing the environment as well as the individual. A highly differentiated and consistent environment is thought to be resistant to change in that its strongest tendency is to reinforce itself. The same can be said about an individual whose characteristic profile is highly focused (differentiated) and consistent. Therefore, when a highly focused individual is placed in a highly focused, but incongruent environment, that individual is most likely to leave and seek a new, more congruent environment, as may eventually be the case with Randall, the African American student in the opening scenario who expressed concerns about seeing only white faces while in between classes. However, as Holland (1983) hypothesized, "Persons with undifferentiated and inconsistent personality patterns tend to adapt to incongruence by changing their own behavior and personality pattern to achieve greater congruence with their environment" (p. 42). The option of remaking the environment is most likely to be selected by a differentiated and consistent individual who finds him or herself in an unfocused environment.

These hypotheses underscore the importance of aggregate characteristics for influencing members' behaviors, that is, whether they are likely to adapt to, leave, or try to change an environment. Although these formulations were derived specifically from the study of vocational interest behavior, Holland concluded that they appear, as well, to be "applicable to other phenomena, to educational and social behavior" (Holland, p. 42). It seems reasonable then to expect, for example, that Clark and Trow's (1966) Vocational subculture would be more congruent in some institutional cultures than others and that the closer a student resembles that subculture the less likely adaptation would occur in a culture dominated by a different type (such as Academic), and likewise with the other models of human environments presented here. Collectively they illustrate the potential power of homogenous groupings on campus and the importance of person-environment congruence as a source of attraction to the institution, and satisfaction and stability once within.

In summary, the human aggregate models and concepts examined in this chapter offer useful descriptive, as well as prescriptive, tools for identifying and constructing, to educational advantage, the patterns campus environments acquire as a result of the various types of people who occupy them. Development of personal identity is a major life task associated with the college experience (Chickering & Reisser, 1993), and these various aggregate models, in particular, have much potential for informing the design of educational environments, from residential settings (for example, living-learning centers and theme houses) and freshman interest groups to student organizations and special student services. Furthermore, these concepts (as discussed in subsequent chapters) can help in unraveling the significant challenges of diversifying institutional profiles and in responding more successfully to the needs of underrepresented students.

3

Organizational Environments
How Institutional Goals Are Achieved

Consider the following scene as Fran, a junior earth sciences major, returns to campus following a summer term away to discover that a few things had changed since the time she was elected to a leadership position for an undergraduate student organization.

Scenario: That's Not How We Do Things!

"But that's not what we're about!" said Fran in frustration with the university's new procedures for registering student activities. As the newly elected chair of an undergraduate women's environmental advocacy group, Students for a Healthy Environment (SHE), Fran had just returned to campus following a summer internship with the Department of Interior in Alaska to discover that the system for organizing and funding campus organizations had changed drastically since the previous semester.

"If we have to do all these forms and go through this review process each time, we'll never be able to complete the programs we planned for this semester. What was wrong with the way we used to do things around here?!" Apparently, the new director of campus organizations and activities had restructured her administrative unit to reflect a new emphasis on efficiency and accountability in the allocation of student fees. Implementation of new application materials and forms, as well as an additional and time-consuming review process, placed more responsibility on student leaders to submit plans and proposals one semester in advance. "I have nothing against being responsible for what we do," Fran reasoned with the new director, "but this really discourages us from suggesting ideas if we have to complete all those materials and wait that long before we get approval."

Fran's experiences with her introductory sociology course weren't all that good either that semester. She was finally able to get into a class that she deferred her first year due to scheduling conflicts. "You wouldn't believe it!" she exclaimed in a conversation with her advisor, "two hundred and sixty of us in a room with 225 seats; you can hardly see the board!" She continued, "What the professor has to say is really interesting, but we never have time to discuss any of her ideas or what we read about that week in one of our books. Most of the students standing in the back leave before the end of the class period."

Back in Williams Hall, though, Fran was at home. One of the five living-learning experiences available to students on campus, it was a place where her leadership skills were frequently challenged as a "wing convener," whose responsibility it was to coordinate the agenda and activities of the community team members on each of the floors in her wing of the building.

"My hands are going to be full this semester," she commented to her advisor, "with all the goals we've set for getting people involved." Fran looked forward to and enjoyed these kinds of opportunities, finding them to be a good fit for her skills and interests in planning and organization. Communication and problem solving were also two areas she enjoyed but had not had much experience with prior to assuming her current responsibilities in Williams. "Around there, everybody gets a chance to make a difference; it just wouldn't work if people weren't involved," she said.

The surprise, frustration, challenge, and excitement in Fran's observations on returning to her college betray the effects of dimensions not accounted for in the environment thus far in our analysis.

In all settings are found varying degrees of organized patterns of structure and process that evolve for purposes of achieving specific goals. "Getting organized" is a common practice in colleges and universities that shapes and influences the behavior of staff in administrative units, faculty in academic departments and classrooms, students in residence halls, student groups, and campus services. Whether in the form of expectations for greater efficiencies, as with the new registration procedures imposed on Fran's student group, the economies of scale in her sociology class, or the complexity of roles and responsibilities available in her residence hall, decisions about the goals to be achieved and the resources to be allocated to them create organizational infrastructures that significantly shape and influence the behavior of individuals in environments. Developing a language for identifying and assessing the effects of these organizational dimensions is the purpose of this chapter.

The Nature of Organized Environments

The notion that human environments, such as schools, workplaces, hospitals, clubs, and churches, are often characterized by planned, systematic, and organized structures that affect their functioning is an idea perhaps first explored systematically in the work of the German sociologist Max Weber (1947). Weber articulated a series of observations and propositions about modern bureaucracies that formed much of the groundwork for understanding how organizations function (at least from a conventional-bureaucratic perspective). Organizations, unlike other social groupings, are "deliberately constructed and reconstructed to seek specific goals" (Parsons, 1960 cited in Etzioni, 1964, p. 3).

As organizations, colleges and universities seek to educate students (typically measured, for example, by numbers of courses taught, students graduated, or increased test scores), to construct and disseminate knowledge (as indicated by research grants and faculty publications), and to serve the community (reflected in consultation with and participation in professional and related groups).

Etzioni (1964) framed his discussion of organizations by reference to three key characteristics.

> Organizations are characterized by: (1) divisions of labor, power, and communication responsibilities, divisions which are not random or traditionally patterned, but deliberately planned to enhance the realization of specific goals; (2) the presence of one or more power centers which control the concerted efforts of the organization and direct them toward its goals; these power centers also must review continuously the organization's performance and re-pattern its structure, where necessary, to increase its efficiency; (3) substitution of personnel, i.e., unsatisfactory persons can be removed and others assigned their tasks. The organization can also recombine its personnel through transfer and promotion. [Etzioni, 1964, p. 3]

Thus, colleges and universities exhibit these characteristics as academic departments are organized, and units and offices report to deans and administrators about assigned responsibilities and allocated resources (division of labor); administrators, staff, and faculty plan, guide, and implement policies, programs, and practices designed to meet institutional goals (distribution of power); and procedures for peer and administrative review provide for the evaluation of personnel and their promotion or dismissal when appropriate. On a typical college campus most students spend a good deal of time in implicitly or explicitly purposeful environments. For Fran in the opening scenario, these environments included the student organization she led, the sociology class she attended, and the residence hall where she lived. These environments are all designed to achieve certain ends, and their success is often gauged by the extent to which they do so, or in other words, by their effectiveness.

The tendency to "get organized to get things done" is a natural one, and in accomplishing such a task there are a number of decisions that must be made along the way. Who is in charge? How will decisions about distributing resources be made? By what rules, if any, will the organization function? What must be accomplished and how fast? The decisions made with respect to these questions create a variety of organizational structures or systems in an environment that, in turn, affect an environment's overall design and functioning as well as an individual's attraction to, functioning, and satisfaction within that environment.

Anatomy of Organized Environments

Organizations can be thought of as environments with a purpose. In that sense, all environments have purposes, some expressed and some implied. Whether an organized environment is defined by a clearly stated mission, complete with targeted goals and objectives, or just an intuited, consensual understanding about its overall purpose, decisions about where the organization is going and what and how various resources should be expended must be made.

Some of the most revealing moments in organized environments (whether tightly or loosely arranged) come when resources are cut, boundaries of authority are ignored, or someone proposes the development of new programs and practices. Such moments in an organization always seem to stimulate discussions about organizational purposes and traditions as well as the inevitable questions about whether it can afford to maintain current programs or implement new initiatives. This backdrop of collective purposes, decision making, and resources gives rise to the organized infrastructure of any purposeful environment, such as a college or university, a classroom, a residence hall, an academic department, or a student organization.

Organized infrastructures take on many different forms depending on what aspects are examined in the environment (Kuh, 1996). For example, a conventional, rational-bureaucratic view may focus on a description of the formal functions, responsibilities, and reporting lines of the infrastructure; other conventional perspectives, such as the collegial and political views, might focus respectively on mechanisms of representation and persuasion or power and conflict resolution. From the perspective of postconventional views, including organized anarchy, organizational culture, and learning organizations, the organizational infrastructure may be described as points of disjuncture, informal channels of communication, the influence of consensual values, traditions, history, and various tensions of fluidity and structure. Regardless of the lens used to understand it, what ultimately comprises this environmental infrastructure is a function of the kinds of concerns often raised by participants and illustrated in the following questions: How shall we divide up the work? How will decisions be made? By what rules will we function? How shall members be rewarded for their work? How much should we be expected to do? How much should it cost to do what we do? How do members feel about their involvement and work?

Each of these questions presents the opportunity to consider options, which, in turn, will result in certain structures being imposed on the environment. Those structures create the organizational dimensions of the environment. Consideration of each structure is important for understanding the nature of intentional systems and how organizational aspects shape the character of human environments. Seven of these structural components are overviewed here: complexity, centralization, formalization, stratification, production, efficiency, and morale. Varying emphases on these organizational components lend themselves to the creation of different characteristic environments, from fixed to fluid, ultimately affecting the extent to which environmental goals are achieved.

Complexity

Questions about the division of work and responsibilities in a setting can lead to numerous options of environmental design. Should assignment of duties be fixed or rotated? Should some individuals assume responsibility for certain functional specialties or certain whole projects? Who should work with whom? Which arrangements more clearly communicate organizational purposes, goals, and functions? What sort of preparation, credentials, or ongoing training, if any, is required to complete these assignments?

Such questions have to do with the degree of organizational complexity present in an environment. Organizational complexity concerns the number of occupational subunits and specialties present, as well as the intensity and extensity of the knowledge and expertise required in them (professionalization) (Hage & Aiken, 1970). Obviously, colleges and universities are characterized by high degrees of complexity, where a variety of highly credentialed professionals conduct the business of postsecondary education. Many different departmental subunits require a variety of specialties dedicated to meeting the needs of campus constituents. Departments of natural sciences require advanced training and preparation of appropriate personnel in order to meet the goals, for example, of teaching chemistry and biology courses. Career planning and placement offices require the services of professional counselors who can effectively assist students in sorting through the maze of academic and occupational interests, skills, and choices. In the context of various campus subenvironments, such as student organizations or departmental classes, complexity might be apparent in the number of discussion groups created in a classroom or the number of specialized task groups in student organizations or residence hall governments.

Just how many units and subunits serve the purposes of the organization and how should they be arranged? This is the fundamental concern of organizational complexity. This dimension is also evident in "the degree to which members of an organization attempt to gain greater knowledge about their respective work activities and the overall activities of their organization" (Hage & Aiken, 1970, p. 18). Colleges and universities are organizations that generally place a good deal of emphasis on staff development and continuing education. Often, decisions have to be made in complicated contexts that require judgment and knowledge of many aspects. In that sense, educational institutions and their various subunits are high in complexity, an inherent quality of professional work environments.

Centralization

Concerns about decision making in an environment also lead to various design options. Who has the power to make decisions for others in the organization? What kinds of decisions require greater participation? Do we decide by majority vote or by consensus? Who decides which way to go when there are two competing interests? How do we respond to two equally compelling choices? Such questions are concerned with the use of power in an organization, that is, its degree of centralization.

> Organizational centralization refers to the way in which power is distributed in a setting. Power is the "capacity of one social position to set the conditions under which other social positions must perform, that is, the capacity of one social position to determine the actions of other social positions . . . ." Every organization needs to make decisions about the allocation of its funds, the promotion of its personnel, and the initiation of new programs. Responsibilities for these decisions must be allocated to some jobs; this helps ensure coordination of many different occupations. [Hage & Aiken, 1970. p. 19]

Thus colleges must decide what courses will be offered and when they will be scheduled, the number, type, and due date of assignments for individual classes, and how various budgets will be allocated, spent, and accounted for. Organizations vary widely in how such decisions are made. Those in which few individuals share this power are said to be highly centralized (or autocratic and authoritarian); organizations where many share formal power with respect to such decisions (as might be the case, for example, under an egalitarian collegial model) are described as having a low degree of centralization or are said to be "decentralized." In the context of a classroom setting, for example, a high degree of centralization might be evident when an instructor makes all decisions about the course syllabus, such as assigned readings and papers, and relies principally on lecture methods of presentation. In contrast, a seminar format where students and instructor work collaboratively to create the syllabus around emerging student interests and learning styles, where grading practices are negotiated, and where an open discussion format is preferred might be described as a decentralized learning environment. Likewise, a student organization or a residence hall association might exhibit similar characteristics depending on how decisions are made about various programs and resources. Highly centralized organizations simply have fewer participants making various decisions.

Formalization

The focus on rules and regulations goes hand in hand with a discussion of power and centralization in an organization. Power is often formalized and distributed through established rules. Some rules are very explicit and found in formal, written documents; others are more implicit, general in scope, and at times only verbally communicated in passing or conveyed symbolically (such as those imbedded in organizational culture). What sort of rules will guide the organization? How specific will they need to be? What concerns will the rules address? How will members know the rules? How will they be enforced? Will there be any exceptions to them? What are the consequences of rule infractions? All of these concerns reflect issues of the degree of formalization present in any organized system.

Getting organized often means developing a set of guidelines and rules for operating, thereby establishing an organization's degree of formalization. More specifically, formalization refers to the importance of rules and regulations (whether formally written or customarily understood) in an organization (Hage & Aiken, 1970). Three aspects are contained in this concept: the number of rules (highly formalized organizations are characterized by many rules); the specificity of established rules (highly formalized units establish rules that are explicit and specific in nature); and the extent to which such rules are enforced (highly formalized organizations place greater emphasis on rule enforcement).

Rules are thought to provide guidelines for efficient functioning and, in doing so, they lend a certain degree of predictability to organizational efforts. Thus for example, course catalogs and registration materials codify when and where classes will meet. Evidence for the degree of formalization in various campus environments might be reflected, for example, in the nature of student codes, administrative manuals and job descriptions, college catalogs, course syllabi, organizational constitutions and bylaws, or customary understandings of "how things are done." High degrees of formalization are associated with organizational rigidity and inflexibility (a common limitation of the rational-bureaucratic model). Low degrees of formalization lend themselves to organizational fluidity and flexibility. Recall in the opening scenario that it was the increase in formalization instituted by the new director of campus organizations and activities that Fran found most frustrating on her return to school.

Stratification

Questions about rewards in an organization often reveal conditions of status, position, and favor. Whose work is given greater priority and esteem? Are there differing levels of remuneration associated with differing functions? What are the perks of power and position in the organization and how are they used? How do individuals lower in the organizational structure gain access to those higher (in the case of a hierarchical arrangement)? Are rewards used to maintain the status quo or to stimulate change? These are all questions about the degree of stratification in an organization, that is, the differential distribution of its rewards (Hage & Aiken, 1970).

Highly stratified systems have many different levels of status, distinguished by differential rewards (such as income, esteem, and prestige). Those at higher status levels receive higher recognition and rewards (such as parking spaces!) than those at lower status levels. Stratification is also a reflection of the degree of mobility members have in moving from lower to higher status levels in the organization. Highly stratified systems tend to preserve status distinctions for purposes of maintaining current reward structures; they also tend to restrict mobility of members. While the application of power and rules exert a conforming influence on an organized system, stratification tends to be more divisive since reward structures are often cast into a competitive framework.

The relevance of this concept can be further understood in applying it to the various organized systems that affect students' campus experiences. For example, classrooms might appear to be highly stratified where distances between students and instructor are maintained by use of formal titles and invocation of formal academic authority. Likewise, high stratification might be apparent in a student organization where rewards (such as access to office space and equipment, titles, and campus recognition) are differentially distributed to leaders of the group. So too, an emphasis on stratification might be evident in a residence hall system where head residents and resident assistants are distinguished significantly from others by higher status and appreciably better living arrangements. Other analogous reflections of stratification in a college setting are typically associated with factors such as class level (seniors have greater claim on campus than freshman students), major (students majoring in "hard" sciences may be perceived by peers to possess greater intellectual acuity than students majoring in education), or status (athletes may have access to preferential course schedules and special living arrangements on campus). Organizationally, environments characterized by high degrees of stratification tend to divide members, and those who share disproportionately in the accrued rewards of such a system have a vested interest in maintaining the status quo.

Production

The value of any organization is often assessed by what it does, most frequently in terms of what it produces (especially from the perspective of a rational-bureaucratic model). To justify any organized unit that does nothing, particularly in times of restricted resources, is to ask the impossible. Since organizations are purposeful systems, success is more times than not measured in terms of how many "this-and-thats" have been achieved, produced, or discovered in reference to whatever index seems appropriate to those who must make such decisions. A fair year is "doing about the same as last year"; a good year is "exceeding last year's output"; and a great year means "doubling projected goals." Trouble can be nearby when the year ends in something less. So academic departments must produce graduates, faculty must publish papers, and staff must offer more programs to more people. Such issues relate to the relative emphasis on quantity or quality of an organization's products or services, that is, its level of production (Hage & Aiken, 1970).

All organizations need to produce, for reasons of justifying their existence, for maintaining current resources or attracting additional ones, and for creating a sense of accomplishment among members who contribute to the organization's goals. When quantity of production is high, or at least sufficient, it is presumed that the system is functioning well. A drop in quantity of production often signals a need for reexamination and evaluation. As organized systems, colleges are also often driven by production mandates, whether from student consumers, who request certain classes to be held more frequently, or from trustees, who look at the number of graduates placed from various programs as an indicator of fulfilling institutional mission. Student credit hours, program enrollments, FTE faculty, retention rates, proportion of students of color, graduation figures, placement goals, students served, advisee contact appointments, hours devoted to teaching, research activities, public or professional service, number of research grants, manuscripts published, programs sponsored, term papers assigned, and books read, to list a few, are all familiar indicators of production in an academic environment. Annual reports teem with such data, the assumption often being that an increase from year to year on many of these measures is indicative of organizational improvement. Further, especially as budgets decline, such measures are invoked and examined for purposes of reallocating resources to units that are perceived to have a greater need, that is, ironically those units that are most productive.

How much to produce, though, is often a trade-off with the quality of production. Student credit hour production can be stimulated by increasing enrollments and increasing class size. Such strategies, in lowering the ratio of students to faculty and thus using resources (faculty salaries) more efficiently, take advantage of an economy of scale. Allowing one hundred students in a classroom increases production fourfold in comparison to restricting enrollment to twenty-five. A higher number of students admitted to a program usually results in a higher number of graduates from the program. In both examples, however, questions about the quality of student experiences must figure in any formula of institutional success. Does having more students in a particular classroom affect the quality of intellectual exchange known to contribute to the development of their critical reasoning abilities? Will students have fewer opportunities to communicate in the form of written papers and essays in such a setting? Will there be sufficient time for the instructor to give quality feedback to all students enrolled in the class? In terms of overall program enrollment, will the quality of advising and student-faculty contacts be adversely affected by a significant increase? Answers to such questions have implications for not only the productivity of various institutional environments but also their ability to meet educational goals.

Efficiency

Concerns about "what and how many" an organization produces are usually accompanied by questions about costs. Are we getting our money's worth? Can more be produced for the same overall cost? Can we save with less? How do we cut back? What is the bottom line? These are all concerns about organizational efficiency and reflect the relative emphasis on cost reduction of an organization's products or services (Hage & Aiken, 1970).

Similar to the assumptions about productivity discussed in the previous section, maximum efficiency is presumed to reflect a smooth functioning system. If the highest production levels are being realized from the fewest resources, then why tinker with a system that works so well? Like other complex organizations, colleges and universities emphasize the efficient use of resources by a variety of institutional strategies. For example, restricting access to copying machines, raising minimum quotas on enrollments before a course is allowed to be offered, and assigning lower salaried graduate teaching assistants to large introductory courses all have the effect of lowering the cost of production. Ensuring full occupancy rates in residence halls, usually by over-booking space 10 to 15 percent, and keeping classrooms full also reduce the cost of physical plant investments.

Although cost reduction is a necessary goal in any organized system, it is particularly difficult to measure and evaluate in the context of an academic setting. Colleges and universities are in the business of creating new ideas and programs responsive to changing conditions and needs. New ideas and programs are inherently risky inasmuch as they may or may not succeed. Failures are detrimental to the efficient use of resources because productivity is interrupted and resources are apparently diminished. In that respect, should a different standard of efficiency apply to an educational institution where the mission itself often challenges conventional norms of productivity and resource use? What is an efficient number of resources to produce a graduate of a program? A publication in a professional journal? A grade of B in a particular course? What is the cost of a new idea? Benchmarks are notoriously absent in such discussions.

Furthermore, without a clear and succinct definition of the goals of an organized system, how can successful accomplishment of such goals be demonstrated? What exactly are the goals of a college? Is there agreement on such matters? Whose point of view counts? Does a graduate of a teacher education program who fails to gain employment as a teacher but who uses transferable skills to pursue a career in another area, or rather chooses to become a full-time parent, count as a failure or success? Answers to such questions are inherently messy and value laden, and serve to complicate discussions about efficiency in higher education. Unfortunately, vague and elusive outcomes of the college experience (such as development of personal autonomy or tolerance for ambiguity) are often reduced to convenient measures that may or may not capture the essence of such goals. That immediately raises questions about what is or is not an efficient use of resources, to which satisfactory answers simply may not exist. Nonetheless, like all other organized systems, colleges and universities are held accountable and must address concerns of efficiency, however challenging they may be.

Morale

Somewhere in the mix of these concerns lies a fundamental question about the satisfaction of the members and participants in an organized system. Are members excited about their assignments and work? Do they respond positively to those with whom they work? Is there a general feeling of goodwill and satisfaction among participants? Although not an organizational structure in itself, morale, or satisfaction, is a summary measure of many aspects associated with participating in any particular organized system, and it is usually reflected in the rate of turnover in the system.

Higher morale is usually associated with lower turnover, and higher turnover is often reflective of lower morale. For example, high student absenteeism in a particular class, or lack of student involvement in a particular student organization, might be indicative of general dissatisfaction with various aspects of those organized systems. At the institutional level, attrition rates provide a measure of turnover, and an increase on such indicators warrants serious concern on the part of campus administrators to identify sources of student dissatisfaction and low morale. Human organizations, if they are to survive, must "maintain a minimal level of morale and loyalty" (Hage

& Aiken, 1970, p.27) among their members. Failure to do so may lead to other difficulties (such as lower efficiency, violations of rules, subterfuge, and a general lowering of productivity). These consequences may ultimately undermine the purposes and goals of the organized system, as members cease to fulfill their roles and eventually withdraw from the system. This may be the impending fate of many students in the opening scenario as they grow tired of the anonymous atmosphere in Fran's large sociology section. As learners in a purposeful classroom environment, the lack of opportunity to engage in discussion of the topics may continue to challenge their morale to the point that some simply withdraw from the setting and get notes from somebody else.

Dynamics of Organized Environments

The organizational structures and characteristics discussed above combine to create certain styles, readily described in varying degrees of environmental flexibility or dynamism. Hage and Aiken (1970) posited that organized systems can be characterized generally along a continuum from dynamic to static. At one end are dynamic environments that are flexible in design and respond easily to change; at the other end are static environments that tend to be more rigid in design and therefore resist change. The extent to which any environment, whether a classroom, a department office, a student organization, or a residence hall, is likely to exhibit dynamic or static organizational characteristics can be understood with reference to the above structures and features—complexity, centralization, formalization, stratification, production, efficiency, and morale.

Of particular importance is understanding how these organizational structures contribute to the nature of dynamic systems most often associated with successful educational experiences. According to Hage and Aiken (1970), the structural arrangements of dynamically organized environments combine a higher degree of complexity with lower centralization, formalization, stratification, efficiency, and a relative emphasis on the quality (in contrast to quantity) of their products or services. In the context of a classroom environment, high complexity may be apparent in references to multiple perspectives on topics and in the nature and complexity of assignments and learning tasks. The degrees of centralization and formalization (two aspects that often work hand in hand) may be lowered by engaging students actively in the planning and determination of the course syllabus and by encouraging a variety of creative options for completing course goals (for example, cooperative projects, independent assignments, or multiple formats). This, of course, is a very labor-intensive process for instructors and students alike. Evaluating essay exams and other unique learning products, such as multimedia web pages, requires much more time and effort on the part of the instructor than evaluating machine-scored, multiple-choice exams and therefore lowers the degree of efficiency in the setting. However, such environments are highly conducive to change and innovation, the essence of powerful educational systems responsive to individual needs (Strange, 1981; 1983b).

Static environments, on the other hand, tend to discourage change and innovation and are characterized by lower degrees of complexity, higher centralization, formalization, stratification, efficiency, and a relative emphasis on the quantity of their products or services. Applying this template again to a classroom setting, it becomes apparent how such an arrangement might discourage creativity and innovation, and therefore active learning. A course syllabus where only the instructor has input exacts little investment from students with respect to their learning interests and goals; class assignments that are highly structured, and explicitly and rigidly formatted, are less likely to be responsive to individual learning styles and needs; insistence on formal titles and status diminishes the kind of personalized atmosphere supportive of the risk-taking inherent to learning new ideas; and an overemphasis on efficiency ("We just don't have time to explore that.") and quantity of readings and assignments (at the expense of quality) tends to invoke a "just get it done" attitude among students as the course unfolds. A key point in this analysis is that powerful developmental environments, whether in the classroom, student organization meeting, or residence hall association, are those that exhibit characteristics of dynamic organizations, where individual differences are appreciated, participation is expected, interactions are personal rather than functional, and risk-taking is encouraged (see Exhibit 3.1) (Strange, 1983b).

The degree to which any organized environment is static or dynamic can also potentially affect the morale of participants in the setting, depending on individual differences. For example, consider

Exhibit 3.1. Complex Organizations Versus Developmental Environments

Complex Organizations	Developmental Environments
• Uniformity, simplification, and routinization of procedures	• Appreciation for the unique and creative
• Minimize conflict and variance	• Encourage complexity, diversity, and controversy
• Centralize substantive decisions	• Maximize responsibility of participants in making decisions (role-taking)
• Clear stratification of authority and responsibility	• Encourage personalism and community by minimizing status and power
• Formalize and specify regulations for accurate accountability	• Minimize formality to create levels of ambiguity and flexibility in response to individual need
• Maximize achievement per unit of time and resource	• Maximize time and resource per unit of achievement
• Interactions based on functional responsibilities	• Interactions based on personal modeling and mentoring
• Minimize risk-taking to maximize efficient use of resources	• Encourage opportunities for risk taking to maximize educational effectiveness

Source: Strange, 1983b, p. 5.

the case of a static classroom environment (rational-bureaucratic) where the professor makes all the decisions about the timing and content of what is taught (high centralization), where assignments are governed by highly specific and inflexible rules (high formalization), where few questions or comments are encouraged for fear of wasting time (high emphasis on production and efficiency), and where examinations assess simple recall of information (low complexity). This classroom environment may be comforting to some students, who, for example, hold assumptions reflective of a dependent-conforming (Harvey, Hunt, & Schroder, 1961) level of development, but it may also be very boring and unchallenging to other students with a different set of assumptions about what it means to learn, such as those reflective of a relativistic (Perry, 1970) or independent self-reliant (Harvey, Hunt, & Schroder, 1961) stage.

Various personality styles may respond differently to this same environment as well. Sensing and judging Myers-Briggs types (Myers, 1980), with their emphasis on specificity and closure, or Conventional and Realistic Holland types (Holland, 1973), whose orientation is toward order and organization in their environment, might enjoy the routine and standardization of such a class, but the consequent high structure may frustrate intuitive perceivers and Artistic or Social types, who share many different and opposing preferences. As another example, student organizations structured around a hierarchical model of constitutionally based roles and powers (often rational-bureaucratic in style) may be less attractive to female students socialized in an ethic of care and "connectedness" (Forrest, Hotelling, & Kuk, 1986; Gilligan, 1982), preferring a more heterarchical, fluid, and less legalistic arrangement.

A similar person-environment dynamic may apply to understanding attraction and satisfaction of students in a residence hall setting. The overall degree of organizational structure in the hall, as is reflected in the manner in which goals are set, rules implemented and enforced, policies decided, and resources expended, may or may not be compatible with the characteristics of those students living there. For example, residents who are limited in their knowledge of organizational leadership and participation, or who are simply inexperienced, may not be ready to assume the responsibilities of an intentional democratic community (Crookston, 1974). A more highly structured and static organizational environment may be appropriate in such cases. On the other hand, a more advanced student group, whose talents and styles have been tested in a variety of settings, may become disinterested and turned off by a highly structured system that allows for little student input and involvement. It is therefore critical for residence life professionals, along with faculty and other student affairs administrators, to have an accurate understanding of the developmental characteristics of students as a source of information for encouraging an appropriate organizational environment (Strange, 1983b).

Organizational Performances

We conclude this discussion of the organizational dimensions of human environments with reference to what Hage (1980) has argued are the essential four performances of organizational functioning: innovation, efficiency, quantity of production, and morale.

These indicators are "central to any theory involving how well an organization is doing . . . [and] are necessary for the survival of [any] organization. If all the workers [e.g., staff, faculty, students] quit or costs skyrocket; if there is never any product [service] change or worst of all, there is no production [service] whatsoever, then the organization presumably ceases to exist" (Hage, 1980, p. 35). Although the language of his comments ("production") may reflect an exclusive focus on business-like organizations, the importance of Hage's four performances is also clear within the context of an educational institution. Obviously, colleges or universities could not exist if low morale led to high attrition among students, faculty, and staff. Turnover is unsettling to any organization, and it contributes further to a sense among those remaining that perhaps "something is wrong." From the human relations tradition in organizational research comes the importance of member morale and satisfaction in understanding organizational functioning. Satisfied members tend to remain productive in the organization longer; dissatisfied members are at risk for becoming unproductive or just dropping out.

Innovation, too, is an important performance criterion for colleges and universities. As dynamic institutions, colleges must be responsive to societal conditions, reflecting changes in programs and curricula in order to continue to attract a sufficient student enrollment base. The foundation of any institution of higher learning must support the creation and implementation of new ideas and practices for purposes of expanding our understanding of the world around us and for improving its functioning. In that sense, colleges and universities, in addition to their role as transmitters of culture, are institutions dedicated to innovation. Resistance to change and innovation threatens the very ethos of any organization committed to learning.

Educational institutions must be productive. Programs must be offered, courses must be taught, students must graduate, grants must be procured, research must be conducted, and manuscripts must be published. Annual reports typically highlight increases on various measures (students served, graduates placed, student credit hours generated) over the previous year and bemoan any decreases ("enrollments are down"). Finally, as important as all of our institutional goals are, they can only be accomplished with finite resources. Striving for efficiency is a mandate of public and private trust for colleges and universities, as the competition for support increases and pressures for accountability persist, both from sources that fund them and consumers that use them. Indeed, being responsive to change, being productive and efficient, and supporting the morale of members is a useful template for successful performance in any organizational subunit of a college or university, whether a classroom, an administrative office, a service center, a student organization, or a residence hall.

Challenges of Organizational Size

Whether or not an organization is able to maintain a dynamic or static quality, and how well an organization functions with respect to the above performances, has much to do with organizational size. As size increases, an organization develops a different set of characteristics that distinguishes it from smaller, human-scale systems. These characteristics, in turn, have certain effects on organizational performances, including the morale of members.

Among key organizational issues that challenge and shape collegiate environments today are those related to organizational size. Size of institutions has become a concern only recently in the history of American higher education. Since World War II, and especially during the 1960s when the higher education community responded to unusual demands for access and opportunity, colleges and universities grew rapidly, fed by an "economy of scale" and the infusion of federal dollars. Institutional growth became the order of the day. Classrooms grew larger, new high-rise residence halls were built, and faculty and staff were hired in unprecedented numbers to accommodate quickly expanding enrollments. By the end of the 1960s, large campuses of over 10,000 students enrolled the majority of college students. This expansion, both in the number and size of postsecondary institutions, resulted in tremendous strides forward in the higher education community. New populations were served (Cross, 1971); campus-based research continued to fulfill its promise of unraveling the secrets of the universe; and graduates emerged with the key to the Information Age, ready to participate as members of a society on the verge of great things. At the same time, however, American higher education also began to reveal itself as increasingly impersonal, bureaucratic, and indifferent to the many and varied needs of individual students, features principally related to its new size. Boyer (1987) found this issue to be related to institutional mission:

Class size, like so many other aspects of teaching and learning, varies from one type of institution to another. Twenty-nine percent of the students at research universities report that "most" or "all" of their classes have more than one hundred students enrolled; at liberal arts colleges only 1 percent of the students report having most or all classes of this size. At the other end, only 5 percent of students at research universities said they had no classes larger than one hundred students. At liberal arts colleges, it was 80 percent. [p. 145]

Boyer went on to conclude that "one important way to measure a college's commitment to undergraduate education is to look at class size in general education" (p. 145).

Because of this increased reliance on an economy of scale for efficient use of resources, larger institutions are typically "overmanned" settings (Wicker, 1973), where too many people compete for too few opportunities for meaningful involvement and achievement. Chickering (1969) identified this as a condition of "redundancy." Generally speaking, larger institutions tend to be "overmanned" and "redundant," and smaller institutions tend to be "undermanned," that is, there are more opportunities for meaningful achievement than there are people to take advantage of them.

The issue of institutional size is a particularly crucial organizational concern in higher education with no easy solution. Blau (1973), in his classic study of academic organizations, identified the dilemma institutions face in that respect:

The ability of a university or college to recruit good faculty and good students and to attain and maintain a high academic reputation depends on conditions that in turn depend to a considerable extent on the large scope of the academic enterprise. High academic standing requires

specialized academic pursuits in a large number of diverse
fields, which simply cannot be developed in a small college. It also requires competing with other institutions for
the best faculty and the best students, and the financial
resources for doing so can rarely be mobilized by a small
academic institution. Once a top reputation has been
achieved, it attracts financial contributions, outstanding
students, and great scientists and scholars, helping to sustain the elite standing of the academic institution, and at
the same time fostering further growth. [p. 99–100]

The other side of the coin, Blau (1973) recognized, is imprinted
with the deleterious effects large size invariably brings to education
and that "endanger the quality of academic work. It [large size]
inevitably makes the academic institution more impersonal and
engenders bureaucratic developments in it, both of which reduce
its attraction for the best students and faculty members" (p. 100).
The trade-off, then, for an economy of scale in higher education is
the challenge educators face in supporting conditions known to be
related to a successful educational experience, such as a sense of
community, opportunities for involvement and creativity—in effect,
conditions that contribute to an "economy of learning" (Strange &
Hannah, 1994). Overall, as institutional size increases, such conditions are simply more difficult to create and maintain.

Organizational size also has implications for how people function and evaluate their experiences in a system. In a discussion of
organizational environment factors related to size, Moos (1986)
drew attention to one empirical conclusion: "As group size
increase[s], morale and attitudes become less positive, and absenteeism is more frequent" (p. 410). He went on to suggest that these
forces might have particular deleterious effects on "marginal individuals in large schools (i.e., schools with relatively overmanned
settings) [who] have a much lower sense of obligation to the school
than do non-marginal students" (p. 408). Banning (1989) con-

curred in his analysis of the impact of college environments on freshman students.

> [T]he ratio of persons per setting is critical to what happens to the people within the setting. In the undermanned setting [see Wicker, 1973], people more frequently serve in responsible positions, engage in actions that are challenging, perform activities that are important to the setting, engage in a wide range of activities, see themselves as important and responsible for the setting, and work hard to maintain the function of the setting. [p. 59]

The college campus offers numerous illustrations of the organizational dynamics highlighted in these observations. "Fighting the bureaucracy" becomes a rallying cry for all too many students attempting to negotiate the barriers inevitable in the organized systems of a large modern day university. Endless long lines, numbers instead of names, forms in triplicate, all take their toll on the human spirit at a time in students' lives when questions of identity and purpose (Chickering & Reisser, 1993) demand, and are better served by, a higher degree of individualization, personalism, and support (Widick, Knefelkamp, & Parker, 1975). Even the expressed goals of the academy—the development of intellect and reason—are jeopardized by the limitations of size. As Fran inquired with frustration in the opening scenario, what are the chances of any individual student posing a question, offering a comment, exchanging a point of view, or writing a position statement in a classroom with 200 students? What are the chances of any individual student assuming a position of responsibility in a residence hall where 900 students compete for only six available governance committee vacancies? The implications of this conclusion on organizational size are clear and consistent: Bigger is not better when it comes to education and learning. Perhaps it is no secret why large institutions tend to have higher attrition rates than smaller ones. The challenge to many institutions is to compensate for the problems of overmanning with the intentional development of smaller subenvironments, such as cluster colleges (Blau, 1973), residence hall units, student organizations, and class discussion sections.

This chapter began with the recognition that many features of human environments reflect the composition of various organizational structures that emerge in social systems for purposes of meeting specific goals. Dimensions of complexity, centralization, formalization, stratification, production, efficiency, and morale contribute to varying degrees of flexibility or rigidity in the environment. The resultant degree of environmental dynamism then, in turn, affects the organizational performances of innovation, efficiency, production, and morale, as mediated by the impact of organizational size. Finally, to be more responsive to students' individual learning needs, educational environments must be flexible, encourage innovation, and engage students as meaningful participants within the boundaries of various human scale designs.

4

Constructed Environments
Different Views Through Different Eyes

Scenario: There's Something About This Place

Returning from the first-year convocation ceremony where the president, several faculty members, key administrators, and the student body president explained some of the history and traditions of Adams College, Clare, a first semester pre-med major, was impressed with what she heard and experienced that day.

"There's something about this place; it just feels really neat to me," she said in a phone conversation with her parents that evening. "They're really serious about hitting the books early here. But I get a sense that they really care about how we do, too." Earlier that day, Clare was introduced to her "faculty coinvestigator," Dr. Williams, in the natural sciences division where they spent some time going over the curriculum and discussing the Adams program with a small group of other science majors.

"It was really interesting to hear about the research projects we can get involved with; they even have you over for dinner once a month to talk about how things are going!" she continued, amazed and excited.

Adams College had always considered the natural sciences to be among its strengths, and through recent grants from the National Science Foundation and Ford Foundation, had established an innovative, collaborative research program where interdisciplinary teams of students and faculty pursued various projects relevant to regional concerns.

"They asked me to join a project looking at some of the effects of acid rain here," Clare explained. "We even have a faculty member from philosophy and one from sociology on our team." Clare had worked on a few small projects before in high school lab with one of her science teachers. "But nothing like this!" she exclaimed. "It seems like they really emphasize working together as a team here and getting out and doing things, not just reading about things." Pictures of past teams and descriptions of the projects they completed lined the entry hallway in the Fischer Science Building where several of Clare's classes were held.

"It's exactly how I thought it would be, from the first day I spent here last March," she said, acknowledging her first impressions of the challenging but very supportive atmosphere she felt while participating in a campus visit weekend at Adams. "I'm really looking forward to the end-of-the-year banquet they have to celebrate what each team accomplishes!"

Out-of-class life also evoked distinct impressions at Adams College. Clare's orientation group became a key involvement group for her once matriculation was under way. "They really encourage us to join a student organization on campus and get involved. The first week I was here, someone asked me to become part of a committee whose job it was to talk to other freshman students about leadership opportunities. I was amazed at all the things you get to do in these groups."

Special value seemed to be placed on serving the needs of the community adjacent to Adams too. Clare remembered reading in a welcoming letter from the chair of the natural sciences department that "understanding of the world must be balanced with action to improve the world."

"It seems like everyone spends some of their time each week volunteering for something; I need to think about that myself, once I get all my schedule worked out," she thought.

For almost a decade, Adams College has offered a developmental transcript system whereby students are encouraged to identify, evaluate, and record their various campus involvement experiences with the guidance of a senior student peer advisor and a retired faculty mentor. At the completion of the degree, this transcript becomes part of the student's official academic record, complete with the college's seal and motto: "In Omni Experientia Eruditio" ("In Every Experience There Is Learning"). Clare's final note, after only one week at Adams, was "This place is really special!"

Clare's early experiences at Adams College in this scenario are less about the formal materials she was given to read as part of her orientation than they are about the specific impressions and intuited understandings communicated to her through conversations with others on campus, stories she heard, and artifacts, symbols, and rituals she observed and participated in. She felt compelled to work hard as a new student and, at the same time, she experienced a strong, positive atmosphere of caring and support in the process. What came through clearly were the values Adams College espoused, as well as the manner in which they were enacted. Emphases on academically challenging work, interdisciplinary teams, personalized relationships with faculty, whole learning, leadership opportunities beyond the classroom, and the need to serve others all merged to create a distinctive campus ethos that proved attractive and very satisfying to Clare, as she came to understand quickly that she had found a special place. She had always dreamed of college being like this. The notion that environments exert their influence on behavior through the mediated and subjective perceptions, or social constructions, of those who participate in them is the touchstone for this fourth perspective on human environments.

Perceptual, or socially constructed, models of the environment recognize that a consensus of individuals who perceive and characterize their environment constitutes a measure of environmental press or climate. These perceived characteristics of the environment, in turn, exert a directional influence on behavior (Moos, 1986). For example, inferred from the perspective of Clare, the press and social climate at Adams College is directed toward achievement in the natural sciences and a supportive atmosphere that encourages faculty-student collaboration in research and learning. A consensus of similar perspectives from other participants would suggest that such characteristics pervade the campus environment at Adams. Thus developing an understanding of any environment entails asking participants what they see and feel.

Seeing Is Believing

Differing from the physical, human aggregate, and organizational models discussed in the previous three chapters, constructed models of the environment focus on the subjective views and experiences of participant observers, assuming that environments are understood best through the collective perceptions of the individuals within them. Thus, although an environment can be measured independently as being seventy degrees Fahrenheit (a physical fact), it may seem "warm" to one person and "cool" to another, leading one individual to put on a sweater and another to take one off. Likewise, identically composed human aggregates may seem "friendly" to one person but "overbearing" to another. Similarly a high degree of formalization (many explicit rules), a feature of the organizational environment, may be reassuring to one participant yet restricting to another, with obvious consequences for their respective satisfaction.

At the core of these various perceptual approaches to human environments is the notion that examining collective personal perspectives of an environment (from inside participants as well as from outside observers) is critical for understanding how people are likely to react to those environments. Thus, whether individuals are attracted to a particular environment, or satisfied and stable within that environment, is a function of how they perceive, evaluate, and construct the environment. In effect, their perceptions are the reality of that environment for them. In that sense, these approaches espouse a phenomenological orientation to human environments that seeks what participants see in the environment as a basis for understanding and predicting their behavior. These models of constructed environments share conceptual roots with the early work of Murray (1938), Pace and Stern (1958), and Stern (1970) on the interaction between individual need and environmental press, and the social climate frameworks developed by Moos (1974; 1979). More recently, a renewed interest in phenomenological perspectives has emerged in the current focus on campus culture (Kuh, 1993; Tierney, 1993) as a tool for describing and understanding institutional environments.

Environmental Press

Murray (1938), Pace and Stern (1958), and Stern (1970) are among those who first articulated this approach to human environments. According to Stern an environmental "press" can be inferred from consensual self-reports of activities by either participants in or observers of an environment. For example, if 80 percent of a representative sample of students on a particular campus report that students frequently spend time studying in the library, a significant press toward academic achievement might be inferred. The various identified presses in an environment may or may not correspond to participants' needs or those "organizational tendencies that seem to give unity and direction to a person's behavior" (Stern, 1970, p. 6). For example, an academic achievement need might be inferred from an individual's self-report of a high level of studying and engagement in additional intellectual activities, such as Mortar Board and an honors student organization. Close correspondence (or congruence) between individual need and environmental press is presumed to be growth producing. Such a match would be apparent in the case of a student who, like Clare in the above scenario, has a high need for achievement, affiliation, and involvement and finds herself in an opportunity-rich environment, like Adams College, that encourages and allows her to do so. Significant dissonance between need and press is presumed growth inhibiting, usually contributing to dissatisfaction and turnover.

Pace and Stern (1958) defined press as "the characteristic demands or features of the environment as perceived by those who live in the particular environment" (Walsh, 1973, p. 114). They developed the College Characteristics Index (CCI) to measure the nature of environmental press within a need-press framework. The CCI is a self-administered questionnaire of three hundred items about the respondent's environment organized into thirty scales of ten items each. A CCI factorial structure of eleven factors capable of differentiating among college environments was developed by Saunders (1969) as a descriptive tool in discerning the basic features, or presses, of an institution. Although the specific measurement tool used in the assessment of these campus dimensions is dated, the conceptual features of each subscale are worth noting as a framework for understanding various impressions a particular campus environment might engender (see Exhibit 4.1).

Collectively, these factors might be grouped to yield a profile of the general intellectual and nonintellectual climate of an institution. For example, a limited emphasis on play-work and vocational climate, in combination with a significant press toward aspiration level, intellectual climate, student dignity, academic climate, academic achievement, and self-expression may result in an overall higher intellectual climate image for an institution. These various presses were perceived by Clare as she learned about the Adams College experience in the beginning scenario. An institution's overall nonintellectual climate might also be apparent in its relative press toward self-expression, group life, academic organization, social form, play-work, and vocational climate. In summary, the extent to which participants intuit these factors constitutes the environmental press of an institution and serves to distinguish fundamental differences between institutional types. For example, a consensus among students at a two-year community college might emphasize a press toward vocational climate, consistent with the educational mission of such an institution. In contrast, a small selective private

Exhibit 4.1. College Characteristics Index Factor Descriptions

Aspiration Level Environmental press for intellectual and professional achievement. High scores indicate students' awareness of their being expected (and being able) to perform at a high level; there is emphasis on preparing for graduate work.

Intellectual Climate Stresses scholarly activities in the humanities, arts, and social sciences; emphasis on pure scholarship and basic research, as well as an interest in poetry, music, painting, architecture, and the like.

Student Dignity Emphasis on student self-determination and personal responsibility. High scores suggest that the environmental climate is non-authoritarian, and students tend to be treated with respect and consideration.

Academic Climate Environmental concern for academic excellence in the traditional areas of humanities, social sciences, and natural sciences. High scores reflect outstanding course offerings as well as well-equipped libraries and laboratories.

Academic Achievement Emphasizes high standards of achievement. Students are encouraged to take part in honors programs, tutorials, special courses, independent study, and so on. Competition for grades is intense.

Self-Expression Assesses environmental opportunities for the development of leadership potential and self-assurance. Students are encouraged to participate in public discussions, debates, student drama, and so on.

Group Life Reflects an environment with numerous opportunities for group activity; a concern for the welfare of fellow students, including the less fortunate members of the community.

Academic Organization Environmental press for organization and structure in the academic environment. Activities tend to be purposeful and planned. Students tend not to resist authority.

Social Form Environmental emphasis on the development of social skills; general student awareness of social position and role.

Play-Work Dominant press toward social life. The environment exhibits many opportunities for parties, dancing, drinking, and informal dating. Students frequently participate in demonstrations.

Vocational Climate Emphasizes practical activities; press for orderliness and conformity in student-faculty relationships; opportunities for aesthetic experiences are limited.

Source: Walsh, 1973, pp. 115–117.

liberal arts college, like Adams, might be recognized for its competitive press toward academic achievement. Yet another distinction might be noted in the press toward social form and play-work
often found in large public universities.

A similar approach to understanding campus environmental press
is found in the conceptual framework for the College and University
Environment Scales (CUES) (Pace, 1969). Again, although dated as
a specific assessment tool, the scale descriptions lend themselves to a
current understanding of campus environments. Accordingly, respon-
dents indicate whether they believe a specific item (each attached to
a specific scale) to be "generally true" or "generally false" of a particular institution. Thus, the general impression of an institution is
described in reference to seven distinctive presses (see Exhibit 4.2).
It is only a small step to transfer these scale descriptions to an understanding of many of today's campuses that, in the interest of increasing marketability and retention, are placing considerable emphases,

**Exhibit 4.2. College and University
Environment Scale Factor Descriptions**

Scholarship Characterized by intellectuality and scholastic discipline, intellectual achievement, and the pursuit of knowledge.

Awareness Encourages concern about social and political problems, individuality and expressiveness through the arts, and tolerance of criticism.

Community Friendly, cohesive, and group-oriented environment.

Propriety Mannerly, considerate, proper, and conventional environment.

Practicality Characterized by enterprise, organization, material benefits, social
activities, vocational emphasis, and orderly supervision.

Campus Morale Characterized by acceptance of social norms, group cohesiveness, friendly assimilation of students into campus life, and a commitment
to intellectual pursuits and freedom of expression.

Quality of Teaching (faculty-student relationships) Professors are perceived
to be scholarly, to set high standards, and to be clear, adaptive, and flexible
[and] at the same time, the teaching is infused with warmth, interest, and help-
fulness toward students.

Source: Baird and Hartnett, 1980, pp. 226–227.

for example, on community, propriety, campus morale, and quality of teaching (faculty-student relationships), especially during campus orientation programs and first-year experiences.

Another useful conception of campus environments in this genre, building on the earlier work of Pace and Stern (1958), is the College Characteristics Analysis (CCA) discussed in Pace and Baird (1966). Consolidating the thirty press variables included in the initial development of the CCI, Pace and Baird identified four overall directions of institutional press (Exhibit 4.3): an intellectual, humanistic, aesthetic emphasis (IHA); a friendly, group welfare emphasis (W); a scientific, independent emphasis (SI); and a practical, status-oriented emphasis (PS). In addition, their framework identifies the "source of press as well as the direction of press, and it measures the press of specific academic and student subcultures as well as the press of the environment as a whole" (p. 217). Thus, environmental press can be attributed to one or all of three different sources: administrative sources of press "are ones describing conditions (rules and procedures, facilities, and overall features) which exist primarily or probably because of the actions or decisions or attitudes of administrators"; academic sources of press are "ones describing conditions (curricula, classroom procedures and expectations, etc.) which exist primarily or probably because of the characteristics, actions and attitudes of faculty members"; and student sources of press refer to "extracurricular programs, informal activities, and the characteristics and attitudes of students" (Pace & Baird, 1966, p. 217).

Most helpful in this model is its suggestion that various environmental presses can be a function of different campus subenvironments. Thus, for example, while the overall campus environment may exhibit a press toward intellectual and aesthetic qualities, particular subenvironments, such as certain departments, or even groups of friends, may exert a force in another direction, as would be apparent in a practical, status orientation. Information about a range of features (physical, aggregate, and organizational) can assist in developing a more complete picture of the total tapestry of a particular campus environment.

Exhibit 4.3. Illustrative College Characteristics Analysis Items

Sources of Emphasis	Direction of Emphasis			
	Intellectual, Humanistic, Aesthetic	Friendly, Group Welfare	Independent, Scientific	Practical, Status-oriented
Administrative				
Rules and protocol	Students are allowed to help themselves to books in the library stacks	The student government has a responsible role in regulating student behavior	Students who don't make passing grades are quickly dropped from school	Student organizations must get administrative approval to take a stand on controversial issues
Facilities	There is a theater on or near the campus specializing in foreign films	Dormitories are nicely arranged for small informal gatherings	Laboratory facilities in the natural sciences are excellent	Athletic facilities are modern and well equipped
Overall features	The school has an excellent reputation for academic freedom	The school helps everyone get acquainted	Students here are encouraged to be independent and individualistic	There is a lot of fanfare and pageantry in many of the college events
Academic				
Faculty	Many of the professors are actively engaged in writing	Many faculty members are active in community work: churches, charities, schools, service clubs, and so on	Many of the professors are actively engaged in research	Faculty members always wear coats and ties on the campus

Curricula	There are good opportunities for students to study and criticize important works in art, music, and drama	Many courses are designed to prepare students for well-informed citizenship	Accelerated or honors programs are available for qualified students	Many courses stress the concrete and tangible rather than the abstract or speculative
Instruction	Class discussions are typically vigorous and intense	Students who are having difficulty with a course are encouraged to talk with the professor about it	Frequent tests are [not] given in most courses	Students almost always wait to be called on before speaking in class
Students				
Student characteristics	Students set high standards of achievement for themselves	Students have a lot of group spirit	Many students are planning careers in science	Students are more interested in specialization than in general liberal education
Extracurricular programs	Many students belong to departmental clubs, such as French Club, Philosophy Club, Math Club, and so on	Many upper-classmen play an active role in helping new students adjust to campus life	Receptions, teas, or formal dances are seldom attended	Student elections generate a lot of intense campaigning and strong feeling
Informal activities	Many students are attracted to concerts and art exhibits	Students often have small parties to celebrate pleasant events	Most students [do not] dress and act pretty much alike	There is very little studying here over the weekends

Source: Pace & Baird, 1966, p. 217.

Social Climate

Consistent with the assumptions of environmental press models discussed above, Moos (1979, 1986) and his colleagues at Stanford University authored a social climate model, describing the nature and effects of various "environmental personalities" as perceived by participants. According to Moos, social climate is comprised of three social-environmental domains, each with a respective set of dimensions contributing to that particular domain: relationship dimensions, reflecting "the extent to which people are involved in the setting. . . support and help one another, and . . . express themselves freely and openly" (Moos, 1979, p. 14); personal growth and development dimensions, measuring the "basic goals of the setting . . . areas in which personal development and self-enhancement tend to occur" (Moos, 1979, p. 16); and system maintenance and change dimensions, assessing "the extent to which the environment is orderly and clear in its expectations, maintains control, and responds to change" (Moos, 1979, p. 16). These three domains guide the understanding and assessment of key aspects of any social climate, and they manifest themselves in specific ways depending on the type of environment being examined. For example, in terms of residence hall living environments, Moos (1979) identified ten aspects important to understanding the environmental impact of specific residence units (see Exhibit 4.4). Classrooms, another significant environment in students' lives, can also be understood in terms of Moos' social climate model (see Exhibit 4.5).

To complete this picture of the various interactive social climates that affect students' lives, Moos' model also provides descriptions of the social climate dimensions of social or task-group environments, helpful for understanding students' experiences as participants in various campus groups and organizations; work environments, important for examining the experiences of many students who hold jobs either on or off campus; and family environments, a basic set of relationships that students, traditional and nontraditional alike, bring with them as a foundation for the college experience (see Exhibit 4.6).

Exhibit 4.4. University Residence Environment Scale Dimensions and Subscales

RELATIONSHIP DIMENSIONS:

Involvement Degree of commitment to the house and residents [and] amount of interaction and feeling of friendship.

Emotional support Manifest concern for others in the house, [the extent of] efforts to aid one another with academic and personal problems, [and] emphasis on open and honest communication.

PERSONAL GROWTH
AND DEVELOPMENT DIMENSIONS:

Independence Emphasis on freedom and self-reliance versus socially proper and conformist behavior.

Traditional social orientation Stress on dating, going to parties, and other traditional heterosexual interactions.

Competition Degree to which a wide variety of activities, such as dating and grades, are cast into a competitive framework.

Academic achievement Prominence of strictly classroom and academic accomplishments and concerns.

Intellectuality Emphasis on cultural, artistic, and other intellectual activities.

SYSTEM MAINTENANCE
AND SYSTEM CHANGE DIMENSIONS:

Order and organization Amount of formal structure, neatness, and organization (rules, schedules, established procedures).

Student influence Extent to which student residents formulate and enforce rules and control use of the money, selection of staff, roommates, and the like.

Innovation Organizational and individual spontaneity of behaviors and ideas [and] number and variety of new activities.

Source: Moos, 1979, p. 29.

**Exhibit 4.5. Classroom Environment Scale (CES)
Dimensions and Subscales**

RELATIONSHIP DIMENSIONS:

Involvement Extent to which students are attentive and interested in class activities, participate in discussions, and do additional work on their own.

Affiliation The friendship students feel for each other, as expressed by getting to know each other, helping each other work with homework, and enjoying working together.

Teacher support The help and friendship the teacher shows toward students; how much the teacher talks openly with students, trusts them, and is interested in their ideas.

PERSONAL GROWTH
AND GOAL ORIENTATION DIMENSIONS:

Task orientation The emphasis on completing planned activities and staying on the subject matter.

Competition How much students compete with each other for grades and recognition and how hard it is to achieve good grades.

SYSTEM MAINTENANCE
AND CHANGE DIMENSIONS:

Order and organization The emphasis on students behaving in an orderly and polite manner and on the organization of assignments and activities.

Rule clarity The emphasis on establishing and following a clear set of rules and on students knowing what the consequences will be if they do not follow them; the extent to which the teacher is consistent in dealing with students who break rules.

Teacher control How strict the teacher is in enforcing the rules, the severity of the punishment for rule infractions, and how much students get into trouble in the class.

Innovation How much students contribute to planning classroom activities, and the extent to which the teacher uses new techniques and encourages creative thinking.

Source: Trickett & Moos, 1995, p. 3. Used by permission.

Exhibit 4.6. Social Climate Dimensions and Subscales Across Environments

	Relationship Dimensions	Personal Growth Dimensions	System Maintenance and Change Dimensions
Residence environments	Involvement, emotional support	Independence, traditional/social orientation, competition, academic achievement, intellectuality	Order and organization, student influence, innovation
Classroom environments	Involvement, affiliation, instructor support	Task orientation, competition	Order and organization, rule clarity, instructor control, innovation
Social/task-oriented group environments	Cohesion, leader support, expressiveness	Independence, task orientation, self-discovery, anger and aggression	Order and organization, leader control, innovation
Work environments	Involvement, peer cohesion, supervisor support	Autonomy, task orientation, work pressure	Clarity, control, innovation, physical comfort
Family environments	Cohesiveness, expressiveness	Independence, achievement orientation, intellectual-cultural orientation, active recreational orientation, moral-religious emphasis	Organization, control

Source: Moos, 1994a. Used by permission.

As illustrated, specific dimensions may vary according to the environment being assessed. For example, relationship dimensions of social task-groups include degree of cohesion, leader support, and expressiveness; for work environments they include involvement, peer cohesion, and supervisor support; and for family environments, cohesiveness and expressiveness.

Each of these many social climate dimensions may vary along a continuum, from low to high, depending on the characteristics of the setting. Also, the particular combination of dimensions in any environment may create a special focus or orientation in that setting. For example, with respect to campus residence environments, Moos (1979) identified, by assessment with the University Residence Environment Scale (Moos & Gerst, 1988), six characteristic environments or "personalities" he attributes to various living groups: relationship-oriented living environments, that is, units characterized by a supportive relationship orientation that strongly value emotional support and involvement, with some stress on dating and cultural pursuits but little emphasis on engaging in new and different activities; traditionally socially oriented living environments, units that "give priority to dating, going to parties, and other traditional heterosexual interactions, as well as to aspects of formal structure and organization, such as rules, schedules, established procedures, and neatness" (p. 55); supportive achievement-oriented living environments, those that place "their highest emphasis on the relationship dimensions of involvement and emotional support and on the personal growth dimension of academic achievement . . . [in a] noncompetitive context . . . [but with] very little focus on independence" (p. 56); competition-oriented living environments, where there is "high stress on competition [with] very little involvement or emotional support" (pp. 56–57); independence-oriented living environments that "encourage a wide diversity of student behaviors without specific social sanction and do not value socially proper or conformist behavior" (p. 57); and intellectually oriented living environments, relatively rare units consisting "primarily of theme houses and living-learning and cooperative units composed largely of students in the humanities and social sciences" (p. 58) and emphasizing intellectuality and independence. Likewise, varying emphases on certain aspects in classrooms, social-task groups, work settings, and family environments may create a combined characteristic effect toward one orientation or another. For example, one classroom may be very innovation oriented, while another is control oriented; one work environment might be very competitive and another oriented toward supportive relationships; one family's social climate may express itself in a strong supportive achievement orientation while another emphasizes independence.

These various environmental orientations have been found to be a function of differing aggregate and physical configurations as well, at least in the context of living environments. For example, Moos (1979) found that predominately male units tend to be more competition oriented, female units more traditionally socially oriented, and coed units independence and intellectually oriented. Furthermore, supportive achievement and relationship oriented units tend to be almost exclusively female and coed. Living units comprised of a greater proportion of single rooms tend to be more oriented toward competition and less toward supportive achievement, independence, intellectuality, or relationships. Thus, variations in the differing aspects of students' environments yield a constructed milieu that, in turn, further influences students' attraction, satisfaction, and stability within the environment.

Campus Culture

Another approach for assessing institutional environments from a perceptual, or constructed, approach is found in the literature on organizational and campus culture. Researchers such as Chaffee and Tierney (1988), Horowitz (1984, 1987), Kuh, Schuh, Whitt, and Associates (1991), Kuh and Whitt (1988), Matthews (1997), and Moffatt (1989) have all drawn attention to applications of this approach to understanding colleges and universities. "Culture," with

roots in anthropology, sociology, and social psychology, is inherently
a perceptual construct in that the culture of any environment reflects
the assumptions, beliefs, and values inhabitants construct to interpret
and understand the meaning of events and actions. Schein (1985)
referred to culture as "a pattern of basic assumptions—invented, discovered, or developed by a given group as it learns to cope with its
problems of external adaptation and internal integration—that has
worked well enough to be considered valid and, therefore, to be
taught to new members as the correct way to perceive, think, and
feel in relation to those problems" (p. 9). In their introduction to
the concept of campus culture, Kuh and Hall (1993) defined it as
the "confluence of institutional history, campus traditions, and the
values and assumptions that shape the character of a given college
or university" (pp. 1–2). Culture, then, is essentially "a social construction" (Chaffee & Tierney, 1988, p. 10) reflected in traditions,
stories, ceremonies, history, myths, heroines and heroes, interactions
among members, policies and practices, symbols, and mission and
philosophy. It was precisely these aspects of Adams College that most
powerfully impressed Clare in the opening scenario of this chapter.

Drawing on the work of others (Dyer, 1986; Lundberg, 1985;
Schein, 1985), Kuh and Hall (1993) described four levels of culture:
artifacts, perspectives, values, and assumptions. Cultural artifacts
include those tangible aspects (physical, verbal, and behavioral)
"the meaning and functions of which may be known [only] by members" (Kuh & Hall, p. 4). Virtually all campuses have some distinctive physical artifacts, usually buildings, landscape features, or
various other physical attributes, which mark points of interest on
a typical admissions or orientation tour. An historical quadrangle,
a state-of-the-art recreation center, a well-manicured green space,
a "Founders' Hall," a majestic library, or a technologically advanced
classroom building can all serve to convey to members and non-
members alike some of the core values that shape institutional culture and the historical roots from which they came. Verbal artifacts
include language, stories, and myths. Language often incorporates

"terms of endearment" (Kuh et al, 1991) associated with specific institutions, as well as slang terms typical of traditional college-age cultures and subcultures (Hancock, 1990). Stories about significant campus leaders, personalities, and even mythical figures convey key moments of institutional history and offer personal models of emulation consistent with institutional values and assumptions. Behavioral artifacts might include a host of celebratory activities and events (such as orientation and convocation) that serve to connect members with the institution, acknowledge their participation in institutional subcultures and groups (sorority and fraternity pledging), or send them on their way following completion of their institutional experience (commencement). Various campus rituals, another form of behavioral artifact, also serve to connect the past to the present (Masland, 1985), as happens annually, for example, when anniversary classes are remembered at homecoming or alumni week.

Perspectives, or "the socially shared rules and norms applicable to a given context" (Kuh & Hall, 1993, p. 6), constitute a second level of institutional culture. As "social conventions manifested through behavior," perspectives define the "way things are done" and "determine what is 'acceptable behavior' for students, faculty, staff, and others in various institutional settings. They are relatively easy to determine, and the members of various groups who adhere to perspectives are usually aware of them" (p. 6). Thus, students quickly become aware of appropriate campus customs, attire, and ideologies associated with, for example, an Earlham College (Krehbiel & Strange, 1991), where consensus is the way in which decisions are made; an Iowa State University (Schuh, 1991), where participation in departmental clubs and organizations is the norm from the first day on campus; or a University of Louisville (Strange, 1991), where a history of social consciousness and causes contributes an air of political liberalism to many campus discussions. Members of the campus community and subcommunities come to recognize certain perspectives as typical of those who reflect and construct institutional culture.

Values, a third level of institutional culture, are more abstract than perspectives and reflect the "espoused as well as the enacted ideals of an institution or group, and serve as the basis on which members of a culture or subculture judge situations, acts, objects and people" (Kuh & Hall, 1993, p. 6). College catalogs, convocation speeches, campus philosophy and mission statements, and core planning documents are important sources for understanding institutional values in their espoused forms. At Earlham College, an institution built on Quaker principles and practices, specific institutional documents underscore the importance of shared governance and responsibility as its principal operating value, which is conveyed to each new member upon entering the college (Krehbiel & Strange, 1991).

Assumptions comprise the fourth and deepest level of institutional culture and are implicit, abstract axioms or "tacit beliefs that members use to define their role, their relationship to others, and the nature of the organization in which they live" (Kuh & Hall, 1993, p. 7). Schein (1992) suggested that various other artifacts of organizational culture, such as organizational missions, primary tasks and goals, and the means chosen to achieve and measure goals, all reflect these fundamental assumptions:

1. The nature of reality and truth: The shared assumptions that define what is real and what is not, what is a fact in the physical realm and the social realm, how truth is ultimately to be determined, and whether truth is revealed or discovered.
2. The nature of time: The shared assumptions that define the basic concept of time in the group, how time is defined and measured, how many kinds of time there are, and the importance of time in the culture.
3. The nature of space: The shared assumptions about space and its distribution, how space is allocated

and owned, the symbolic meaning of space around the person, the role of space in defining aspects of relationships such as degree of intimacy or definitions of privacy.

4. The nature of human nature: The shared assumptions that define what it means to be human and what human attributes are considered intrinsic or ultimate. Is human nature good, evil, or neutral? Are human beings perfectible or not?

5. The nature of human activity: The shared assumptions that define what is the right thing for human beings to do in relating to their environment on the basis of the foregoing assumptions about reality and the nature of human nature. In one's basic orientation to life, what is the appropriate level of activity or passivity? At the organizational level, what is the relationship of the organization to its environment? What is work and what is play?

6. The nature of human relationships: The shared assumptions that define what is the ultimate right way for people to relate to each other, to distribute power and love. Is life cooperative or competitive; individualistic, group collaborative, or communal? What is the appropriate psychological contract between employers and employees? Is authority ultimately based on traditional lineal authority, moral consensus, law, or charisma? What are the basic assumptions about how conflict should be resolved and how decisions should be made? [Schein, 1992, p. 95-96]

How institutional participants respond to these questions yields various assumptions that define and shape the core elements of institutional culture, which, in turn, form a powerful milieu within which the processes of education ensue.

According to Schein (1985), organizational culture serves to solve group problems of both external adaptation, that is, what a group must do to maintain survival in a changing environment, and internal integration, that is, what the group must do to maintain internal relationships and functioning. The character Tevye in *Fiddler on the Roof* responds emphatically to the question "How do we keep our balance?" "That I can tell you in one word," he says, "Tradition!" Problems of external adaptation include establishing a core mission, specific goals derived from that mission, a means to attain the goals, criteria for measuring success, and strategies for remediation when goals are not being met. Internal integration tasks include establishing and maintaining a common language and set of concepts, determining criteria for membership, deciding how power is used, delimiting relationships, discerning the nature of rewards and punishments, and defining an ideology that helps the group face unexpected events (Schein, 1985).

From the paradigm of organizational culture, it can be argued that residence halls, classes, informal student groups, and formal campus organizations are all cultures that assist participants, staff as well as students, in making meaning of the college experience. In effect, they are powerful tools in socializing students to the goals and purposes of higher education, what it means to be a member of a community, and how to go about the business of being a college student. At times, these cultures can be at cross purposes with the educational goals of an institution, as in the case of the stereotypical "zoo" or "animal house" culture evident where students place a premium on hedonistic and disruptive activities (Moffatt, 1989). At other times, they can be expressly supportive of institutional goals, as in the case of honors halls or living-learning programs.

Understanding campus environments from a cultural perspective entails application of the tools of qualitative inquiry—personal interviews, participant observation, and document analysis—in the form of a culture audit (Kuh et al., 1991). The meaning of various events, personalities, regulations, programs, traditions, symbols, stories, and interactions are discovered, described, and understood from the perspective of the members of those environments as reflections of a core set of beliefs and assumptions that is organizational culture. For example, at the University of Michigan, it is important to understand the assumptions of selection, membership, and participation in Martha Cook Hall where formal sit-down dinners, rather than the more usual cafeteria-style, are regular fare for its all-female occupants. At the University of Virginia, fourth-year students vie for the prestige of living in one of forty-seven, nine-by-eleven foot single rooms on "the Lawn," forsaking the convenience of a personal bathroom, as recognition for their academic achievements and overall contributions to the university. Also, at Morehouse College in Atlanta, room numbers assigned to Martin Luther King, Jr. and other noted alumni ("Morehouse Men") who were once undergraduates in Graves Hall are committed to memory by many students.

To understand the intent of Xavier University of New Orleans' six "ladder" programs, designed to increase the number of under-represented groups in the health professions, one must learn of the "Xavier way," which means "high expectations for academic performance within a highly structured and supportive academic and social environment" (Kuh et al., p. 233). Likewise, to understand Earlham College requires an understanding of Quaker values and beliefs, and to know Mount Holyoke is to know the history and expectations of its founder, Mary Lyons. That places, too, are important pieces of the campus cultural fabric becomes clear when one understands the significance of Red Square at the Evergreen State College, the Forum at Grinnell College, the Red Barn at the University of Louisville, and the bicycle repair shop at the University of California-Davis. Participant perceptions and understandings of campus organizational culture are an important source of information for designing responsive educational environments, and educators must be particularly sensitive to any discrepancies between their views of the institution and those of students.

———————

The concepts of environmental press, social climate, and campus culture reviewed in this chapter share a common focus on participant perceptions, impressions, and systems of meaning making in understanding the nature of campus environments. They all stress the importance of illuminating consensual interpretations and constructions of various elements of campus environments as key sources for understanding behaviors of individuals within those environments. In addition, these models offer conceptual templates, useful in deciding which aspects of various campus environments might warrant greater attention than others, and what resources to prioritize for purposes of environmental redesign.

Part II

Creating Environments That Foster Educational Success

The first part of this book illuminated and discussed the principal dynamics of human environments as a function of their physical features, the aggregate characteristics of their inhabitants, their organizational designs, and the perceptions or constructions of those who participate in them. This second part focuses on conditions thought to be seminal to the success of environments committed to educational purposes. They are environmental safety and inclusion, structures for involvement, and conditions of community.

Learning entails engagement with new experiences and opportunities that challenge an individual's current ways of viewing, understanding, and responding to the world. The expected outcome is the replacement of these views, understandings, and responses with new and more adequate forms. For example, research on the cognitive development of students during the college years (Love & Guthrie, 1999) suggests that students' viewing of the world in absolute, categorical terms soon gives way to more complex forms of uncertainty and flexibility—what King and Kitchener (1994) have identified as a shift from prereflective to quasi-reflective thinking.

Inherent to any successful learning process is the element of risk. Acquiring a new system for making meaning and learning new ways of responding to the world is fundamentally a risk. Familiar, tried-and-true ways of thinking and doing offer a sense of personal comfort, and they are not easily forfeited as new situations arise. To do so is to risk a system that has become safe and secure over time. What if the new way of interpreting the world, or the new way of doing things, fails? What is the price of letting go of current ways of approaching and understanding the world? What assurances are there that a new way of thinking will be more effective? Such concerns and doubts are an expected and normal feature of the learning process as educational challenges unfold in the learning environment.

From this perspective, learning may be seen as a progression of steps in meaning making and understanding toward increasingly complex and advanced ways of viewing and interacting with the world. This process requires both the acquisition of new information as well as access to opportunities for the exercise of new skills, competencies, and ways of thinking and acting. Ultimately the goal of learning might be seen as the merging of personal identity, values, beliefs, knowledge, skills, and interests toward a purposeful endpoint of fulfillment and human actualization.

Such a conception is at the heart of the classic model of human development and motivation articulated by Maslow (1968). According to Maslow, the basic needs of all humans form a hierarchy, beginning with physiological, safety, belongingness, and love needs, and progressing upwards toward needs of esteem and self-actualization. A basic assumption in Maslow's model is that needs lower in the hierarchy must be met sufficiently before other needs in the hierarchy can be addressed. Therefore, physiological, safety, belongingness, and love needs take precedence over esteem and self-actualization needs. As issues of basic "security, stability, dependency, protection, freedom from fear, anxiety, and chaos, need for structure, order, law, limits, strength in the protector, and so on" (Tribe, 1982, p. 50) are addressed, greater energy can be devoted to higher-level capabilities.

Furthermore, as the needs to belong and to be loved are satisfied, successful adjustment is imminent. The goal in Maslow's model is the development of healthy people who "have sufficiently gratified their basic needs for safety, belongingness, love, respect and self-esteem so that they are intrinsically motivated . . . to strive toward

self-actualization as an unceasing trend toward unity and integration within the person" (Tribe, 1982, p. 59).

Parallel to and implicit in Maslow's (1968) conception is a cor-
responding hierarchy of environmental purposes and designs,
wherein the need for environments that promote safety and inclusion may precede the need for environments that encourage
involvement and community (see Figure II.1). When fundamental
needs of safety and inclusion are in jeopardy, the effectiveness of
involving and communal environments may be compromised.

We begin our analysis in Chapter Five, Promoting Safety and
Inclusion, with an overview of the basic environmental conditions
of safety and inclusion. According to our model, an educational
institution must present first an inclusive, safe, and secure environment for all students. Without a fundamental sense of inclusion and
security, the pursuit of more fulfilling educational experiences is a
daunting task. Without a basic sense of belonging to the campus
community, free from threat, fear, and anxiety, attempts at other

Figure II.1. A Hierarchy of Learning Environment Purposes

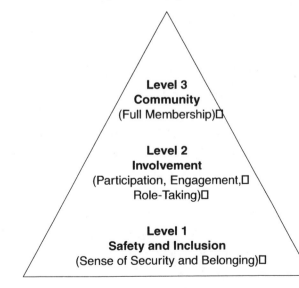

Level 3
Community
(Full Membership)

Level 2
Involvement
(Participation, Engagement,
Role-Taking)

Level 1
Safety and Inclusion
(Sense of Security and Belonging)

more lasting goals will likely fail. The first step for campus leaders, then, is to ensure that the physical, human aggregate, organizational, and constructed aspects of campus environments create such conditions and serve such purposes.

Safety and inclusion are not the endpoints, though, but rather just the beginning steps. As explained above, education is fundamentally about engaging students in a process that calls for risk-taking and challenge (Sanford, 1966). Thus, if campus environments are to be educationally purposeful, they must also involve students in effective learning experiences that require taking on meaningful roles and responsibilities. Without access to environmental structures for participation and involvement, the focus of Chapter Six, Encouraging Participation and Involvement, students remain detached from the kinds of opportunities that call for their investment and responsibility for their own learning, key requisites for powerful educational outcomes.

Finally, it is presumed that, while safety, inclusion, and involvement are all necessary conditions for the achievement of educational purposes, they alone are insufficient to ensure an integrated, whole learning experience for students. This requires, as we discuss in Chapter Seven, Building a Community of Learners, conditions of community, where goals, structures, values, people, and resources come together in a seamless experience for purposes of self-actualization and fulfillment. It is within a community, whether in the form of a class, a student organization, a peer training program, or a residence hall floor, to cite a few examples, that participants experience a complete sense of membership in a setting. They become part of the history and culture of the setting such that, when they leave, they are missed, for they have imprinted the environment with their unique mark, in effect, leaving a trail for others to see.

Each of the four dimensions of campus environments discussed in Part One (physical, human aggregate, organizational, and constructed) has the potential for contributing to or detracting from the safe, inclusive, involving, and communal experience of students.

Furthermore, as the implications of the electronic campus, connected to the Internet and World Wide Web, are further explored and understood, the dynamics of educational environments promise to change significantly the way students attend to their educational needs, a point of discussion in Chapter Eight, Considering Computer-Mediated Environments. The following chapters discuss and illustrate the nature of each environmental condition, and then suggest various design strategies or options for effecting a resolution of each, based upon findings and examples noted in the literature.

Finally, in Chapter Nine, Designing for Education: Campus Assessment and Action, we argue for the systematic incorporation of this environmental knowledge base in considering the impact of and response to the total campus ecology. Rather than an exact prescription for achieving the above conditions, the intent here is to offer broad strategies, the specifics of which must be determined within the context of each campus.

5

Promoting Safety and Inclusion

Although safety and inclusion are distinct concepts, they are related in the sense that both reflect campus conditions thought to be important requisites for development and learning to occur, and contributing to one will undoubtedly enhance the other. It can also be said that failure to address one can easily jeopardize the other. For example, insufficient outdoor lighting on campus (a safety issue) may make it less attractive to some students (an inclusion issue), and failure to successfully attract and retain sufficient enrollment of some students (for example, gay, lesbian, bisexual, and transgendered students), an inclusion issue, may make it psychologically unsafe for those few who do matriculate. Therefore, both concerns are addressed here as necessarily integrated conditions.

Campus attempts to provide safe environments date back to the early beginnings of campus-based education. Turner (1995) suggested that the placement of the early American colleges in the countryside outside the towns was an attempt to remove the students "from the corrupting forces of the city" (p. 4), and the early use of the quadrangle for campus design served the purpose of campus safety in two important ways: "the enclosed quadrangle functioned as a defense against potential enemies, who were the townspeople themselves as much as outside armies" (p. 10); and "the ability to close off a college at a few gate-points also gave college authorities the advantage of greater control over students, a concern that was a major factor in the growth of the collegiate system" (p. 10). Smith and Fossey (1995) noted that the custom of having the sheriff of Middlesex County attend Harvard graduation ceremonies stemmed from early Harvard commencements where the sheriff was needed to help control students and to make ceremonies safe. Dating from these early concerns about campus safety has been the continuous and growing perception that the traditional view of campuses has eroded and there are now "cracks in the ivory tower" (Hopkins, 1994). The safe haven image has been replaced by an awareness that the college campus is a "microcosm for a larger increasingly violent society" (Whitaker & Pollard, 1993, p. xi).

Recognition of the need to increase campus safety is reflected not only in the many recent books, journal articles, and institution-based publications on campus crime and safety (Siegel, 1994; Sherill & Siegel, 1989; Smith & Fossey, 1995; Wensyel, 1987; Whitaker & Pollard, 1993), but the concern has also found its way into federal legislation (for example, the Drug-Free Schools and Communities Act Amendments of 1989, Public Law 101-266; and Students Right-to-Know and Campus Security Act, Public Law 101-542). As noted by Schuh (1993), failure to comply and to provide the information required by these laws (level of campus safety and criminal activity) places at risk an institution's student financial aid. Furthermore, institutions have a duty to warn especially if there is a measure of forseeability with respect to safety and can be held liable for injury.

The federal government has also addressed the issue of inclusion. According to Gehring (1993), federal laws that relate to the inclusion and treatment of all students include the Civil Rights Act of 1964, Title IX of the Higher Education Amendments of 1972, and Section 504 of the Rehabilitation Act of 1973. These laws, in addition to the Americans with Disabilities Act of 1990, place an increasing emphasis on including individuals who have been left out (Schuh, 1993) and treating all who have entered in a manner that they are not excluded from participation, denied benefits, or subjected to discrimination on the basis of race, color, national origin, sex, or disability.

Whether motivated by educational goals or mandated by legal constraints, strategies to promote campus safety and inclusion involve aspects that are physical as well as psychological in nature. Freedom from physical harm is one thing; feeling safe is another. Being physically present may meet the technical requirements of inclusion, but experiencing a sense of belonging may require another standard. Both physical and psychological aspects can detract from environmental safety and inclusion, and both can contribute to their attainment. The conceptual link between safety and inclusion is that the lack of either can create a potentially hostile environment for the activities of personal development and learning. If one fears for personal safety or if one feels unwelcome, either condition is detrimental to the individual and to the campus community.

Drawing on the environmental components discussed in Part One of this volume, the challenges and solutions related to campus safety and inclusion derive from the physical dimensions of the environment, the composition of human aggregates, the arrangement of organizational structures, and the meanings attributed to the constructions and artifacts of campus culture. Each of these components can be a potential source of exclusion and insecurity, depending on the characteristics of those interacting with the environment, and each can enhance the sense of safety and belonging.

Physical Dimensions of Safety and Inclusion

Recent publications and reports reveal that American colleges have increasingly become places of risk in terms of campus violence and crime. A major newspaper survey of 494 colleges and universities in the fall of 1990 revealed that "larceny occurs every four minutes; vandalism every 13 [minutes]; drinking violations, every 24 [minutes], violent crimes every two hours 12 minutes; and rape, every 21 hours. Overall, crimes on campus occur at a rate of 26 per 1,000 students, roughly one-half the 57 per 1,000 for the population at large" (Lipman, 1991, as cited in Hopkins, 1994, p. 21). Clearly, such a profile is cause for concern for the capacity of colleges and universities to carry out their educational missions. Crime, violence, vandalism, harassment, and hazing all make it very difficult for any institution to foster learning and development. The role of the campus physical environment in addressing issues of safety and inclusion is illustrated in a consideration of two key concepts: the effects of various campus design features and the importance of territoriality and defensible space.

Campus Design Features

In a list of environmental dimensions, Moos (1974) included geographical, meteorological, and architectural design variables. Campus geographic variables pertain to both macro- and microdesign features. At the macro level, issues related to regional location emerge. For example, patterns of campus violence in terms of type and time of year may vary with regional conditions such as climate, terrain, and urban versus rural location. Strange (1993) suggested that a campus in a natural wooded setting may influence student behavior differently than a campus located in the "middle of a massive urban metropolis" (p. 137). Although rural areas are not without crime (Phillips, 1982), census data suggest that felonious assaults against persons are strongly related to city size, underscoring a simple fact: "There is more crime per person in urban areas than rural areas" (Martin & O'Connor, 1989, p. 28). Although these data do not directly speak to campus environments, they do describe the nature of the institutional environment for many campuses.

The relationship between climate, weather, and specifically heat and aggression, has been a long-standing research interest of environmental psychologists. Bell, Greene, Fisher, and Baum (1996) concluded their review of the topic suggesting that moderately uncomfortable heat increases aggression. They also pointed out that the Federal Bureau of Investigation itself "has listed climate as a variable of importance in explaining the incidence of crime" (Bell, Greene, Fisher, & Baum, p. 203).

Microgeographic design variables, such as placement of buildings on campus, also influence campus crime. Outlying buildings on school grounds, those located in poorly lit areas, and buildings that are not easily seen are most likely to be a target of vandalism (Pablant & Baxter, 1975). The relative location of rooms can also influence social contacts and therefore indirectly predispose some individuals to safety risks more so than others. For example, rooms next to elevators or stairwells, or in remote sections of the building, are much more likely to expose occupants to contact with others, friend or foe.

The role of architectural design in the affording of campus safety, particularly its role in the reduction of vandalism, is well documented. A rather interesting position is found in Weinmayer (1969) where the author claimed that the real vandals in our environment are the designers. Concurring with this perspective, Zeisel (1976) suggested that about half of the vandalism that occurs in schools results from poor design. Many of these features will be discussed later in this chapter.

In addition to the initial design and layout of buildings, there is evidence to suggest that vandalism is also a function of buildings' physical appearance and maintenance (Pablant & Baxter, 1975). Given that American postsecondary institutions will need to spend over $60 billion to upgrade and replace aging campus facilities (Rush & Johnson, 1989), the relationship of poor building appearance and maintenance to vandalism and other crimes becomes an urgent campus environment management concern. This is especially the case as we come to understand more about the connections between various microlevel design features of aging buildings and the perceptions of insecurity and fear they may evoke from users. Three factors associated with such perceptions are victim prospect (how far, how well, and how much they can see); offender refuge (the availability of places for offenders to hide); and victim escape (access to an escape route from the area) (Nasar & Fisher, 1992). Fear is heightened by "poor prospect for the passerby due to inadequate lighting, blocked escape for the passerby, and conceal-ment for the offender" (Nasar & Fisher, 1992, p. 48).

Macrodesign issues, that is, those involving campus layout and location, are equally troublesome. This is especially the case at insti-tutions in large urban areas where there may be an "opportunity for victimization presented by potential targets (students, faculty, and staff), a supply of motivated offenders nearby (neighborhoods with poor socioeconomic conditions), and poor guardianship (open access with varying levels of security among students)" (Nasar & Fisher, 1992, p. 48). Ironically, some of the same characteristics that contribute to the richness of possibilities campuses offer to students also render them especially vulnerable to victimization. As Fisher and Nasar (1992) observed: "Campuses tend to have easy access, free movement at all hours, and the diversity that allows offenders to remain unnoticed, all of which contribute to a lack of guardian-ship" (p. 36). In sum, the authors cautioned about the broader enrollment implications of these concerns, noting that, "if parents or students believe that a campus is unsafe, they may voice demands for greater security or simply decide to go elsewhere. At a time when universities face safety issues, due, in part, to an increase of fear of crime on campus, the design of the physical environment should not be overlooked as a safety strategy" (Fisher & Nasar, 1992, p. 63). Based on their assessment, Fisher and Nasar (1992) recommend the development of design criteria and audit processes focusing on the three aspects of victim prospect, offender refuge, and victim escape:

> Specifically, campuses might try to improve areas that have low prospect, high refuge, or poor escape. This might involve reducing the height or increasing the permeability of visual barriers, such as shrubs and walls, and eliminat-ing or opening up alcoves and other confining areas.

These changes have particular importance near heavily
used paths [adjacent to] an offender population . . .
because of the coincidence of offenders and innocent
passersby make such areas likely targets for crime. [p. 63]

While the effects of architectural design variables in campus living environments have been reviewed broadly in the literature (see
Blimling, 1988, Heilweill, 1973; Moos, 1979; Schuh, 1980; Strange,
1993), one feature important to the reduction of vandalism due to
rowdiness is related to the concept of behavioral zoning (Jackson
& Schroeder, 1977). This concept underscores the need for stimulation behavior zones, particularly in the design of residence halls. If
not accommodated in the original design, students will create their
own, and usually in ways that are unproductive or that inflict damage on the facilities, for example, using a corridor for an impromptu
bowling alley or hockey match.

The literature on campus environments suggests that physical
design variables also relate directly to the goals of environmental
inclusion. While some features lend themselves to a sense of exclusion, others serve to include. Wilcox and Holahan (1978) found that
students living in low-rise facilities are likely to feel greater commitment toward fellow residents than students living in high-rise
facilities, and even students on the upper floors of high-rise facilities
are likely to express less concern and support for other students in
the building (Nadler, Bar-Tal, & Drukman, 1982). Student density,
as measured by number of students per square footage, is another
design "culprit" (Banning, 1997). A body of research (Baum &
Valins, 1977; Bell, Greene, Fisher, & Baum, 1996) suggests that high
density leads to behaviors less likely to foster inclusion or to build
community. For example, these research reviews suggest that high
density in residence halls is associated with less positive attitudes
toward people and places and that it leads to social withdrawal,
interrupts social networks, reduces a sense of neighborliness, and

encourages more aggressive behaviors. Perhaps the same criticism can be leveled at large classrooms where anonymity often encourages higher absenteeism among students.

The relationship between campus physical design and the safety and inclusion of students encountering mobility challenges is significant. It stands to reason that without fundamental access to the campus, its facilities, and opportunities, students' sense of inclusion is clearly jeopardized. Jones (1996) pointed to the "social construction of disability" as an important perspective in campus modification efforts when addressing access and other challenges, calling for the inclusion of both those with and those without disabilities. Campus design in both its ecological and architectural dimensions has impact on campus safety and inclusion, but the concept of territoriality and defensible space sharpens the focus.

Territoriality and Defensible Space

Territoriality is a set of behaviors and thoughts persons or groups exhibit, underlying their perceived ownership of physical space. This concept includes both claiming and defending the identified space (Bell, Greene, Fisher, & Baum, 1996). Newman (1972) expanded on the concept of territoriality in his development of the idea of defensible space. Accordingly, a design "which makes use of semi-private and private space, as opposed to public space is more defensible" (Newman cited in Jeffrey, 1977, p. 193). Bechtel (1997) summarized Newman's four characteristics of defensible space:

> [T]erritoriality, as manifested by architectural barriers and markers; surveillance, as defined by what people can see from windows, or lines of sight; image, which is conveyed by architectural design, presence or absence of trash and vandalism, and evidence of maintenance; and milieu, which is the numbers and kinds of people and the frequency of their habitancy. [p. 190]

There are three basic processes by which defensible space contributes to campus safety (Bell, Greene, Fisher, & Baum, 1996). First, if campus spaces look "defended" then potential offenders have to assume that their inhabitants will likely respond to intrusions. For example, a campus building that is well lit and showing signs of activity is less likely to be vandalized than a remote, unlit, and unoccupied unit. Second, defensible campus spaces may also encourage inhabitants to develop closer relationships and therefore a greater awareness of potential offenders from outside. For example, traffic patterns associated with housing complexes can be designed to bring people into social contact with one another through a common, centrally located entrance, rather than individual ones. Third, defensible space may inhibit crime by increasing inhabitants' feelings of territoriality and the desire to protect their space. For example, Schroeder (1978-1979) and Phelps (1990) both suggested that encouraging students within a residence wing or floor to paint a wall mural leads to greater group identity and personalization, increasing their sense of territoriality and their willingness to protect the facility against potential intruders. The same can be said for other facilities such as student organization offices in a university union. Encouraging students to make their mark on the space enhances their sense of ownership and therefore their willingness to defend.

Given the importance of architectural design in the creation of defensible space, the positions of Weinmayer (1969) and Zeisel (1976), emphasizing the role of designers in campus vandalism, become more evident. The importance of this design issue is being recognized by campus housing personnel across the United States. In a 1995 survey (Banning, McGuire, & Stegman, 1996), housing officers reported that, next to the cost, designing for security was their highest priority in future building projects. In Smith and Fossey's (1995) major work on campus crime they concluded with strong support for Newman's theory of defensible space, encouraging campus administrators to give serious consideration to parking, lighting, locking systems, key control, and building maintenance. It is clear that campus physical design plays a crucial role in campus safety and inclusion, but also important is the collective role of persons within the campus environment.

Influence of Campus Aggregates

From the perspective of human aggregates, campus environments take on unique features due to the collective characteristics of their inhabitants (Strange, 1993). Dominant campus features reflect the influence of dominant groups. The essential challenge in the achievement of campus safety and inclusion is the fact that those who share the dominant characteristics are more likely to feel safe and included, while those whose characteristics differ may be at risk.

The composition of campus human aggregates may also contribute indirectly to campus violence. Goldstein (1996), in a comprehensive review of the related research, concluded that "at the university level also, males are more vandalistic than females. [First-year students] commit more vandalism than [upper-class students], and regardless of class level, alcohol consumption is a frequent concomitant of such behavior" (p. 24). A similar pattern is found in other crime forms. Men, usually Caucasian, are cited the most in hate crimes, rape, and sexual harassment. Finley and Corty (1993) reported in their study that approximately one-third of men on campus indicated being perpetrators of nonconsensual and pressured sexual penetration. More often than assault by physical force alone this group also implicated the involvement of alcohol. Kilmartin (1996) noted as well the serious problem of campus sexual assaults and domestic violence perpetrated by males. Several authors (Dietz-Uhler & Murrell, 1992; Koss, Gidycz, & Wisniewski, 1987; Warshaw, 1988) concurred on the importance of sex-role attitudes in these matters. Not all men make the campus unsafe for women, but as the above studies suggest, college men who have less respect for women, see them as inferior, and have callous attitudes toward rape victims do create a hostile environment for women.

The characteristics and dynamics of human aggregates are particularly relevant to understanding the challenges of creating inclusive campus environments. Groups less welcomed on campus are seldom in the numerical majority but are usually in the minority in terms of overall membership. This majority versus minority dynamic often sets up conditions that promote a "chilly climate" for those in the minority, similar to the experience reported by many women on campus (Hall & Sandler, 1982; 1984). These conditions for women often include a variety of behaviors from men in the majority, including their lack of recognition, their devaluing of women's abilities, giving them less opportunity to participate, and subjecting them to hostile and harassing remarks.

Ethnic minorities also face a less than welcoming environment that is often the antithesis of inclusion (Gunnings, 1982). The "chills" can occur in admission policies, distribution of financial aid, academic programs, housing programs, and various campus incidents (Hawkins, 1989). Gay, lesbian, bisexual, and transgendered students also face hostile campus environments (D'Augelli, 1989; Evans & Rankin, 1998; Evans & Wall, 1991). Not only is minority status antithetical to inclusion, it also usually limits the availability and visibility of role models for purposes of mentoring and support (Sandeen & Rhatigan, 1990). The majority versus minority distinction, while illuminating the noninclusive nature of the environment, often brings with it serious problems that may hinder rather than enhance necessary environmental changes. For example, Jones (1996) suggested that "minority group thinking," while often used to identify issues related to the unjust distribution of power, status, and privilege in the campus environment, also lumps members together, forfeiting their individuality, and builds on a deficit model, too often justifying the setting apart of minority groups, ultimately jeopardizing the goal of inclusion. Although this seemingly separatist approach (such as minority student orientation) is important for creating an initial opportunity for maximizing congruence, it may, in the long run, result in greater exclusion from the campus environment.

Organizational Dimensions of Safety and Inclusion

Organizational features of the environment may also affect behaviors and attitudes (Strange, 1993), among them inhabitants' sense of security and inclusion. Organizational dimensions are relevant to the safety and inclusion of individuals primarily through organizational size and organizational mission.

Organizational Size

The concept of manning theory presented in Chapter Three is important to understanding the impact of campus size. When the number of inhabitants in any environment exceeds the number needed to complete the various tasks in the environment (a condition described as overmanned), those not engaged feel little commitment to or responsibility toward maintaining the environment (Wicker, 1973). Studies of secondary school settings have found that the larger the school environment the more incidents of vandalism per capita (Garbarino, 1978; Goldman, 1961). High density or crowding, often a consequence of environmental overmanning, "has been found to result in less liking for others (especially in males), and . . . is associated with withdrawal from interaction . . . [greater] aggression and . . . lower incidence of prosocial behavior" (Bell, Green, Fisher, & Baum, 1996, p. 365). Such effects can indirectly influence the overall organizational climate for safety and inclusion. Overmanned environments may simply place individuals at risk (a safety issue) and may do little to engage them in the activities of the environment (an issue of inclusion). Current emphasis on the organization of small freshman interest groups on many campuses suggests that administrators are becoming more sensitive to and are responding to the challenges of oversizing.

Carry capacity, or the ability of an environment to sustain itself with current resources, is also affected by oversizing. As campuses or living units become larger in terms of the number of inhabitants, there is seldom the necessary increase in support staff or programs to accompany the larger environment. Goldstein (1994) points to school size as a correlate to school violence noting that in larger school settings violence and vandalism increase due to "nonparticipation in governance, impersonalness, and crowding" (p. 38). These concepts are descriptive of the condition of "deindividuation" (Zimbardo,1969). Accordingly, when individuals lose their identity and begin to feel anonymous, because they are "small or unknown fish in a big sea," their inhibitions toward antisocial behavior are lowered. While this phenomenon has been most often associated with high-density urban settings, it may be relevant in examining the effects of size as a campus organizational feature.

Organizational Mission

Institutional missions vary across a number of dimensions (Lyons, 1993), and what the mission statement of the campus says about inclusion, multiculturalism, and diversity is important to the interface between organizational concepts and the inclusion of all persons in the campus environment. Kuh, et al. (1991) outlined the fourfold commitment necessary for a campus to become an inclusive multicultural learning community: "advance knowledge and intellectual understanding of differences among groups of people"; "encourage interaction among members of different subcommunities (ethnic, cultural, gender-based, academic living groups)"; "promote the appreciation and valuing of commonalties across all students"; and "build on commonalties while acknowledging the importance different groups can make to the academic community" (p. 294).

Constructed Dimensions of Safety and Inclusion

While the physical, aggregate, and organizational dimensions directly shape conditions of campus safety and inclusion, it stands to reason that how these dimensions are constructed, or given meaning by participants, is also a predictor of their consequences. A case

in point may be found in the growing concerns over campus vandalism and graffiti. Students from large urban areas may react more
benignly to vandalism and graffiti than students whose backgrounds
have not exposed them to such conditions, or who are themselves
targets of the noninclusive messages embedded in these acts (for
example, when windows in an adjacent Jewish synagogue are bro-
ken, or the doors to the campus women's center are defaced with
sexist remarks). Campus graffiti often target race, ethnicity, religion,
gender, and sexual orientation, and through various social constructions, can evoke feelings of insecurity and exclusion. Banning
(1992; 1995) and Banning and Luna (1992) have published photographs of campus graffiti that target women, Latinos, gay, and lesbian students. The content of such graffiti often includes messages
telling the targeted students that they don't belong on campus, threatening their safety, and suggesting that they will have limited equal-
ity and opportunities within the campus environment (Banning &
Bartels, 1993). Vandalism in all its forms is destructive to all groups
and diminishes the ability of the campus to foster learning and development. In effect it "is like a cancer of bricks and mortar. And the
side effects are erosion of campus spirit as well as public confidence
in the institution" (Taming Campus Vandals, 1980, p. 44).

Verbal harassment, including the use of spoken or written language, is another category that warrants attention in a discussion of
campus safety and inclusion (Palmer, 1996). "It may take many different forms, including (but not limited to) racist, sexist, homophobic, or anti-Semitic slurs or other comments that are obscene,
demeaning, intimidating, [and] threatening" (Palmer, 1996, p. 270).
Although hate crimes and graffiti may send similar messages,
Palmer's verbal harassment category focuses on the verbal nature of
the communication. While every student on campus is a potential
victim for harassment, nevertheless the most likely targets for verbal
harassment are groups distinguished by race, ethnicity, religion, gender, and sexual orientation.

According to Paludi and Barickman (1991) as many as five million female college students may have experienced sexual harass-

ment. Although harassment is found in dating relationships of college women (Sugerman & Hotaling, 1989), it is also found in other parts of the campus environment. Dziech and Weiner (1984) reported that 30 percent of college women were sexually harassed by academic instructors. Two reports by Hall and Sandler (1982; 1984) and again by Boyer (1987) support these general findings regarding the sexual harassment of women on campus to the point that Hall and Sandler's "chilly climate" critique, applied originally to describe the experience of women on campus, has become part of the standard discourse on campus safety and inclusion.

Psychological safety and inclusion is not only the absence of threat or harassment; it also involves a positive sense of mattering (Schlossberg, 1989) and validation (Rendon, 1994), especially among those who may differ significantly from the dominant campus culture or are marginalized in some manner. Mattering includes five aspects: feeling noticed, feeling important enough to be cared about, feeling empathy from others for accomplishments or failures, being needed, and feeling appreciated for one's efforts (Rosenberg & McCullough, 1981; Schlossberg, 1989). Feeling that one matters is an important "precursor to students' becoming involved in activities and academic programs that would facilitate development and learning" (Schlossberg, 1989, as cited in Evans, Forney, & Guido-DiBrito, 1998, pp. 27–28). Rendon (1994) underscored the need for validation, especially in the early stages of a student's experience, and for creating safe space for those whose diverse racial, ethnic, and cultural backgrounds have predisposed them to doubts or low self-esteem concerning their abilities and experiences on campus. This process of "enabling, confirming, and [supporting]" (Rendon, 1994, p.46) can occur in any campus setting (classroom, student organization, advisor's office) and be offered by any campus agent (classmates, instructors, staff). Again, active interventions in that respect are important for encouraging nontraditional students to become involved in campus life.

The interaction of campus culture and the goals of environmental safety and inclusion can be seen in the issues surrounding various recent challenges to the appropriateness of campus mascots and symbols at some institutions. For example, at the University of Illinois, where Chief Illiniwek has been an institutional symbol for seventy years, controversy has embroiled the campus since 1989, pitting alumni, state legislators, congressional representatives, and the governor against representatives of Native American tribes. At stake is the meaning of Illiniwek's display and ritual at various sporting events on campus. Alumni cling loyally and fiercely to the mascot, which they claim to be a symbol of honor, elevating the sacred qualities and history of the Native American tradition. Native American students, on the other hand, under the leadership of Native American graduate student, Charlene Teter, have challenged the authenticity and decorum of the costume and dance, suggesting that such displays during sporting events are demeaning, humiliating, and an affront to their peoples' culture, spirituality, and heritage. One Native American student specifically commented on the effect of seeing Chief Illiniwek crests, in full headdress, hanging in storefront windows of area merchants in Champaign, Illinois, particularly during homecoming events. While these crests were a symbol of pride for the majority of Caucasians, they reminded her of the time in Illinois history when bounties were placed on the heads of banished Native American tribes ($7 for males, $5 for females, $3 for children) by advertising with similar storefront effigies. While both groups claim high motives for their objections (to either keep or eliminate the current mascot), for the fewer in number Native American students, this controversy has created a campus environment that threatens not only their inclusion in it but their safety as well. Acts of hostility have become regular fare among some students and alumni when they return to campus to face the protests of these offended groups. Pride confronts pride, and what elevates one group denigrates the other. A more recent version of this same debate concluded with the replacement of the Redskins logo at Miami University of Ohio with Redhawks, a decision resulting in the resignation of a board of trustee member. Traditions run deep and are not easily changed.

A similar example, with consequences of social exclusion for African American students, continues to raise concerns of campus administrators at the University of Mississippi. Although the university has officially disassociated itself with the confederate flag as an official institutional symbol, throngs of alumni and students continue to wave it at various sporting events while the fight song "Dixie" and the cane-toting, mustachioed, Southern gentleman mascot, Colonel Rebel, lead the charge. Again, what is at stake here is the meaning and interpretation of history as reflected in these symbols. For some of the Caucasian majority such symbols embody the university's heritage but, for students of color, these same symbols may provide painful reminders of deep racial division, social exclusion, and oppression. Once again, tradition conflicts with sensitivity. An interesting consequence of this debate has spilled over into the academic arena where the institution's scholarly reputation is being questioned by a panel of external reviewers considering its application for installment of a chapter of Phi Beta Kappa. Apparently this prestigious academic honor society has reservations about affiliating with an institution where such symbols threaten to exclude some constituents. Symbols create powerful images that carry their messages in forms of pervasive social constructions, regardless of their high intent.

Concerns for safe and inclusive environments are not just about racial and ethnic differences. Images and symbols related to gender distinctions and religious traditions also have captured the attention of campus constituents, with considerable debate. For example, at Southwest Missouri State University, recent charges of sexism were leveled at proponents of the Sugar Bears, a female cheerleading squad. Also, the use of the mascot, Princes, has been questioned at Heidelberg College in recent years as perhaps insufficiently masculine or aggressive to be supportive and symbolic of the male athletic teams. The placement of Christmas holiday decorations and the recognition of Easter break at many campuses draw concerns from those whose religious traditions do not share these practices. The point of all of these examples is that symbols of campus culture serve to wall-in some constituents and wall-out others. What any particular symbol actually means is indeterminate, although its effects on various campus groups can be readily observed. It is the nature of constructed environments to emerge from consensual interpretations. Inclusion for one group often rests on the exclusion of other groups, ultimately challenging their sense of safety and security, physical or psychological.

Campus Assessment and Response

Issues of campus safety and inclusion are complex and require a variety of institutional responses to succeed in creating conditions that promote a sense of belonging and security. Perhaps the place to begin, in terms of campus policies and practices, is an audit of current conditions both in terms of how they contribute to or detract from a basic sense of security and safety, as well as their potential for making students of all backgrounds feel that they belong and are valued. A number of institutional checklists and policy statements exist for informing this process. For example, the American Council on Education (1985) issued a report on campus self-regulation initiatives, making many recommendations, including the appointment of an explicitly designated administrator who will ensure that security needs are considered in the design, maintenance, and operation of buildings, grounds, and equipment, that students and others are informed about security risks and procedures, that security staff are properly screened, trained, equipped, and supervised, that the number of security staff is adequate to perform necessary functions, and that security data are collected and periodically reviewed.

Among the concerns for campus design, maintenance, and operation are the provision of adequate lighting, accessible campus telephones and escort services, clearance of obstructions to pathways and entrances, and monitoring of campus access through selective issuance of keys and heightened sensitivity to unauthorized visitors. In addition to the importance of adequate numbers of well-trained and supervised security staff, professional and paraprofessional alike, the report calls for informed communication with campus constituents concerning various security procedures and incidents, and cooperative arrangements with local law enforcement personnel.

Strategies for campus assessment might include

Postoccupancy evaluation. Postoccupancy evaluation (POE) is retrospective evaluation of physical environments and buildings where the results are used to suggest modifications for improvement (Bell, Greene, Fisher, & Baum, 1996). Elements of POE for monitoring safety might incorporate some of the environmental design issues noted in Goldstein (1994): target hardening, that is, the use of devices or materials, such as security screens, to obstruct vandals; access control, such as placement of reception desks in residence halls, making it more difficult to enter a space; deflecting offenders, that is, redirecting behavior to more acceptable outlets, such as providing graffiti boards in campus restrooms; target removal, that is, removal of potential crime targets, such as returning outdoor tables and chairs after special events; and removing inducements, that is, physical alteration of potential targets, such as quickly removing graffiti to help prevent its spread.

Archival records review. Institutional archival records, from police, disciplinary proceedings, and other campus incidents, should be reviewed on a periodic basis for trends, events, and issues related to safety and inclusion. After a complete debriefing of the records, more insightful intervention strategies can be planned.

Photographic assessment techniques. Banning (1992) presented a series of pictures of campus artifacts that could send messages of sexism. Photographs can be taken and then presented to various campus groups for their interpretation of messages and suggestions for interventions, if necessary. More recently, Banning (1997) conducted an assessment by photographing a housing system and using the photographs for training purposes. One item of the housing system's mission statement was to ensure resident safety. These photographs served to expose both compliance and contradictions of mission. For example, one photograph demonstrated a security door properly locked, conveying a message of security. Another exposed a dislodged window screen, calling into question the safety of the setting. The photographs were assembled into a slide show and presented to the housing staff personnel for discussion and recommendations, serving to sensitize staff to issues of safety and to more effective solutions.

With respect to potential intruders, Smith (1988) argued for the "erection of perimeters of protection that can deter, hinder, or prevent penetration of the facility. . . . Appearances are important; discouragement of would-be intruders is of greater value than apprehending those who do intrude" (pp. 110–111). Citing Territo (1983), Smith recommended consideration of several potential campus safety concerns: surveillance of problem locations (where incidents have occurred); maintaining recommended lighting standards; checking groundskeeping with a focus on placing and trimming shrubs or hedges to eliminate hiding spots; scheduling classes to avoid secluded locations at night; checking for availability of emergency phones that do not require coins near walking routes, parking lots, and recreational areas; providing adequate protection in residence halls; arranging after hours and weekend work schedules so that staff are not left in isolated areas; organizing rape prevention programs; and offering crime prevention programs for security personnel.

How campuses are responding to these assessments and suggestions for intervention is captured in a framework of five types of campus safety and security initiatives reported in a survey of 701 institutions (Beeler, Bellandese, & Wiggins, 1991):

- Traditional services: campus police, patrols, security services, outreach programs, prevention and response services, security technology and communications

- Educational and support programs: from general security precautions to in-depth crime victim advocacy, including orientation programs, class meetings, residence hall programs and symposia

- Planning, policy, and information strategies: crime reports, safety studies and reviews, research and use of broad-based safety information to guide decision making

- Environmental and technical modifications: construction or landscaping to minimize crime opportunities, reducing places where crime is likely to occur; electronic technology (phones, personal entry device [PED] access, cameras)

- Community action: use of campus and community groups to enhance safety strategies

These initiatives suggest that the goal of securing campus life is multifaceted and requires the application of a wide range of strategies.

Finally, recommendations from the Council of Ontario Universities (1991) are instructive concerning the importance of student characteristics in achieving a sense of security. Their report concludes that "the environment is experienced differently according to a person's ethnicity, race, class, age, ability, and sexuality" (p. 10). Thus, campus safety audits should be conducted with the needs of various campus groups and constituents in mind. For example, concerns about sexual harassment and assault are more apparent among women. In such cases, "The goal of safety audits is to improve the physical environment in ways that reduce the opportunities for sexual assaults and to effectively make the campus a more equitable environment" (p. 9). "An environment designed to discourage sexual assault will minimize the opportunity for other kinds of assaults and for crimes involving property" (p. 4). A focused audit of this kind might include:

- Surveying places where people feel most unsafe or uncomfortable.

- Visiting these identified places in different seasons and times of day.

- Using an audit checklist at each site to focus on general impressions, lighting, signage, sight lines, degree of visual and sound isolation, number of people in the area at different times, distance from emergency services, frequency of security patrols, predictability of movement along routes and paths, availability of alternate routes, location of hiding places, location and security of possible assault sites (indoors and out), availability of escape routes, nature and usage of adjacent land, maintenance of facilities, sense of care displayed for the location, overall layout and design.

- Considering aspects of the nonphysical environment as well (policies and programs). Do the people around seem trustworthy? Would they respond sensitively to an assaulted person? Is information about assaults in the vicinity publicized? What are the lengths of wait for transportation or escort service? Are there policies on sexual assault and harassment on campus? Policies to deal with racism? Sexism? Homophobia? Are free self-defense courses available? Is there an escort or walk-home service available?

The authors concluded that "women's safety is affected not only by the physical design of spaces but also by a variety of other design factors such as policies, practices and services. Universities and colleges must examine environments that encourage a climate of sexual exploitation and must challenge social values, attitudes and practices which are prejudicial to women" (Council of Ontario Universities, 1991, p. 10). Implicit in these suggestions is that measures taken on behalf of one campus group (women) might also improve conditions of safety and inclusion for other groups (gay, lesbian, transgendered students, students of color, students with disabilities).

Safe and inclusive environments are created physically (in the class-room, residence halls, campus offices, campus grounds), in human aggregate groupings (targeted services and programs focusing on the needs of particular types of students), organizationally (the cur-riculum, student organizations, departments), and perceptually (through images, symbols, cultural variations). Being free from phys-ical threat and harm and experiencing a fundamental psychologi-cal sense of belonging on campus are important conditions for the pursuit of opportunities to learn, develop, and grow. At the very least, student time and energy spent on coping with feelings of inse-curity and exclusion can only detract from efforts applied to more positive growth experiences.

Although identification of problems associated with campus safety and inclusion is rather straightforward, implementing solu-tions is a much greater challenge. The dilemma created by many of these suggested strategies is that an approach designed to attend to one concern may actually create another concern of equal propor-tion. Sometimes the trade-off is between strategies that ensure anonymity and strategies that support identity. Such is the case where special theme housing arrangements (by hall or floor) on some campuses (such as the University of Massachusetts) are designed to meet the needs of particular groups of students (racial and ethnic minorities, gay, lesbian, bisexual, and transgendered stu-dents). The emphasis on identity recognition and support for pur-poses of inclusion and safety might also expose students, rendering them ready targets of vandalism and other forms of abuse.

Target hardening, another often recommended strategy to secure campus facilities, also serves to illustrate this dilemma. As educa-tional settings, colleges and universities traditionally have been committed to openness and accessibility, encouraging the free flow of diverse peoples and ideas in a rich mix of intellectual pursuit. That mix contributes to the unique and powerful qualities of edu-cational institutions, but it also renders them highly vulnerable. Securing the campus environment tightly (target hardening) with

PEDs (personal entry devices) and other mechanisms also diminishes its openness and accessibility. The price of these approaches is perhaps not yet well understood, but the direction charted by such strategies certainly raises significant questions about institutional purposes and goals.

A balance or compromise of strategies may be inevitable in addressing these concerns. Whatever the case, the importance of safe and inclusive environments is that they free individuals to pursue more active engagement and higher purposes in a setting, that is, to become involved as participants in the educational environment.

6

Encouraging Participation
and Involvement

Whether in the form of classrooms, student organizations, department offices, residence halls, or a complete campus, educational environments exert their influence long before students enter them. Such influence is recognized in the degree of attraction or repulsion a student may feel for any particular setting, and those environments found most attractive are presumed to exert the greatest influence in terms of encouraging individuals to join them. Environments seen as least attractive are most likely to repel individuals.

This theory of attraction is a fundamental dynamic of every institution's efforts to successfully recruit students who can benefit from its educational programs and opportunities. Providing the right kind of student-institution match that is further supported by features of inclusion and safety, as Chapter Five discussed, maximizes the chances that personal satisfaction and stability will result. Thus, retention is encouraged and attrition is minimized.

However, creating conditions that support the desire of students to remain in a particular setting is only the first step. If active learning is the goal, institutions must also look beyond issues of belonging, stability, and comfort to consider the nature of environments that might encourage engagement and the investment of time and effort, in other words, those that call for participation and involvement. The National Institute of Education report (1984) concluded that "The most effective education is one which most fully involves the student in the learning process and the opportunities for enriching experiences in the college setting. . . . The quality of education can be improved by three critical conditions: student involvement, high expectations, and assessment and feedback" (Pace, 1990, p. 7–8).

This chapter characterizes and discusses features of campus environments, from the perspectives of physical design, human aggregates, organizational structures, and constructed aspects, that encourage student involvement and participation in learning, both within and beyond the classroom. At the heart of current debates about institutional effectiveness are issues of student learning. What conditions promote student achievement and learning? It is clear from numerous studies that the benefits of learning are related directly to degrees of student participation and involvement. Students who engage themselves as active learners, regardless of setting, show greater gains from the learning experiences encountered. What are the environmental conditions and mechanisms that promote involvement of students in their learning?

A Theory of Involvement

The key to successful learning and, indeed, to developing students' talents, can "be simply stated: Students learn from becoming involved" (Astin, 1985, p. 133). According to Astin, involvement is recognized more by actions than by attitudes:

> Involvement is neither mysterious nor esoteric. Quite simply, student involvement refers to the amount of physical and psychological energy that the student devotes to academic experience. A highly involved student is one who, for example, devotes considerable energy to studying, spending a lot of time on campus, participates actively in student organizations, and interacts frequently with faculty members and other students. Conversely, an uninvolved student may neglect studies, spend little time

on campus, abstain from extracurricular activities, and have little contact with faculty members or other students. [p. 134]

Although a person's motivation is a potentially important indicator, Astin (1985) concluded that "it is not so much what an individual thinks or feels but what he or she does that defines and identifies involvement" (p. 135). Likewise, Pace (1984) concluded that "what counts most is not who they [students] are or where they are but what they do" (p. 1). Thus, involvement is most clearly manifested in actions such as joining, participating, attaching, committing, engaging, immersing, and volunteering.

Astin (1985) outlined five basic postulates of his involvement theory:

1. Involvement refers to the investment of physical and psychological energy in various "objects." The objects may be highly generalized (the student experience) or highly specific (preparing for a chemistry examination).

2. Regardless of its object, involvement occurs along a continuum. Different students manifest different degrees of involvement in a given object, and the same students manifest different degrees of involvement in different objects at different times.

3. Involvement has both quantitative and qualitative features. The extent of a student's involvement in, say, academic work can be measured quantitatively (how many hours the student spends studying) and qualitatively (does the student review and comprehend reading assignments, or does the student simply stare at the textbook and daydream?).

4. The amount of student learning and personal development associated with any educational program is

directly proportional to the quality and quantity
of student involvement in that program.

5. The effectiveness of any educational policy or
practice is directly related to the capacity of that
policy or practice to increase student involvement.
[pp. 135–136]

Pace's and Kuh's (1998) work with the College Student Experiences Questionnaire offers a systematic inventory of 142 activities,
reflective of a range of undergraduate experiences constituting forms
of student involvement. These activities are arranged within fourteen
different categories (or subscales) providing a useful map through various arenas of student participation on a typical college campus,
including course learning; library experiences; activities related to science and technology; use of cultural facilities, student union, and athletic and recreation facilities; experiences in residence halls and
fraternity or sorority houses; experiences with faculty; writing activities; participation in clubs and organizations; personal experiences;
student acquaintances; and topics and information in conversations.

The six to twelve items within each category offer a descriptive
litany of observable activities that students may engage in and that
indicate the quantity and quality of their campus involvement. For
example, within the category of experiences with faculty, students
report on the frequency with which they "talked with a faculty member," "discussed career plans and ambitions," or "worked with a faculty member on a research project." Exemplar items from other
arenas include, for purposes of further illustration, "heard a speaker
at the student union or center" (student union), "asked other people to read something you wrote to see if it was clear to them" (experience in writing), and "had serious discussions with students whose
philosophy of life or personal values were very different from yours"
(student acquaintances). The items in each subscale vary in intensity of activity, ranging from those more passive to those more active.
Implicit in this scheme is that each of these activities is presumed to

contribute to students' learning and development. Therefore, campus environments that make available and encourage such activities are thought to be "involving." What is it that characterizes such environments? According to Pascarella and Terenzini (1991): "The environmental factors that maximize persistence and educational attainment include a peer culture in which students develop close on-campus friendships, participate frequently in college-sponsored activities, and perceive their college to be highly concerned about the individual student, as well as a college emphasis on supportive services (including advising, orientation, and individualized general education courses that develop academic survival skills)" (p. 64).

The National Survey of Student Engagement (Kuh, 2000), a joint undertaking of the Indiana University Center for Postsecondary Research and Planning and National Center for Higher Education Management Systems, employs the College Student Report (Kuh, 1999) to assess institutional quality in reference to how students report using their time (in terms of activities and experiences inside and outside the classroom) and what instructors and student affairs staff do to engage students in empirically proven good educational practices. Much like its predecessor (Pace, 1990; Pace & Kuh, 1998), this survey evaluates campuses on a range of involvement indicators or best practices known to be related to powerful educational outcomes.

We now turn to a consideration of a range of physical, aggregate, organizational, and constructed environment concepts that illuminate the dynamics of environments that may promote student involvement.

Physical Dimensions of Involvement

Several key concepts emerge from the study of physical environments relevant to a discussion of student involvement. Among the more salient are notions of campus location, human-scale design, layout, and flexibility.

Campus Location

The location of an institution itself is perhaps the most obvious factor in considering the degree of involvement encouraged among students. Although the dynamics of a small rural campus differ significantly from those of a large urban campus (to cite two variations among others), opportunities abound in either type of setting. As Kuh, Schuh, Whitt, and Associates (1991) observed in their study of fourteen exemplary institutions recognized as "involving colleges," "No matter where a campus is located—geographically isolated, a short distance from a city, or surrounded by a metropolitan area—that location can be used to educational advantage" (p. 307).

For the small rural, residential campus, in spite of predictable student complaints about nothing to do, motivation for involvement may emerge from physical isolation and the need to create a whole, meaningful life as full-time students. Much like the workings of a small village or town, decisions need to be made with respect to purposes and goals of programs, allocation and expenditure of resources, the social and intellectual needs of citizens, and the nurturing of a sense of pride of place. Each of these aspects offers numerous opportunities for students to become engaged in practices of good citizenship and assuming responsibility for the quality of life encountered. Grinnell College, for example (see Kuh et al., 1991), located in a small Iowa town sixty miles from the nearest city of any size, perhaps works best in involving its talented students precisely because of the fewer distractions demanding student time and energy in its immediate environs. Students there take great pride in the creation of their own involved learning environment. Berea College in rural Kentucky and Earlham College in southern Indiana are other examples of this same dynamic. Isolation becomes the occasion for participation.

On the other end of the spectrum, the location of a large urban campus, ensconced in a thriving, or in some cases deteriorating, metropolis presents a different challenge. On the one hand, issues of campus safety and security may mitigate against access of students to various resources and locations in limited ways. Evening hours, traditional times for student meetings, events, and gatherings, may be especially risky in such settings, particularly for female students who are often cautioned not to venture out across campus at night. On the other hand, such settings may offer a wealth of opportunities for students to participate in a wide range of community activities, from cooperative learning positions to group service learning programs. In fact, an understanding of involvement in such settings may need to be expanded to include those activities and roles students bring with them to campus, particularly nontraditional age students (Schuh, Andreas, & Strange, 1991). Whether internal to the institution or a combination of campus-based and community-centered programs and leadership opportunities, the key is to identify those initiatives with potential for drawing students into them both as a means of complementing classroom learning as well as contributing to the quality of life in the institution and its environs.

Human-Scale Design

Another principle derived from the physical dimensions of an environment has to do with its overall scale. As Nock (1943) observed, "All Souls College, Oxford, planned better than it knew when it limited the number of its undergraduates to four; four is exactly the right number for any college which is really intent on getting results" (p. 51). Clearly, settings characterized as human-scale in design tend to encourage greater participation and involvement of members. Just as their locations serve to generate opportunities for involvement, the human-scale physical properties of "involving colleges" further encourage participation and investment of time among students (Kuh et al., 1991).

> The concept of human scale is multifaceted. Taken together, human-scale properties permit students to

become familiar with and feel competent in their environment. In this sense, human-scale environments engender a sense of efficacy and confidence. . . . Human-scale environments are not over-crowded, blend in with the natural surroundings, and accommodate small numbers of people in structures usually no more than three stories above the ground. . . . For example, smaller, low-rise dormitories seem to be more cheerful, friendly, relaxing, and spacious than larger, high-rise dormitories. A greater sense of community and increased incident of helping behavior are exhibited by residents of low-rise units when compared with counterparts in high-rise units. In addition, cohesion and social interaction characteristic of small living units seem to mediate tensions and stress common to academic communities. [Kuh et al., 1991, p. 110]

The importance of human-scale design to the central purposes of higher education becomes quickly evident when considering the experiences of students in a typical large-scale, introductory course often encountered during the first year of college, especially at large public institutions. From the literature on intellectual development during the college years (for example, King & Kitchener, 1994), it is clear that students bring varying assumptions about knowing and appropriate sources of knowledge to any learning experience. The economies of large-scale classes, not to mention the potentially intimidating qualities of such settings, all but preclude many of the conditions related to active learning. Given the standard fifty-minute time period, it is practically and physically impossible to include all students in the type of active learning strategies known to promote intellectual development (such as constructing, presenting, and defending a point of view in the presence of peers; leading a group discussion about a significant issue; or authoring a paper synthesizing a range of resources on a particular topic). Too often such conditions dictate the use of standardized, objective assessments and generally a much more passive format than smaller, human-scale settings.

Design Layout and Flexibility

Finally, it is clear that the design, layout, availability, and flexibility of campus settings (see the distinction between "soft" and "hard" architecture in Chapter One) also have much to do with their ability to encourage involvement. The extent to which the design and layout facilitates interaction of participants is thought to be an important antecedent to involvement. Spaces that encourage individuals to spend time interacting with others are described as "sociopetal" or "socially catalytic" spaces. Intentionally planned or not, these designs support the social qualities of campus life and mitigate against the personal isolation that may evolve over time in a competitive academic milieu. Kuh et al. (1991) underscored the importance of these institutional spaces.

> Interaction among community members is fostered by the availability of indoor and outdoor spaces where people can come together without much effort. Institutions should consider whether their campuses have adequate places that encourage spontaneous, informal interaction among students. Examples include: accessible departmental lounges; alcoves, benches, and chairs in the hallways of classroom buildings which allow faculty members and students a convenient place to continue class discussions; residence hall and union areas that encourage impromptu interaction, such as lounges with comfortable furniture, wide hallways, and side stairwells; and meeting facilities with space dividers that permit the creation of small, quiet gathering spaces. [p. 309]

In addition to public spaces, providing personal space may be equally important for purposes of involvement. Students need places to call their own, where a sense of ownership, personalization, security, and identity offer a base from which to venture out and seek engagement and involvement with others. In the words of Virginia Woolf, a person needs "a room of one's own" to be creative and successful. Again, most involving colleges

> provide places to which students can escape and find solitude if desired. . . . Escape places are more than a library carrel or a single room in a residence hall. The availability of personal space—such as the foothills at Stanford, the Miller farm and back campus at Earlham, the pond at Western College at Miami University, the river at Mount Holyoke, and the organic farm and Puget Sound at The Evergreen State College—allows students to relax and to think. [Kuh, et al., 1991, p. 120]

Related to this notion of personal space is the importance of a "third place" (Oldenburg, 1989) in students' lives. A third place is distinguished by its characteristic setting, that is, a place where one neither lives nor works, but where one goes to relax and enjoy the moment. Much like a familiar hangout, a third place tends to bind people together in a defined space where typical roles and responsibilities are lifted temporarily while new relationships and connections are explored in a unique and comfortable culture. The corner pizza pub, coffee shop, or bookstore has served such purposes for many. On college and university campuses the need for a third place is often met in the facilities of a student union or commuter center.

Ultimately, space most likely to contribute to involvement must be flexible in its design. The ability to move walls and to rearrange seating capacities and designs allows for the maximum use of space and the accommodation of the greatest number of needs. Thus, a small tiered lecture room by day becomes a comedy club stage by evening, encouraging students to share time and talents. The availability of multiple spaces amenable to multiple uses seems to be the key to an involving physical design.

Aggregate Dimensions of Involvement

Concepts from human aggregate theory (see Chapter Two) suggest that individuals are most attracted to and involved in groups of people who share interests and activities and that such groups are most likely to reinforce those interests and activities as congruence between personal needs, skills, and environmental rewards is maximized. In Holland's (1973) terms, highly differentiated (dominated by a single type) and consistent aggregates (comprised of similar compatible types) create characteristic environments that have greater potential for attracting, supporting, and retaining those most similar to the aggregate's dominant features. Thus, person-environment fit is presumed to encourage involvement and engagement. This basic dynamic of human aggregates is evident in the synergy of any student organization or activity group where individuals of like minds and spirits come together in the interest of a common goal, program, or event.

A principle worth exploring here is the potential connection between homogeneous groupings and degree of student involvement. The use of common interest groupings is on the rise among academic and student affairs planners. On some campuses this takes the form of establishing living-learning communities where students are assigned rooms, floors, wings, or entire residence halls based on a commonality of academic interests (such as women in sciences or business majors). In other places (such as the University of Missouri and Bowling Green State University) freshman interest groups (FIGs) are organized around a core set of learning experiences. In many ways the standard academic department reflects a similar dynamic, as faculty and students come together in a curriculum designed to focus on a particular set of interests.

Specialized offices and organizations serving the needs of particular students (adult learners, students of color, women, gay, lesbian, and bisexual students) also function as supportive aggregates that, in turn, encourage involvement. In Spitzberg and Thorndike's (1992) analysis, these centers sustain the "community of the parts" in an institution, in effect, offering homogeneous groupings of individuals who share common cultures, experiences, and values that distinguish them from others in the setting. This is particularly important when considering involvement of those who differ from the dominant culture and characteristics of the campus at large. Thus, the Latino student union, multicultural affairs office, and the gay, lesbian, bisexual, and transgendered student organization become important not only as a source of support and security for select students but also as a base from which to become involved within the larger campus.

Organizational Dimensions of Involvement

Involvement entails the engagement of individuals in significant roles and activities. As participants assume responsibilities, settings make greater claims on them, exacting commitments and uses of time and energy in support of specific goals. This is the nature of organized behavior, a dynamic basic to learning and involvement whether in the classroom, conference room, or student activities planning room. What aspects of the organizational environment contribute to or detract from involvement? Answers to this question may lie in an understanding, once again, in the consequences of organizational scale and in the dynamics of organizational structure.

The overall organizational scale of a setting has significant impact on the level of involvement in that setting. According to Moos (1986, p. 410) "The results on organizational size are highly consistent. As . . . group size increase[s], morale and attitudes become less positive, and absenteeism is more frequent." From this perspective it becomes clear why large-scale organizational settings might discourage involvement indirectly through attenuating participants' enthusiasm and morale, and ultimately their retention.

Simply stated, if individuals have few reasons to "show up," they have even fewer reasons to become involved in the setting. For example, large settings encounter the problems of overmanning (Wicker, 1973) or redundancy (Chickering & Reisser, 1993). Redundant and overmanned environments simply have too many people for too few opportunities for meaningful achievement among participants. The opposite condition, undermanning (too many opportunities for too few people) also has consequences for involvement. As Moos (1986) observed:

> People perform more activities in undermanned settings, and they are required to accept more positions of responsibility. These settings have a greater "claim" on people, because they require more effort and because relatively more difficult and important tasks are assigned to the occupants. It is less likely that a person will achieve great proficiency at any one task, since each person must fulfill several tasks. Each person has greater functional importance in the setting, more responsibility, and a greater feeling of functional self-identity. However, there may be greater feelings of insecurity, since each person is in greater jeopardy of failing to carry out the tasks assigned, and the tasks are more important for the maintenance of the setting. [p. 408]

In order to encourage involvement in an overmanned setting, either the overall size of the membership needs to be reduced (perhaps by starting another group) or the number of opportunities must be increased. In undermanned settings, increasing the number of participants or reducing the number of tasks and responsibilities becomes the challenge. In essence, it is the overall ratio of number of individuals to number of opportunities in a setting that is most important for consideration in creating an involving environment.

Related to this discussion of the effects of organizational scale is the design of organizational structures (see Chapter Three). The degree of organizational complexity and the way in which power is distributed in an organization often determine the level and significance of involvement for participants. Insufficient structural complexity, combined with centralization of power and decision making and maintained by higher degrees of formalization and stratification, usually means that fewer individuals become involved. In such cases, a minimal number of individuals do most everything, leaving little room or reason for others to participate. On the other hand, as structural complexity increases (to a point) and power and decision making are distributed more equally throughout, greater opportunities emerge for the participation of greater numbers of individuals. For example, the history of most new student organizations can illustrate this dynamic. Although functioning as a committee of the whole might be quite satisfactory initially while the group is small, success in attracting additional members depends on the extent to which the organization can create multiple tasks and assignments establishing a need for additional members. This goal is typically achieved by the creation of subcommittees with their respective charges and functional responsibilities within the organization. In effect, this step increases structural complexity (horizontally), and, as long as this change is accompanied by a decentralization of power and decision making, opportunities for significant involvement increase.

An interesting parallel is seen in the growth and development of churches, particularly among the rapidly growing evangelical sects. As church membership increases, greater and varying needs emerge, calling for the establishment of new ministries (increasing horizontal complexity), which in turn engage additional members in the decision making and work of the church. When optimum size is surpassed, additional churches break off from the larger body to form a new smaller scale unit, and the process continues.

Perhaps the key to any involving organizational environment has most to do with the distinction between a dynamic and static organizational design. Recall from Chapter Three that the structural arrangements of dynamically organized environments combine a higher degree of complexity with lower degrees of centralization, formalization, stratification, efficiency, and a relative emphasis on the quality (rather than quantity) of the organization's products or services. An organization oriented toward the status quo might be characterized by lower degrees of complexity but higher degrees of centralization, formalization, stratification, and efficiency, and a relative emphasis on the quantity (in contrast to quality) of the organization's products or services. In general, a dynamic organizational design encourages and supports innovation, while the static design tends to discourage change (Hage & Aiken, 1970).

Both forms might contribute to involvement, to some extent, at differing points in the life cycle of the organization. For example, any organization (residence hall government, student activities club) that is up and running, complete with an array of clearly delineated structures, functions, and programs, offers an identifiable framework for potential members to become involved with, especially as vacancies occur. The familiar request "We need someone to take over this responsibility this year" becomes a direct invitation to participate and get involved. Simply stated, there's something to join. A dynamic structure, on the other hand, might also encourage participation through its potential for innovation. Change brings opportunities for program development and leadership, especially for those who are more capable of functioning within ambiguous and fluid leadership situations. Perhaps an extreme of either design might discourage involvement, the static organization through its limited flexibility, and the dynamic through its limited definition of direction and structure.

Support for these notions of a dynamic and involving organizational design is reflected in the recent growing interest in models of classroom teaching, variously labeled cooperative, collaborative, and peer learning. These forms of academic teamwork call for a restructuring of the more traditional centralized, formalized, and stratified classroom to include group-oriented strategies, with students assuming major responsibilities for their own learning in collaboration with peers and instructors. Benefits of these pedagogical designs have included greater student achievement, more positive relationships among students, and greater psychological well being.

Constructed Dimensions of Involvement

The notion that constructed (or perceived) aspects of a setting contribute to the degree of participant involvement is immediately recognized when consideration is given to the consequences of various social climate and organizational culture features of the environment. From a social climate perspective (see Chapter Four), Moos (1986) concluded that those settings emphasizing relationship dimensions "exert a consistent positive influence on morale and satisfaction in all environments" (p. 415). Whether in work settings (where involvement, peer cohesion, and staff support form the components of this dimension), task-oriented groups (emphasizing cohesiveness, leader support, and expressiveness), or living environments (emphasizing involvement and emotional support), relationship dimensions serve to invite participation and to sustain those who do become involved. From an institutional view, the importance of relationship dimensions may lie in their capacity for evoking a sense of attachment from students. As Moos (1986a) observed, "Colleges with a high sense of Community and Awareness (Relationship dimensions) have a high proportion of students who feel a strong emotional attachment to the college. In addition, it is rare for students to report not having participated in any extracurricular activities in college environments that are high on Cohesion" (p. 337).

The effects of this dynamic are apparent in specific institutional subenvironments as well: "Students express greater satisfaction, show more interest in their course material, and engage in more course-relevant activities in classes that are high on Relationship dimensions" (Moos, 1986a, p. 338). The pervasive influence of relationship dimensions on involvement makes sense given the social nature of human beings and the potential for reinforcement gained by joining a group. Clearly, a group that alienates others has little potential for attracting, satisfying, or sustaining involvement of members. Thus, taking the time to build and nurture connections and relationships in a setting may be the single most important strategy a group leader can pursue if continuing involvement and satisfaction of members is the goal.

The role of customs, symbols, beliefs, values, and other artifacts of organizational culture must also be considered in this discussion of involvement. Cultural artifacts not only invite others to join and participate but they also instruct members on how to participate successfully. The study of Amish society has yielded some interesting observations in that respect (Hostettler, 1993), underscoring the power of nonverbal communication in shaping member's behavior.

Among the strongest communities are those that emphasize nonverbal modes of communication—a practice, a style, an expression, a tradition, a ritual. Those communities most at risk of losing their identity tend to emphasize verbal communication. The same might be said about colleges and universities that promote involvement. Those institutions most successful at enculturating a tradition of involvement among students are culturally distinctive in the sense that they create an attractive and powerful "feel," apparent immediately to prospective participants in the setting. Perhaps this is why such campuses concentrate many of their resources (recruitment materials, orientation programs) at the beginning of or prior to the college experience in the interest of communicating to prospective students the nature of those cultural artifacts.

Campus culture creates a signature impression on students prior to their enrollment, inviting them to join the legacy that has served others well. Recall the opening scenario in Chapter Four when Clare learned about the unusual involvement history and tradition of Adams College at the freshman convocation ceremony. There is something special about such places that encourage students to become part of the experience. This is the tacit power of institutional culture.

Involving Campuses

Colleges and universities most successful at inviting students to get involved seem to do so through offering a continuous and seamless experience of learning, both within and beyond the classroom. After visiting fourteen exemplar institutions perceived to engage students in out-of-class involvement as a complement to the academic mission, Kuh, et al. (1991) concluded the following about what characterizes such places:

1. Institutions that have a clear mission, kept plainly in view, encourage involvement (p. 341).
2. Institutions that value and expect student initiative and responsibility encourage involvement (p. 345).
3. Institutions that recognize and respond to the total student experience encourage involvement (p. 347).
4. Institutions that provide small, human-scale environments and multiple subcommunities encourage involvement (p. 351).
5. Institutions that value students and take them and their learning seriously encourage involvement (p. 359).
6. Institutions that are able to generate feelings of loyalty and a sense of specialness encourage involvement (p. 363).

What Kuh et al. (1991) observed in whole institutional settings is concurrent with many of these same environmental strategies discussed in this and previous chapters. Physical design and layout, human aggregate groupings, organizational structures, and collective constructions all come together to leave little doubt as to the purposes of the setting—to join, participate, and get involved.

Institutional Assessment and Response

To promote more active involvement, institutional leaders must first become aware of the extent to which the environments they create and participate in exhibit the kinds of characteristics most likely to capitalize on students' sense of belonging and security. The following might serve as institutional probes for identifying factors that encourage or inhibit involvement.

1. Involving environments contain physical features of human scale dimension, flexible design, and the capacity for encouraging interaction as well as providing for individual needs. Is there sufficient meeting space? Where do students and faculty gather? How accessible are these places? What spaces isolate individuals? What spaces encourage individuals to gather informally? What are the traffic patterns of those who participate in the setting?

2. Involving environments encourage the development of campus subgroupings characterized by a commonality of purposes and interests. To what extent does the institution support and sustain its "community of the parts" (Spitzberg & Thorndike, 1992, p. 145)? Are various campus groups given adequate resources for sustaining an ongoing agenda of educational purposes? How do students learn of the various group participation options? How is participation in campus groups facilitated, recognized, and rewarded?

3. Involving environments offer an optimum ratio of individuals to opportunities, with sufficient structure to allow for the identification of significant roles and sufficient flexibility to accommodate the imprint of participating members. Are there sufficient opportunities for students to join and participate in various leadership roles on campus? In residence halls? In student organizations? In classrooms? What is the average class size? What is the ratio of faculty to students? Are resources available to cover start-up costs of new student initiatives?

4. Involving environments tacitly encourage participation through cultural artifacts that signal the availability, importance, and value of involvement. What nonverbal messages are communicated to prospective students about the role of campus involvement? What would a campus culture audit (Whitt, 1993) say about the prevailing value placed on participation and involvement in classes? In student organizations? In campus governance? Who is included in campus culture? Who is excluded?

Depending on what information is generated from such assessments, campus policies and practices can be directed more intentionally toward the development of involving milieus. For example, where overmanned settings prevail (such as large introductory classes), small, human-scale subgroups can be organized to promote greater participation and investment of time and energy. Democratic and collaborative decision-making practices can be modeled to create opportunities and expectations for involvement. Gathering spaces can be identified and enhanced through new construction or renovation of current facilities (as is happening with student union buildings and recreation centers on many campuses) to encourage interaction of various campus constituents. Social events (such as a campus-wide picnic) can be featured to enhance the relational and hospitable qualities of campus life. Last, campus traditions, practices, and symbols can be highlighted in ceremonies and publications for purposes of enhancing student identification, attachment, and engagement.

Involvement in an environment extends beyond mere physical presence and sense of security. While such conditions promote participant fit and stability, they may do little to encourage the level of engagement required for learning, growth, and development. The latter outcomes are more effectively addressed by more active modes of participation. Thus, involvement includes the investment of time and energy in significant roles and responsibilities, where individuals' skills are called upon under conditions of challenge and support to contribute to the processes and outcomes of the setting (Sanford, 1966). Physical scale, design, flexibility, the affiliation and organization of people, and the integration and support of campus culture can all serve in the interest of promoting this degree of environmental response. However, as the next chapter suggests, involvement is just the beginning of yet another level in this model—the development and maintenance of community.

7

Building a Community of Learners

W e have suggested in previous chapters that environments that offer inclusion and safety, and involve participants in significant and meaningful roles, fulfill two primary conditions for promoting learning, growth, and development: a sense of belonging and security and a mechanism for active engagement. We also suggested that if the learning potential of any environment is to be realized, a third and more complete condition is proposed: the experience of full membership in the learning setting. This last condition is present most powerfully in an environment that is characterized by the dimensions of community.

A recurrent interest in the importance of community has emerged recently within society in general and within higher education in particular. Etzioni (1993) charted a "communitarian agenda" as the means to restore a civil society in America; the Carnegie Foundation for the Advancement of Teaching (1990), noting earlier the historical tension between individuality and community in the undergraduate experience, called for a "larger, more integrative vision of community in higher education" (p. 7) that is purposeful, open, just, disciplined, caring, and celebrative; Spitzberg and Thorndike (1992) presented a theory of campus community to guide institutional renewal in the form of a "Compact for a Pluralistic Community"; and Tierney (1993) used ethnographic case studies to illuminate the challenges of building "communities of difference" on college campuses.

Indeed, the image of "community" has become deeply embedded in our views of powerful educational environments, and for very good reasons. The concept of community contains all the essential features associated with effective educational environments, as unifying purposes and values, traditions and symbols of belonging and involvement, and mutuality of care, support, and responsibility encourage a synergy of participation and worth, checking and cross-checking, to create a positive human learning environment. It is no surprise then that conditions of community are often prescribed in the literature on higher education reform (for example, the Carnegie Foundation for the Advancement of Teaching, 1990; Chickering & Reisser, 1993; Palmer, 1987). As Palmer (1987) concluded in his observations of the status of higher education: "Community must become a central concept in ways we teach and learn" (p. 25). In fact, Palmer (1998), drawing on the transformed "images of reality—from fragmentation and competition to community and collaboration" found in "virtually every academic discipline over the past fifty years" (p. 96)—takes his recommendation one step further to suggest that "community is the *essential* form of reality" and that "we know reality *only* by being in community with it ourselves" (p. 97, emphases added). Thus community-building and its associated tasks have become a major focus in how we think about the goals of education and the means to achieve them.

Perhaps no one in the higher education and student affairs literature first addressed these issues more directly than Crookston (1974, p. 57) in his proposal for the development of an "Intentional Democratic Community (IDC)" as a model for campus residential living (which is still employed at the University of Connecticut where it was first created). In that proposal, Crookston outlined the essential characteristics of such a community to include (much like Hage and Aiken's dynamic organizational environment) shared power and decision making, open communications, flexibility, and organizational and individual symbiosis. Crookston argued, "as the individual contributes to the enrichment of the community, so the community is able to enrich the individual" (p. 58). Implicit in Crookston's analysis is an understanding that community is as much a process as it is a condition. What is community? What does it mean to build community, to engage in community living, to learn as a community? These questions are addressed in this chapter with consideration of the role and design of physical, human aggregate, organizational, and constructed aspects of campus environments.

Characteristics of Communities

Communities offer a sense of belonging, security, and engagement of participants, but they also do much more. Communities establish a status of full membership for participants in an environment, offering them opportunities to engage over time in a distinct history, tradition, and culture. Historically, the qualities associated with community have included a common location, common ties of purpose and direction, and forms of social interdependence (Gardner, 1990). McMillan and Chavis (1986) have further distinguished a "psychological sense of community" to include "a feeling of belongingness, a perception of one's ability to have influence in the community, a shared belief that members' needs will be met by their commitment to be together, and a shared emotional connection" (as cited in Wells, 1996, p. 4).

The literature on human community is vast and rich, drawing from many disciplines and insights. Wells (1996, pp. 15–16) distilled ten "overlapping and intersecting themes" from this material to include:

> a sense of history and longevity (Bellah et al., 1985; Selznick, 1992) . . . a distinctive identity (Selznick, 1992) with explicit group norms and values (Gardner, 1990) . . . a healthy pluralistic differentiation of personal, family,

ethnic, and occupational groups (Gardner, 1990; Selznick, 1992; Warren & Lyon, 1983) . . . interdependent, reciprocal, genuine, caring relationships (Selznick, 1992) that provide a sense of fellowship and confirm "otherness" (Friedman, 1983) . . . equilibrium between the preservation of individual rights and the maintenance of systems that serve the common good (Boyer, 1987; Etzioni, 1993; Friedman, 1983; Newbrough & Chavis, 1986) . . . full participative inclusion of all people without regard to difference in formal status, race, gender, political ideology, sexual orientation, age, etc. (Palmer, 1977; Peck, 1987) . . . structural mechanisms for conflict containment and accommodation (Cottrell, 1983) . . . institutional provisions and processes for self-regulation (Gardner, 1990) and for facilitating participant interaction and decision-making (Cottrell, 1983) . . . on-going linkages and relationships with the larger society (Cottrell, 1983; Gardner, 1990; McMillan & Chavis, 1986), using it as a reference point for self-examination (Peck, 1987) . . . [and] a celebrative ceremonial life which honors, affirms and renews a sense of shared identity (Boyer, 1987; Dunne, 1986; Gardner, 1990).

Synthesizing this list further it appears that communities, at their most fundamental level, are recognized by their distinct and celebrated historical identities, their balance of interdependent roles and relationships, their norms and procedures for functioning, and their linkages to the larger society.

Successful Communities

Wells' (1996) review is also instructive on the characteristics of successful communities, suggesting that they can be assessed using three criteria: "(a) commitment to the community, (b) a sense of empowerment, and (c) a sense that one 'matters' to others within the community" (p. 18). Genuine commitment, instrumental, affective, and moral (Kanter, 1972), is possibly the most important criterion of successful communities. Commitment is most apparent when members' "(a) observations of how [the community] acts and is acted upon has a vital impact in their lives and their chosen values, (b) they find that they have a significant role in [the community], and (c) they see positive results in their efforts to participate in [the community's] life" (Cottrell, 1983, as cited in Wells, 1996, p. 17). The commitment's manifestations are high retention, cohesiveness, and an acceptance of social control (Kanter, 1972). With respect to empowerment, the second criterion, successful communities influence members to act, in effect, to move beyond a sense of security and belonging to become actively engaged. Successful communities are places where it is "safe for taking risks and trying out new behaviors" (Peck, 1987), where "members participate fully and freely (Cottrell, 1983; Selznick, 1992) and share the tasks of leadership (Gardner, 1990)" (as cited in Wells, 1996, pp. 17–18). The third criterion, mattering (Schlossberg, 1989), is apparent when members move from a marginal (invalid or invisible) state to a feeling that others depend on them, are interested in them, are concerned about their fate, and share pride or empathy for their successes or failures. Crucial to this quality of successful communities is the measure of "responsible concern" members demonstrate, including "not looking away when a member is in need, a known set of community values, and the obligation to confront a member when he [sic] deviates from these values" (Mandell, 1981, as cited in Wells, 1996, p. 19).

Although this analysis thus far draws primarily from the insights of modern behavioral sciences to define the characteristics of successful community, it is interesting to note their similarity to those features that have distinguished an ancient, and one of the most persistent, forms of community life in Western culture—the monastery. Strange and Hagan (1998) identified six hallmarks of monastic communities committed to the Rule of St. Benedict, a defining document for men and women called to this form of life since the sixth century (Fry, 1981). Benedictine community members share a routine of daily life informed by both a written rule and a tradition of practices and customs; a commitment of stability to a specific place, a people, and a teacher (such as an abbot or prioress); a willingness to pursue personal change and growth in the presence of and in relationship with others; a heightened sensitivity to other members expressed in the form of careful listening and mutual obedience; a balance of active work and reflective contemplation; and an openness to and hospitality toward those outside the community. Whether in the form of ancient rituals of prayer or designer artifacts of modern corporate culture, the characteristics of community, however manifested or expressed, elevate individuals to a purpose greater than self. For an institution of higher education that purpose becomes the learning, growth, and development of all involved.

Environmental Dimensions of Community

Not surprisingly, communities evolve from the same components that define inclusive, safe, and involving environments. That is, communities depend on various natural and synthetic physical features of their location, the collective characteristics of their members, the manner in which relationships and tasks are organized, and the distinctive and tacit qualities of their dominant cultures. Thus, each component can potentially contribute to or detract from a sense of community in the environment. Among strong communities there is a synergy of components as physical features define spaces where members pursue common purposes over time in ways that are sustained by their shared characteristics and compatible with their collective, unique qualities. What is impressive about any community is not the nature of any given component, but rather how all components resonate to form a more complex and seamless whole—the community. Nonetheless, there are certain forms of these environmental dimensions that seem to support the development of community more so than others.

Among the physical features that most clearly shape the direction of any community is territory. Communities, by nature, tend to be territorial; they need space in which to exist and to carry out their functions. Territory (in both natural and synthetic forms) serves to orient the community and to create a sense of a home place, a space where artifacts of material culture are maintained and the company of members enjoyed. Proximity establishes the ground from which the community's agenda can grow.

Commonly shared interests are important features of most communities. Human aggregate concepts (see Chapter Two) suggest that the collective characteristics of people in communities are more highly differentiated and consistent, reflecting a higher proportion of similar types. Homogeneous aggregates exhibit clearer characteristics which, in turn, attract, satisfy, and sustain individuals who already share those same interests. Joining in the group then reinforces the characteristics already present, ultimately strengthening its dominant features. This accentuation effect (Feldman & Newcomb, 1969), or press toward conformity (Astin & Panos, 1966), weaves a very tight fabric for most communities, adding to a stability of roles, rewards, and expectations over time. The initial development of a community may depend on the attraction of a critical mass of involved participants whose common interests create a momentum that becomes self-sustaining. As time passes, and a community history and culture emerge, the capacity for incorporating and sustaining a more diverse aggregate improves. The power of this community development dynamic is apparent in the establishment of theme houses or freshman interest groups on many campuses, for example, where students of like majors are assigned to live in one location for purposes of creating a "living-learning community."

Organizationally, communities are often a paradox of design. They must be structured sufficiently to offer a framework of stability for involvement yet be flexible enough to respond and adapt to changing conditions and circumstances. Maintenance of traditions, customs, and practices—the collective memory and life's blood of most communities—requires certain degrees of formalization, stratification, and routine (see Chapter Three). These organizational structures tend to conserve the status quo and mitigate change. Innovation—the capacity of any organized system for responding to changing conditions—depends on a more dynamic design, one that deemphasizes "the way things have always been done." Communities also require structural flexibility as new demands call for changing roles, rewards, and expectations. Long-standing communities can point to "the way things were" and to "the way things are." For them, adaptability ensures continuing viability. This capacity for responsiveness is probably facilitated by a balance of defining authority and a decentralized, democratic distribution of power and decision making within the community.

Finally, in terms of the constructed dimensions of communities, the importance and power of organizational culture cannot be overstated. Strong communities exhibit and are recognized most often by their strong, well-defined presses, climates, and cultures. Values, beliefs, symbols, and artifacts form a seamless and, for the most part, silent synergy of influence over all aspects of community life. How this works is illuminated by the distinction, noted by Hall (1976) as cited in Hostettler (1993), between high-context and low-context cultures.

> A high-context culture is one in which people are deeply involved with one another. Awareness of situations, experience, activity, and one's social standing is keenly developed. Information is widely shared. Simple messages with deep meaning flow freely. There are many levels of communication—overt and covert, implicit and explicit signs, symbols, and body gestures, and things one may and may not talk about. Members are

sensitive to a screening process that distinguishes outsiders from insiders. . . The nonverbal, or unstated,
realms of culture are extremely important as conveyors of
information. High-context cultures are integrated, for
members are skilled in thinking comprehensively according to a system of the common good. Loyalties are
concrete and individuals work together to settle their
problems. If one person has a problem, others are expected to know what is bothering that person. [Hostettler,
1993, p. 18]

Such a description seems highly appropriate in the context of some
departments, classes, or campus organizations where the intensity and
sense of community has been experienced by many. In contrast, Hall's
description of low-context cultures, as paraphrased in Hostettler
(1993), might lend an understanding to the challenges other departments, classes, or organizations face that seem to fall short of the goals
of communal life.

Low-context cultures emphasize literacy and rationality.
Highly bureaucratized segments of culture within American life are "low" in context because information is restricted primarily to verbal communication. Other levels
of awareness are underdeveloped or dormant. Ways of
perceiving are restricted primarily to a linear system
of thought, a way of thinking that is considered synony-
mous with truth. Logic is considered the only road to
reality. Low-context cultures use primarily mathematical
models to explain nature and environment. People are
highly individualistic and somewhat alienated in contexts
that require little involvement with other people. Low-
context culture is fragmented rather than integrated, and
people live more and more like machines. The contradictions that compartmentalize life are carefully sealed

off from one another. Persons in low-context cultures
are prone to use manipulation to achieve their goals and
are also prone to be manipulated. Failures are blamed
on the system. In times of crisis, individuals expect help
from institutions, not from persons. [Hostettler, 1993,
pp. 18–19]

Hall suggests that these differences do not emerge "through conscious design," but rather unconsciously through "the hidden cur-
rents of culture that shape the lives of people living under its
influence. These differences are rooted in how people express themselves, the way in which they think, how they move, how problems
are perceived and solved, . . . and how people arrange their time and
space" (Hostettler 1993, pp. 18–19). Perhaps all of this is to say that
socially constructed dimensions are the glues that hold a community together.

   In summary, communities seem to thrive when space is available
for (or dedicated to) a group of individuals who share characteristics and interests, when organizational designs invite participation,
role taking, and decision making, and when artifacts of culture
express and support a common vision and purpose. This synergy of
environmental components creates a life of its own, recognized by
those within its boundaries, as well as by those beyond, to be whole
and distinctive.

Challenges of Building Community

Understanding the dimensions of community in higher education
is one thing; implementing policies and practices to create and sustain them is another. Yet, as Wells (1996) noted, the "creation of a
sense of community on college and university campuses is viewed
as one of the central tasks of leadership" (p. iv). Spitzberg and
Thorndike (1992) articulated the timely challenge facing higher

education leaders committed to building community in a pluralistic world:

> Those who work to strengthen community on American campuses walk hand in hand with paradox. In the face of increasing complexity and diversity, they seek ways to connect individuals to subcommunities and subcommunities to community of the whole. Those aspiring to community have always possessed the ability to see the promise of wholeness in the apparent contradiction of competing individual and small-group needs and rights. Today the challenge is greater than it has ever been. [p. 145]

The creation and maintenance of community on campus is particularly challenging to educators today, especially at institutions that are overmanned and fragmented by various subgroups. The dilemma is that that which contributes to strong subcommunities usually detracts from the community of the whole, and that which sustains the whole community often does so at the expense of various subcommunities. The solution from Spitzberg and Thorndike's perspective is rather elusive but ever more urgent: "In our travels, we found many people who share our concern that healthy subcommunities are not enough, that in today's complex and diverse world, more than ever, students, and everyone else working on our campuses, must connect with the institution" (Spitzberg & Thorndike, p. 151). However, for large campuses, the structural accommodation of subcommunities is a necessary step in making that connection:

> Such a campus must affirm the centrality of its subcommunities, for it is through these that people are most likely to connect to the whole. In addition, a large campus could

choose to create a variety of cross-cutting learning communities, no larger than five hundred members (students, faculty, staff), in order to reduce the scale of the institution. These intermediate networks could connect the smaller subcommunities to the campus as a whole. [p. 161]

The challenge of building authentic campus communities is addressed by Schroeder (1993) in the context of residentially based programs. For purposes of encouraging and assessing the development of communities, the author applies four criteria: involvement, influence, investment, and identity. He defines these criterion elements as follows:

1. *Involvement*. A true community encourages, expects and rewards broad-based member involvement. The environment is characterized by a high degree of interaction, with students, not staff, assuming a multitude of roles. As a consequence, everyone is important and everyone is needed. Returning residents assume responsibility for orienting and integrating "new" members through formal and informal rites of passage. High-involving floors are characterized by supportive interactions, with students naturally helping one another with personal and academic problems.

2. *Influence*. In floor units that exhibit a high degree of influence, control is vested in members, and students exert maximum control over their physical and social environments. For example, residents are encouraged and expected to personalize their rooms and hallways, through painting and decorating them, and to recruit and assign members. They are also expected to develop a social contract whereby group standards are affirmed, both individually and collectively. In such units, students

feel important, their perspective is valued, and their contributions are essential to the welfare of the group.

3. *Investment.* Investment is a reflection of psychological ownership and flows naturally from involvement and influence. Students care about one another and their group. Boundaries with respect to other groups are clear, and group or institutional property is guarded rather than damaged. Interactions are often characterized by gentle confrontation rather than polite or passive-aggressive behaviors. Students are simply unwilling to have staff assume responsibility for them—they understand and appreciate the need for open, honest, and assertive communication with one another. Finally, there are clear variations in status and roles, as well as longevity of association. Rewards are provided for being a "good" member.

4. *Identity.* Floor units characterized by a high degree of identity are ones that focus on commonalties and transcendent values. Students in such units have shared symbols, similar to those fraternities and sororities use to signify their identities. In such living units, members describe themselves in collective terms such as we and us, not I or they, thereby reflecting their emphasis on common purposes and unity. [pp. 524–525]

The value of these four elements is apparent beyond their specific residential application, as consideration is given to what might characterize a strong academic department, a student activities organization, or a classroom. Certainly, achieving the goals of involvement, influence, investment, and identity as outlined above will go far in terms of building a sense of community in these settings as well.

Schroeder (1994) extended this framework with a six-point prescription for creating learning communities in general. Learning

communities are "generally small, unique, and cohesive units characterized by a common sense of purpose and powerful peer influences." They include "student interaction [that is] characterized by
the four I's—involvement, investment, influence, and identity"; they
"involve bounded territory that provides easy access to and control
of group space that supports ongoing interaction and social stability";
they are "primarily student centered, not staff centered, . . . [that is]
staff . . . assume that students are capable and responsible young adults
who are primarily responsible for the quality and extent of their learning"; they are "the result of collaborative partnerships between faculty, students, and residence hall staff. . . designed to intentionally
achieve specific educational outcomes"; and they "exhibit a clear set
of values and normative expectations for active participation . . .
[with] normative peer cultures . . . [that] enhance student learning
and development in specific ways" (p. 183). The role of physical, human aggregate, organizational, and constructed dimensions
discussed in preceding chapters is apparent in these prescriptions.
Homogeneous groupings, facilitated by defined space, participative
organizational structures, and an integrative culture sustain communities capable of supporting learning in powerful ways.

Chickering and Reisser (1993) also suggested a formula for the
development and maintenance of community, conditions they propose for optimum development of students. They conclude:

> the community, whether it takes the form of residence hall
> unit, sorority or fraternity house, student organization, or
> informal circle of friends, should have the following char-
> acteristics . . . regular interactions between students [as] a
> foundation for ongoing relationships . . . opportunities for
> collaboration—for engaging in meaningful activities and
> facing common problems together . . . small enough so
> that no one feels superfluous . . . [inclusion of] people
> from diverse backgrounds . . . [and] [i]t serves as a refer-

ence group, where there are boundaries in terms of who is "in" and who is "out," [with] norms that inform those with different roles, behaviors, and status that they are "good" members or that what they are doing is unacceptable. [pp. 276–277]

Brower and Dettinger (1998) offer a comprehensive model for learning communities, incorporating academic, social, and physical components in the interest of developing students' professional, ethical, and civic responsibility. These components are defined respectively in terms of the "curriculum content" (academic), "interpersonal relations among students, faculty, and staff" (social), and the "place or facility where the community meets or resides" (physical) (Brower & Dettinger, 1998, p. 17) . They argue that "for a program to create a community effectively and enhance learning . . . it must integrate these three components to some degree" (p. 17). They further describe seven characteristics common to all learning communities.

All learning communities are purposefully designed to do the following:

1. Develop a sense of group identity in which all participants recognize one another as learners, while still valuing the contributions of each individual. Students recognize that participants are neither solely independent nor dependent.
2. Provide facilities or spaces in which people can come together to meet and engage in transformative learning activities.
3. Create a supportive environment that engages new students in the life of the institution. Activities and programs are designed to engage a continual stream of new members.

4. Develop a seamless student experience that integrates social and academic experiences. Although the level of integration will vary, activities and programs are designed to enable students to bring their personal interests into their academic work, as well as to bring their academic work into their personal and social activities.

5. Develop connections among disciplines, recognizing that although ways of knowing may be discipline specific, knowledge and concepts are not.

6. Provide the context for developing complex thinking skills—including divergent, flexible, and critical thinking—and social cognition, creativity, and metacognition, whether the focus is on civic, professional, or ethical responsibility. Programs and activities are designed so that students interact with material at a much deeper level than simply receiving information.

7. Continually evaluate both the process and the outcomes. Modifications should be made as necessary. A learning community continually evolves as new members enter. Although this is essential to the vitality of the community, it also requires that the community be continually evaluated to ensure that its stated objectives continue to be met. [Brower & Dettinger, 1998, pp. 20–21]

The authors' prescriptions closely parallel those of the other observers and theorists summarized in this and preceding chapters, insomuch as they understand the development of community as an integrated process, involving physical, aggregate, organizational, and constructed dimensions along a dynamic, evolutionary path. Successful communities never come "to be," in any fixed formula; rather, as living entities, they must continue to grow and develop in response to their own environs, both internal and external to their boundaries.

Assessment and Institutional Response

In addition to those features contributing to a sense of belonging, security, and involvement, assessment of campus characteristics that support the development of community, whether in the classroom, academic department, student organization, commuter student center, or residence hall should include the following questions:

- Do students, faculty, and staff have opportunities and spaces to connect with others on campus around their common interests, values, and experiences?

- Are differences of interests, values, and experiences accommodated in caring and supportive ways?

- Are decision-making structures and practices facilitative of participation?

- Do symbols, traditions, and other cultural artifacts reflect and celebrate the community of the whole as well as the community of the various parts?

The importance of common interests, values, and experiences in learning underscores the role of identity and affiliation in students' lives. Individuals seek educational experiences in order to explore dimensions of self. Questions such as Who am I?, What can I do?, and Where am I going? all converge in a state of transition (Levinson, 1978; Levinson & Levinson, 1996) as life structures are unpacked, examined, and reassembled for the next phase of life. Experiencing a community of interests during such a time affirms and supports the emergence of a sense of identity, one of the most powerful and consistent outcomes of the learning process.

Institutional administrators should inquire as to what extent gathering spaces and resources are allocated and opportunities created to facilitate multiple communities of interest on campus. How and when are these opportunities communicated to students? What are the expectations concerning these opportunities and their role in student learning goals? The resurgence of first-year experience programs on many campuses may offer the best model for introducing new students to these communal dimensions of education.

The dynamics of selection and identification necessary for developing a community of interests will sooner or later lead to a divergence of interests and inevitable moments of conflict and tension. However, as Palmer (1987) notes, conflict is not the absence of community but rather its heart. In Palmer's analysis, "Knowing and learning are communal acts. They require many eyes and ears, many observations and experiences. They require a continual cycle of discussion, disagreement, and consensus over what has been seen and what it all means" (p. 25). Thus, conflict, rather than detracting from community, energizes it. Parker continues: "At the core of this communal way of knowing is a primary virtue . . . capacity for creative conflict . . . there is no knowing without conflict." In fact, "A healthy community. . .includes conflict at its very heart, checking and correcting and enlarging the knowledge of individuals by drawing on the knowledge of the group" (p. 25). The key, then, may lie in how conflict is embraced and responded to, and therein is the importance of communities in learning. As Palmer concluded: "Community . . . is precisely that place where an arena for creative conflict is protected by the compassionate fabric of human caring itself" (p. 25).

In addition to an ethic of justice and fairness, campus leaders must inquire as to what extent an ethic of care is manifested during moments of conflict. Can individuals disagree with each other without forfeiting relational bonds? In a pluralistic society this ethic of care must extend beyond the community of the parts to also include the community of the whole. Are individuals and groups willing to give up self-interests for the sake of preserving the larger sense of community?

The importance of facilitating learning through participative, democratic organizational structures has long been a part of the philosophical discussions of educational systems (for instance, Dewey, 1916 and Thayer-Bacon and Bacon, 1998). Democratic processes entail the distribution of power and decision making in a setting (a decentralized organizational design) while inviting participants to assume significant roles and responsibilities. This is the essence of involvement—the exertion of energy and time on task toward the achievement of educational goals. Such an approach recognizes, as Palmer (1987) suggests, that without the investment of community members, education quickly reverts to a one-sided, hierarchic, and at best, rote ritual of information giving and receiving.

Learning is a more active challenge, enhanced by the input and processing of a variety of perspectives and points of view. It also involves a level of risk as participants struggle to construct new ways of thinking and being in the company of others. The participative structures of democratic community offer the conditions most likely to support the outcomes of active learning. Institutional leaders, faculty, and staff interested in encouraging participation must develop an ear and an eye for democratic community wherever it may be found on campus. Classroom instructors, directors of student activities and residence hall groups, and department heads can all begin by asking: Who is in charge here? and How are decisions made? In general, the extent to which responses are inclusive of the greatest number of participants in the setting reflects the degree to which this criterion is being met.

The significance of organizational culture in effecting a sense of community on campus has been underscored in numerous studies (for example, Kuh et al., 1991). Engaging communities are mission driven and are recognized immediately by a distinctive array of symbols, values, beliefs, practices, and other artifacts that create a compelling vision of where they are going and how they intend to get there. While accommodating the varying needs of subcommunities (the community of the parts), those settings committed to the goals of community building are successful in identifying that which unites all members, regardless of differences. That is to say, they can visualize the community of the whole.

Questions contained in the Involving College Audit Protocol (Kuh et al., 1991) include several probes appropriate to assessing this criterion, such as: "What traditions and events introduce and socialize students to core values of the institution?"; "What opportunities exist to celebrate the campus community?"; "Are there segments of the campus community who feel they are excluded from participating in such celebrations?"; and "What 'terms of endearment' [that is, words and expressions that have context-bound meanings and encourage feelings of belonging in members and express institutional values and beliefs] are used to communicate the special qualities of the institution to insiders and outsiders?" (pp. 403–404).

A number of different models have served as frameworks for understanding the nature and role of educators in colleges and universities. We've grown accustomed more recently, under increasing pressures for accountability, to assessing inputs and outputs as the managers of educational "industries," where student achievement scores and degrees are written into annual reports as "products," with expectations of increasing various efficiencies from one year to the next. Also familiar to us are the political dimensions of our work. We become monitors and referees in cultural wars on a battleground of ideas, where alliances are struck, persuasions mounted, and power consolidated to effect the outcome of debated concerns. While elements of either of these models are perhaps unavoidable in any educational setting, the engaging and generative qualities of community are preferred here for purposes of defining the character of a learning environment. In community, shared interests, in time, space, and culture, compel individuals to engage one another creatively toward the achievement of specific goals and outcomes. This is the most powerful framework for the pursuit of learning.

Finally, we acknowledge that the elements of community defined here heavily depend on physical proximity for shaping their dynamics. With increasing emphasis on distance learning and the technological capacities of the Internet and World Wide Web emerging on many college campuses, it is becoming a distinct possibility that our thinking about this particular dimension in the lives of students might change significantly in the years to come. The potential for computer-mediated environments to deliver similar conditions of inclusion, safety, involvement, and community suggests that this is an area deserving of our attention.

8

Considering
Computer-Mediated Environments

With estimates of 40 percent of current Internet users being in the eighteen to twenty-six-year-old age range, and over one-third of the thirty million users on-line worldwide logging in from computers with the domain name "edu" (educational institution), it is apparent that computer-mediated communication (CMC) is rapidly ingraining itself into the college campus among faculty and students alike. Marshall McLuhan is reported to have remarked (Kelly, 1998) that the academic community could best understand the implications of these changing communications technologies by keeping one step ahead of their popular use, observing their impact as it occurs. In light of this advice, it is important that a book focusing on understanding and improving campus environments pursue the concept of computer-mediated communication and its impact on campus environments.

The higher education community may not be a full step ahead of other segments of society in implementing activities associated with these new technologies, but enough has occurred that their value is being studied and networks are being implemented on campuses with considerable investment. How is CMC and the multitude of virtual communities it has spawned in recent years reshaping for students the dimensions and dynamics of their college experience, especially with regard to aspects of learning? What is the promise of these new forms of communication on campus? What

are its challenges and cautions? In response to the conceptual structure of this book, what are the implications of this technology for
the inclusion, safety, involvement, and communal experience of students? These are the questions that guide our examination in the
following pages.

Computer-Mediated Communication and Teaching and Learning

Computer-mediated communication (CMC) is an umbrella term for
the use of computers to support human communications (Santoro,
1995). Included are the various communication activities associated
with electronic mail, group conferencing systems, and interactive
communication modes, like chat rooms and listservs. CMC allows
computer networks to be "primarily a mediator of communications
rather than a processor of information" (Santoro, 1995, p. 11).

CMC is unique in that it does not include many of the various
cues that accompany face-to-face communications, such as eye
contact, head nods, proxemics, clothing, body language, smell,
voice inflections, vocalizations, and other forms of emotional
expression (Dunlop & Kling, 1991b; Kiesler, Siegel, & McGuire,
1991). Instead of customary social cues (Walther, 1992), CMC
relies primarily on text; it is the language of the keyboard. The
emotional component of CMC is limited to emoticons or symbols
used to convey general sentiments, ASCII drawings, and a few
agreed upon construction rules (such as the use of uppercase letters
for emphasis). Kiesler, Siegel, and McGuire (1991) outlined some
of the basic characteristics of CMC, noting its speed, efficiency,
distribution options (to either a single person or to many), and
social anonymity, but also its weak nonverbal cues, limited dra-
maturgical cues, and lack of status or position cues. They concluded
that, from a social psychological perspective, CMC has "a paucity
of social context information and . . . few widely shared norms
governing its use" (p. 335). Concurrently though, Kiesler (1987)

also noted that CMC tends to break down hierarchical barriers, is more efficient in its use of words, and that people tend to join in more readily than they do in face-to-face encounters. Furthermore, the impact of CMC on the people who use it includes being "less bound by convention, less influenced by status, and unconcerned with making a good appearance. Their behavior becomes more extreme, impulsive, and self-centered. They become, in a sense, freer people" (Kiesler, 1987, p. 48).

The exponential growth of CMC on the college campus has supported an array of activities, particularly in the service of teaching and learning (Berge & Collins, 1995). Among various forms of computer-assisted instruction (CAI) are found:

- Mentoring, such as advising and guiding students
- Project-based instruction, either within the classroom or in projects involving community, national, or international problem solving
- Guest lecturing, which promotes interaction between students and persons in the larger community
- Didactic teaching, that is, supplying course content, posting assignments, or other information germane to course work
- Retrieval of information from on-line information archives, such as OPACs (Online Public Access Catalog), ERIC, and commercial databases
- Course management, for example, advising, delivery of course content, evaluation, collecting and returning assignments
- Public conferencing, such as discussion lists using mainframe listserv software
- Interactive chat, used to brainstorm with teachers or peers and maintain social relationships

- Personal networking and professional growth and such activities as finding persons with similar interests on scholarly discussion lists

- Facilitating collaboration

- Individual and group presentations

- Peer review of writing, projects involving peer learning, groups or peer tutorial sessions, and peer counseling

- Practice and experience using emerging technologies that may be intrinsically useful in today's society

- Computer-based instruction, such as tutorials, simulations, and drills. [p. 3]

Berge and Collins (1995) further point out that, although there are certain limitations to its support of higher education's teaching and learning mission, CMC holds the greatest promise in "its ability to liberate instruction from the constraints of time and distance" (p. 3).

Computer-Mediated Communication and Virtual Environments

Regardless of any specific contributions it can make to the instructional goals of higher education, the ultimate function of CMC in all its various forms and purposes is to bring people together (Weinreich, 1997). To underscore the significance of this role, Hudson (1997) concluded his historical review of the internet by observing that people are the killer application (referring to software applications that stimulate people to use computers). Despite the compelling quality and quantity of fingertip information available from the World Wide Web (WWW) and other on-line sources, the real attraction to being on-line, Hudson claims, is the basic human desire to be in touch with people. Kiesler (1987) made the same point, calling computing fundamentally a "social activity" (p. 47). The interactive capacities of CMC often lead to the formation of characteristic social aggregations, varying in purpose and structure. For example, some aggregations are primarily social in nature and are referred to as computer-supported social networks (CSSNs) (Wellman, et al, 1996). Computer-assisted instruction (CAI) networks form from aggregations of learners and teachers (Berge & Collins, 1995). Other on-line groups take on various forms as a function of their nature and purpose, including for example, multiuser simulated environments (MUSEs) and multiuser object oriented environments (MOOs), which use CMC to build communities of real people and constructed objects that the group agrees to treat as real (Polin, 1993). The purpose of the MUSEs and MOOs can vary from specific topic exploration to journeys into unique fantasy environments.

It is this coming together of people through computer messaging that is the basis of the concept "virtual community" (Rheingold, 1993), another important aggregation that has surfaced on the college campus in multiple forms. According to Goodman (1994), "messaging is one of the most compelling reasons humans should participate in the information superhighway . . . [it] brings them closer together" (p.20). CMC supports messaging and brings people together via electronic mail, bulletin boards, and conferencing, making possible the creation of various virtual communities. Rheingold (1993) contends that virtual communities exist and serve functions similar to real or "sensual" communities. He points to the millions of people across the world who are currently engaged in these unique technologically enabled social groups. These people communicate on a daily basis as if the computer were an electronic watercooler. Rheingold highlights the array of human activities observed in virtual communities: "People in virtual communities use words on screens to exchange pleasantries and argue, engage in intellectual discourse, conduct commerce, exchange knowledge, share emotional support, make plans, brainstorm, gossip, feud, fall in love, find friends and lose them, play games, flirt, create a little high art and a lot of idle talk. People in virtual communities do just about everything people do in real life, but we leave our bodies behind" (Rheingold, 1993, p. 3).

Johnson-Lenz and Johnson-Lenz (1995) concur with this analysis, noting that we are now using technology in "laying the foundation of a new social structure made of fiber-optic cable, silicon chips, high speed switches, and software through which digital information travels as pulses of light" (p.246). They also caution that the nature of the community produced by this technology still depends on the way we respond to it: "We must choose what we want, with whom we connect, and for what purpose" (p. 246). They conclude that community is a verb, a process, not an end state, and that with deep conversation based on "truth seeking and speaking," respectful listening, and reflection in an atmosphere of trust and safety, with time and committed intent, community will emerge from this new technology.

Some observers are more skeptical of the potential CMC may hold for effecting genuine human communication. For example, Weinreich (1997) concluded his commentary on virtual communities by questioning the quality of these networks: "How far can mediated contacts constitute community? I believe they cannot, because CMC cannot substitute for the sensual experience of meeting one another face to face. Trust, cooperation, friendship, and community are based on contacts in the sensual world. You communicate through networks but you don't live in them" (p. 2). After reviewing the arguments of the proponents of computer-mediated community building, Hunt (1997) concluded that "community on the Net remains the same nebulous term, bandied about all the time but signifying nothing" (p. 3). While our terminology and definition regarding what "community" or "sense of community" may signify lack specification, the use of CMC to establish virtual communities within the campus environment is moving forward holding both promise and precaution.

Virtual Learning Communities

Among the promises touted by those who espouse the many applications of CMC is its capacity for fostering virtual learning communities (Palloff & Pratt, 1999). For example, Ellsworth (1995) reported on using CMC in two courses and concluded that, for many students, CMC provided a new way to learn where time and location of the instructor were not critical. Students, through electronic mail, computer conferencing, and synchronous communication, built, in essence, their own peer-based virtual learning community. Paulsen (1995) identified some of the techniques for increasing student interaction in such learning communities, including the use of a computer conferencing system to facilitate debate activities, simulation, role play, discussion groups, transcript-based assignments, brainstorming, delphi research techniques, nominal group techniques, and project groups. The promise held by CMC and virtual communities to enhance teaching and learning seems to be unlimited.

Using CMC to form a virtual community of common interests among students seems to hold promise for reducing barriers between students' academic lives and their social lives. For example, programmers at Gettysburg College in Pennsylvania designed a computer program called the "Curriculum Navigation Project." Students enter on-line their curricular interests (majors and minors), career plans, and current general interests. The Curriculum Navigation computer program identifies related courses and events scheduled on campus. In addition, it assists students in locating others with similar interests and goals. The program also allows faculty to search in advance for information regarding students who have enrolled in their classes. The program is aiming for a virtual community of 2,500 campus members ("Computer Brings Students," 1997).

Campus e-mail systems are now available at most institutions, with each student having access to an on-line connection from his or her residence hall room. These systems do not sit idle. For example, it is reported that students at Dartmouth College, a campus of 8,000 students, faculty, and staff, send 25,000 e-mails daily (Gabriel, 1996). A recent college graduate said: "E-mail is like the god of every college student. People probably spend easily three hours a day sending and receiving messages. It's the No. 1 way that romances go on at colleges. It's like the dating game on line" (Gabriel, 1996, p. C10).

Students not only use CMC as part of their daily routine, but they are also connecting by way of the Web prior to coming to the institution. Guernsey (1998) reported a very rapid growth in the number of prospective students (from 4 percent in 1996 to 78 percent in 1998) using university Web pages to obtain campus information. Given the extent of current use of CMC on campus in support of teaching, learning, and social activities, as well as the growing promise of virtual learning communities, the essential question regarding CMC in the postsecondary environment is not if or when, but how virtual classrooms might improve on what has traditionally taken place in the familiar physical classroom (Doheny-Farina, 1994).

Although visions of fully computerized college campuses are tied, for the most part, to positive and exciting images (Dunlop & Kling, 1991a), voices of caution are also evident. Concerns seem to focus on the issue of the kinds of persons and communities CMC will produce, particularly whether it will engender addictions and individuals who are nonsocial in the traditional face-to-face sense. The work of Popcorn (1991) and her introduction of the concept of "cocooning" often flags this counterargument to further dependence on campus-based CMC systems. Here she reflects on the alarming levels of isolation observed among users in the recent history of such systems:

> The last gasps of the eighties found Americans huddled in high-tech caves. Cocooning, the trend we first predicted in the late seventies, was in full spin. Everyone was looking for haven at home—drawing shades, plump-

ing their pillows, clutching their remotes. Hiding. It was full-scale retreat into the last controllable (or sort of controllable) environment—your own digs. . . Cocooning is about insulation and avoidance, peace and protection, coziness and control—a sort of hyper-nesting . . . If anything, the early nineties have brought us into a time of heavy-duty burrowing, digging in deeper, building ourselves a bunker—cocooning for our lives. [pp. 27, 29]

Popcorn's description of cocooning raises questions about the impact of CMC and virtual communities on face-to-face social communications among students. Will residence hall rooms become electronic caves? Will students become overdependent on these on-line communities? Rheingold (1993), while very supportive of the virtual community concept, raised a similar note of caution:

Many people are alarmed by the very idea of a virtual community, fearing that it is another step in the wrong direction, substituting more technological ersatz for yet another natural resource or human freedom. These critics often voice their sadness at what people have been reduced to doing in a civilization that worships technology, decrying the circumstances that lead some people into such pathetically disconnected lives that they prefer to find their companions on the other side of a computer screen. There is a seed of truth in this fear, for virtual communities require more than words on a screen at some point if they intend to be other than ersatz. [p. 23]

Are these fears of students retreating to their rooms to find social relationships on-line, rather than through more typical ongoing daily interactions, unfounded? Or is the concern real? Does CMC deserve the moniker of the "addiction of the millennium" as claimed by Kiernan (1998)? In a newspaper article about college students and their use of computers (Gabriel, 1996), one student reported that he spends ten hours a day on-line. Normative data for how much time college students actually spend on-line are not available, and even if they were, there is no consensus as to what constitutes "too much" or what level would signal an addiction. From a University of Texas study of student computer use, Kiernan (1998) reported that 9 percent of those surveyed had three or more of the classic symptoms associated with addiction. In the end the choices are profound, as Rheingold (1993) warns that time on-line could be spent in "amusing ourselves to death" as well as building community.

To summarize the promise and caution of CMC use and virtual community development on campus, Michalski (1995) seems to capture the current state of affairs: "Depending on your point of view, technology is either destroying our way of life by obliterating all meaningful connections between people, or opening new possibilities for connection, new ways of building communities that can enhance and enrich our non-technological lives. There's much truth to both points of view" (p. 259).

Given these points of both praise and precaution, we now turn to a brief discussion of the potential we see in the use of computer-mediated campus environments for promoting the safety, inclusion, involvement, and community experience of students on campus.

Virtual Community and Campus Safety

Do CMC and virtual communities promote a safer campus environment? What are the safety issues associated with these forms of communication? Given the frequency with which topics of computer abuse, computer crime, and computer fraud (Kling, 1991) are featured in our campus newspapers and conversations, virtual communities, like face-to-face communities, are not immune from threats to personal safety. As Goodman (1994) noted in a discussion of virtual community deviants (on-line stalkers, sexual game players, and pornography peddlers): "as in [face-to-face] communities there are people [in virtual communities] you would rather not have contact with" (p. 170). There are, however, a number of issues unique to the safety dimensions of virtual communities. One such concern is related to the maintenance of privacy. Ladd (1991) summarizes the essence of this issue: "The traditional concept of privacy itself, involving, say, control over information about oneself of the sort that formerly was secured by pulling down curtains and locking drawers, has no application in the modern world of computer technology, where detrimental information about individuals can be easily collected without violating physical barriers" (p. 664).

Another issue related to on-line safety involves gender. McAdams (1996) speaks of the increased feelings of safety reported by women using CMC in two respects. First, for example, connecting to a library via computer alleviates concerns about venturing out onto a dark street or walking across a deserted parking lot to gain access to resource materials on campus. The sense of safety experienced while connecting to the world from one's own room is obvious. As McAdams poignantly observes: "Danger to my physical body does not exist on-line" (p. 1). The other side of the picture, though, is apparent too as reports of threats and harassment of lesbian, gay, and bisexual students, for example, emerge from time to time.

Another point related to the environmental conditions of safety concerns the dynamics of gender and interactive conversations. Studies have shown (Zimmerman & West, 1975) that in conventional face-to-face conversations women are interrupted by men more than women interrupt one another. To feel more protected from interruptions and the potential for concomitant degradation and abuse, some women are hiding their gender when they go online. CMC offers an anonymous shield against gender stereotyping, for example, with the use of on-line names that disclose little or nothing about the participant's characteristics, including gender.

Another concern related to the safety of virtual communities extends from the recent rise in incidences of cybersex or virtual sex.

This is the practice, as defined by Anderson (1996), of two or more people typing in graphic descriptions of physical sexual action to simulate sex with words over the computer network. Anderson points to the need to assess the potential effects virtual sex will have on the developmental process of college students. He also observed that due to the "high degree of anonymity and flexibility with which students can engage in virtual sex, some students develop real-life complications as a result of their virtual experience" (p. 16). On the other side of the safety issue, Anderson also points out that virtual sex may permit students to experience sexual behaviors without the associated physical threats of contracting sexually transmitted diseases or risking pregnancy. All in all, as Goodman (1994) suggests, the risks to personal safety associated with on-line communication and participation in virtual communities is quite small:

> Considering the millions of individuals on-line these days, the incidents of truly criminal behavior are infinitesimally small. Today's on-line community does not mirror American society in all proportions, so it's difficult to say how tomorrow's on-line world will fare in this arena when a greater cross section of society is on-line. That's not to say that on-line meeting places don't have their share of otherwise harmless boors and pigheaded oafs, but it's usually easy enough to ignore or bypass those folks once you get to know who they are—just as you do the people you don't like in your real-world community, block or family. [p. 171]

Virtual Community and Environmental Inclusion

Who is excluded from and who is included in virtual communities? Two major sources of exclusion operate in virtual communities: the expense of being connected to a network and the limits of technical literacy required for full participation. Perhaps the most important of these issues on campus is the need for students to have skills in computer-mediated communication. Lanham (1993) underscores this need by arguing that even in the humanities the curriculum of the future will be delivered in a highly digital form. For students to access and interact with this curriculum, they must have highly developed skills in CMC or risk exclusion from rather than inclusion in basic learning opportunities on campus. Goodman (1994) also links the lack of digital literacy to exclusion, noting that literacy will continue to play a significant role in distinguishing the haves from the have-nots. He also emphasizes the importance of a more general form of literacy, warning that on-line "you are judged primarily on your ideas, knowledge, humor, and general contribution to the sense of community within any forum" (p. 133). In order for CMC and the virtual community to provide full inclusion to the campus environment, institutions must provide the means for access, as well as assist students in the literacy required to participate fully in these on-line systems.

In addition to general issues of access and literacy, there are groups of students for whom the role of computer-mediated environments in achieving a sense of inclusion is viewed with some ambivalence. For example, with appropriate access software and hardware (screen readers, screen enlarging programs, touch screens, voice and alternate input devices), students with some physical disabilities may find the virtual community very attractive and easier to access, in comparison to negotiating the real campus physical environment. On the other hand, in the absence of such access equipment, those physically challenged may be abruptly excluded from the campus virtual community. Other student characteristics illustrative of this dilemma may be related to personality differences. For example, Livingood (1995) reported that introverts, as defined by the Myers-Briggs Type Indicator, are much more likely to use CMC and to participate in on-line networks than are extroverts. Livingood noted that "Computers are the friend of the introvert" and "Extroverts often seem too impatient for computers; they get frustrated. They would rather be out talking to someone or performing some action" (p. 1). Finally, Livingood observed that, "Rather than displacing them, today's technology is giving introverts new ways to express themselves. They are connected, they are communicating, and they are comfortable in the new world of cyberspace" (p. 2). If this is the case, it is equally important to be vigilant as to how, if at all, others may be inadvertently excluded from the campus virtual community.

In terms of environmental inclusion, perhaps the most lauded benefit of CMC and virtual community is the potential for further democratization of communities (Michalski, 1995). For instance, Hand (1994) noted the ease with which individuals access and participate in the virtual world of computers:

> One of the great things about meeting in Text Space is that no one can see you. This means that prejudices are left behind on the desktop: people have to judge you on your words rather than on your t-shirt, hair, gender, or body odor. You are what you type. It also means you can crawl out of bed, grab a cup of coffee and log in just in time for a meeting instead of rushing around like an idiot trying to get into the office—you don't even have to bother getting dressed. [p. 2]

In addition to this veil of anonymity and ease of participation, the digital world also allows greater inclusion of citizens into government functions (Langham, 1994), in that CMC and associated networks provide additional ways to create public spaces for discussion. The value of this democratizing force to campus environments is also compelling. Campus issues could be discussed by all constituents using a campus conferencing system. Answers to the proverbial question of What do students think about this issue? are only a few keystrokes away. The inclusive motives of any democracy appear to be quite easily supported by current computer technology. Por (1995) noted that virtual time and virtual place extend opportunities for all members of a community to participate, an essential feature of any productive system. If not, Por (1995) concluded, it "is an unnecessary and unacceptable waste of the community's human capital and self organizing capacity" (p. 273).

Virtual Involvement and Community

Involvement is usually defined in the campus literature as how much time, energy, and effort students invest in their endeavors, whether they be curricular, cocurricular, or extracurricular (National Institute of Education, 1984). How do CMC and virtual community engage participants? Given the above discussion it seems clear that the answer is: very well! It has the potential for involving both a larger number of participants as well as larger amounts of their time and energy. In fact, Rawlins (1996) used the metaphor of "moths to the flame" to describe the seductive nature of how computer technology involves users. For most, the technologies of virtual community are experienced as engaging. Technological uses to involve students in their learning and development continue to evolve rapidly (Engstrom & Kruger, 1997). This inevitable trend, however, raises the question as to whether the time and energy given to being on-line creates for participants a true sense of community. Is a virtual community a "real" community?

Predictably, firm opinions appear on both sides of this concern. Rheingold (1993), Goodman (1994), and Johnson-Lenz and Johnson-Lenz (1995) all make strong cases for a virtual community functioning much like a real community. Strangelove (1994) also concludes an essay with support for the concept of virtual community: "The Internet is not about technology, it is not about information, it is about communications—people talking with each other, people exchanging e-mail, people doing the low ASCII dance. The Internet is mass participation in fully bidirectional, uncensored mass communication. Communication is the basis, the foundation, the radical ground and root upon which all community stands, grows, and thrives" (p. 2).

A counter to this argument is Weinreich's (1997) position that "the idea of virtual community is wrong . . . Communities rely on interaction on a face-to-face basis, and one can't get to know one another when people are limited to mediated contacts" (p. 1). December (1997), acknowledging the existence and meaning of these communities, also cautions those who may applaud too quickly their communal qualities: "To say that the set of all telephone users constitutes a 'community' is like saying that toasters foster a brotherhood/sisterhood of bagel eaters" (p. 1).

In spite of their differences, some will argue that virtual and traditional face-to-face communities share the same basic features. Michalski (1995), drawing from the work of Peck (1987), delineated the essential facets of community to be: "Inclusivity, commitment, and consensus; realism; contemplation; a safe place; a laboratory for personal disarmament; a group that can fight gracefully; a group of all leaders; and a spirit" (p. 263). The concept of virtual community compares favorably with the characteristics of face-to-face community. According to Michalski's (1995) analysis, inclusivity, commitment, and consensus are exactly those characteristics that distinguish virtual community. Our discussion of inclusion and involvement seems to also support such a conclusion.

In further developing this position, Michalski emphasizes the homogenizing effects of CMC and virtual community where hierarchical issues related to status and personal identity apparently do not exist, or at least can be circumvented. The geographical reach of virtual community also supports inclusivity. He also points out that the commitment people make to being on-line often creates an emotional experience at their departure from the group. Finally, he contends, the direction of most virtual groups and their rules are established through consensus.

Realism, another characteristic of community, is evident as real-life situations and crises are often responded to within virtual communities much as they are in face-to-face communities. This is often the case when members acknowledge a birth, marriage, or death of a member. Contemplation is an important part of any community and places are needed to contemplate and be silent. The use of silence in CMC is more difficult to achieve, but Michalski suggests that a simple solution may be the presentation of a screen prior to entering, for example, a chat room that asks newcomers to take a moment for centering themselves and contemplating the topic before entering. A safe place is also characteristic of community.

From the discussion above, we reiterate that virtual community has the potential of providing safety in ways more difficult for a face-to-face community to accomplish. Physical safety is particularly protected in virtual community. Offering a laboratory for personal disarmament includes, according to Michalski, the opportunity to be anonymous and to enter into discussions without personal fear. The virtual community not only provides for a high degree of anonymity but also the opportunity to explore other identities and issues with a broad range of people while maintaining a sense of privacy. The capacity of group members to fight gracefully also characterizes community. Many on-line communities have rules of engagement, or "netiquette," to guide discussants in arguing their points without personal attacks.

A group of all leaders is, in essence, the democratizing feature of being on-line. Without hierarchy, status, and position playing a significant role in who or in what ways one is participating, the virtual community comes closer to a group of all leaders than most face-to-face groups can achieve. Spirit, the final characteristic of community, features the way a group takes delight in its existence. In a sense, the interdependence established in many on-line groups approaches this ideal of enthusiasm and camaraderie associated with belonging to something larger than oneself.

In summary, the features associated with traditional sensual communities are applicable, as well, to virtual communities. Both have strengths and weaknesses associated with each characteristic. Gozdz's (1995) observation regarding these issues is helpful in bringing some closure to this debate. He sees the virtual community as a modern application of the more traditional notion of community, but in the virtual community "connectivity" becomes the "glue that binds" people together rather than geographic proximity. He also asks the question: "How is the use of technology enhancing or detracting from a systemic sense of community?" (p. 241). This question points to the observation that virtual and face-to-face communities need not be mutually exclusive; perhaps each could enrich the sense of community of the other. In a campus environment with an established physical locale, virtual community could serve to enhance rather than detract from its overall sense of community.

Virtual Community as Campus Porch

Gozdz's (1995) position that computer-based technologies can be valuable allies in establishing and maintaining campus community complements Banning's (1997) allusion to the campus "porch" as a metaphor for thinking about the role of computers in college and university residence halls. Mugerauer (1993) refers to the porch as being a "between." It is an architectural feature found between the outside and the inside of dwellings, and it serves a variety of purposes. While it protects from the elements of weather, it also connects dwellers to the outside social world. One can sit and view the social world from a porch (a "lurker" in virtual terms), or one can invite others onto the porch, or perhaps leave the porch to join and participate with others. The porch is a physical structure, but at the same time a sociopetal feature that encourages social interaction. As Mugerauer observes, it is both a "between" and a "joining." To extend the metaphor further, CMC and virtual communities, much like porches, are "betweens" in the campus community, but they also offer opportunities for "joining" or, in virtual language, "connecting." CMC and virtual communities can be reframed as tools for building campus community rather than escaping from it. In concert with other campus features, these new technologies can serve to promote and maintain community in both of its forms, virtual and face-to-face. Synergy between the two promises much toward improving the effectiveness of college and university campus learning environments.

9

Designing for Education
Campus Assessment and Action

Theories and models of human development during the college years have abounded in the higher education and student affairs literature over the past several decades (Evans, Forney, & Guido-DiBrito, 1998; Rodgers, 1980; 1990b; 1991; Strange, 1994; Strange & King, 1990). However, until recently, few conceptual reviews (Baird, 1988; Conyne & Clack, 1981; Huebner & Lawson, 1990; Moos, 1979; Pascarella, 1985; Strange, 1991; 1993) have focused on synthesizing what is known about the nature, dynamics, and assessment of campus environments or how their various features affect student learning. As Evans, Forney, and Guido-DiBrito (1998) have pointed out, the principal focus of the behavioral sciences has limited our perspective, in that "developmental theory has its base in the field of psychology. As such, internal developmental processes tend to be emphasized and insufficient attention is paid to the role of environmental forces that influence development" (p. 283). Without such an overview, our ability to explain students' experiences remains, at best, incomplete. Thus, we have attempted in this volume to fill the gap by organizing a descriptive overview of extant theories and models within a conceptual template that addresses their application to the design of campus learning environments.

Toward an Ecology of Learning

We now understand some of the basic features of human environments, and we are beginning to appreciate more clearly their meaning for the design of higher education systems, policies, and practices. In summary, it appears that environments exert their influence on behavior through an array of natural and synthetic physical features, through the collective characteristics of inhabitants, the manner in which they are organized, and as mediated through their collective social constructions. Our analysis also suggests that a measure of any educational institution's environmental capacity to encourage and sustain learning is the degree to which it provides the conditions (in real and virtual form) for students' inclusion, safety, involvement, and full membership in a community. In effect, these conditions constitute an "ecology of learning," a state of dynamic balance when student characteristics are synergetic with institutional features (physical, aggregate, organizational, and constructed) in support of the outcomes of learning. Campus environments set conditions that affect student learning and, in turn, students influence the shape of campus environments.

The perspective that the relationship between student and campus is a transactional one was articulated first in the form of a "campus ecology model" (Aulepp & Delworth, 1976; Banning, 1978; Banning & Kaiser, 1974; Huebner, 1979; Western Interstate Commission for Higher Education, 1973). This model begins with an assumption that student and campus are mutually shaping forces in the complex balance of institutional life. As Kaiser (1975) and others have framed this approach, eight themes comprise its conceptual core:

- A campus environment consists of all the stimuli that impinge upon the students' sensory modalities, including physical, chemical, biological, and social stimulation.

- A transactional relationship exists between college students and their campus environment, i.e., the students shape the environment and are shaped by it.

- For purposes of environmental design, the shaping properties of the campus environment are focused on; however, the students are still viewed as active, choice-making agents who may resist, transform, or nullify environmental influences.

- Every student possesses the capacity for a wide spectrum of possible behaviors. A campus environment may facilitate or inhibit any one or more of those behaviors. The campus should be intentionally designed to offer opportunities, incentives, and reinforcements for growth and development.

- Students will attempt to cope with any educational environment in which they are placed. If the environment is not compatible with the students, the students may react negatively or fail to develop desirable qualities.

- Because of the wide range of individual differences among students, fitting the campus environment to the student requires the creation of a wide variety of campus subenvironments. There must be an attempt to design for the wide range of individual characteristics found among students.

- Every campus has a design, even if the administration, faculty, and students have not planned it or are not consciously aware of it. A design technology for campus environments, therefore, is useful for both the analysis of existing campus environments and the design of new ones.

- Successful campus design depends on input from all campus members including students, faculty, staff, administration, and trustees or regents. [p.33]

These assumptions underscore the point that college and university environments are complex, dynamic phenomena; any change in one component will likely manifest itself in changes in other components. Likewise, failure to attend to other components may jeopardize attempts to change only one.

These core themes also emphasize the point that campuses exert their effects whether we want them to or not. Campus design is not a matter of choice; a design already exists. The more important question is whether such designs serve intended purposes. In the context of the present discussion, how do they promote student learning or how do they inhibit it? Designs prohibitive of learning need to be altered or eliminated; facilitative designs need to be supported and enhanced. Furthermore, these assumptions suggest that our best intentions will do little in those directions unless campus constituents affected by these designs are involved in their creation and implementation. Campus environments cannot be molded simply to specification for outcomes to emerge on cue. At best, we can only hope to create conditions that set broad limits on behaviors (Michelson, 1970), encouraging those consistent with institutional mission and supportive of educational purposes. However, providing leadership for this ongoing challenge requires a broad understanding of the various design elements capable of contributing to that goal.

A Campus Design Matrix

Drawing from materials presented in the preceding chapters, Figure 9.1 integrates these environmental concepts into a three-dimensional matrix of campus design for purposes of assessment and action. Three essential questions are addressed in this matrix:

- What components are involved in this particular environmental assessment or action?

- What is the impact of the current design?

- What is the intended focus or purpose of this design?

Answers to these three questions can alert educators to conditions of current campus environments as well as the intended design of environments to be created.

With respect to the first question, any campus assessment or action must identify the environmental components of concern. Are the physical dimensions of the campus involved natural (terrain) or synthetic (layout)? Is the composition of particular aggregates (for example, campus affinity groups) at issue? Are there concerns related to the organizational dimensions of the setting (such as decision-making structures)? How do participants construct this condition or phenomenon of interest (social climate or press)?

Figure 9.1. Campus Design Matrix

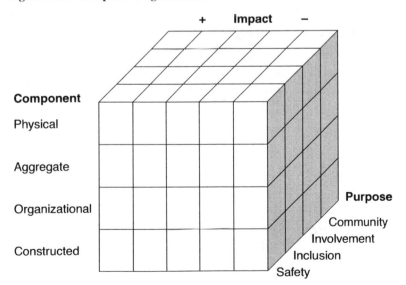

With respect to the impact of current design, the second focus of this matrix, it is helpful to consider a continuum of possible effects (Moos, 1986) (See Exhibit 9.1). At one end of the continuum, environments can be seen as essentially negative, including those that are actively stressful or limiting, resisting, and inhibiting. At the other end are environments seen as essentially positive, that is, those that release capacities, allowing behaviors to occur, and those that actively stimulate and challenge individuals toward growth. In the middle are those environments that neither enhance nor inhibit individuals, but rather select favored characteristics.

Of course, the nature of the impact depends on the characteristics of the individual or persons experiencing the particular environmental condition (Lewin, 1936). For example, a highly differentiated affinity group, such as a student organization or club, may be a very positive force for individuals who share much in common with the group but may be actively stressful for those who don't. Also, it makes sense that environmental selection of certain characteristics depends on what is favored by the environment. Again, those who exhibit certain characteristics (for example, high academic test scores on an honors program application) are most favored in the selection process.

Third, this campus design matrix identifies the intended purpose(s) of the environmental condition. Is the concern one of inclusion or exclusion of certain students in campus life? Is the question

---

Exhibit 9.1. Five Conceptions of Environmental Impact

+   Environments are active and *positive* forces
- Stimulate and challenge individuals toward growth
- Release capacities, allow behaviors to occur
- Select favored characteristics
- Limit, resist, or inhibit behaviors
- Actively engender stress
−   Environments are essentially *negative* and stressful

Source: Moos, 1986, pp. 29–30.

of safety at stake, physical or psychological? Are the environmental components and impacts related in some way to aspects of involvement? To what extent, if any, does the environmental assessment or planned action relate to the establishment and maintenance of campus community?

Identification and assessment of environmental components, impacts, and purposes are important first steps in campus design. The value of this matrix in the process is that it requires consideration of the larger campus ecology, with reference to current impacts and intended purposes. As an evaluative tool, use of this matrix can alert educational planners to conditions that warrant particular attention. For example, a campus retention committee may focus on the role of small orientation groups (an aggregate component) in having a powerful positive impact toward purposes of safety and inclusion in the campus environment; or the lack of participatory structures in a particular department (an organizational component) might signal the limiting, resisting, and inhibiting impact on students who wish to become involved.

Institutional leaders can also use this matrix to systematically plan the design of new or renovated campus environments, considering their impact and purpose. For example, if plans for a new or renovated student union invoke images of a facility for building campus community, then the impact of its current location and proposed design changes must be considered carefully in light of its capacity for including, securing, and involving all students. Such a project is under way at Bowling Green State University where plans for a renovated student union have been attached to the institution's web page to allow observers to take a virtual tour of the building before the first brick is laid.

In this way, potential users can consider the impact and purposes of the facility while there may yet be time for adjustments. Do the plans suggest a facility that is accessible to all (a physical component)? What student groups might be located in the building, for purposes of increasing campuswide involvement (an aggregate component)?

What rules will govern the use of this facility (an organizational component)? What images of the facility are conveyed to students as they consider the facility's space and layout (constructed component)? At each point, campus planners can consider whether the intended designs will add to the stress of some students (such as students with disabilities), and ultimately, whether it will serve as a powerful positive force in campus life. This kind of analysis can assist institutions in anticipating environmental challenges and conditions that, if impervious to alteration or redesign, can at least be responded to in supportive ways.

Campus Policies and Practices

As campus environments are understood in terms of their impact and purpose, as well as their design components, implications for campus policies and practices become clearer. Applications to the college campus of the environmental knowledge base presented here might be considered in terms of five basic strategies (Moos, 1979): maximizing educational information; facilitating and evaluating environmental change; implementing educational consultation; formulating ecologically relevant case descriptions; and enhancing environmental competence. Each of these strategies is considered in light of the policies, functions, and practices of campus educators who, as administrators and staff, faculty, or student affairs professionals, contribute to the learning, growth, and development of students.

Maximizing Educational Information

The knowledge base on human environments presented in this volume offers a conceptual framework for guiding assessment, organization, and communication of information about a college and its various subenvironments. This framework might also prove useful for giving and taking feedback from students with respect to various campus environments. College catalogs and university view-books are full of images and descriptions of campus life, focusing mostly on academic departments, majors, and interest areas. Although such information is certainly important, whether this is the best information to offer prospective students as they make the decision to enroll is questionable, especially if it is the only source of information.

Technical data about departments and curricula rarely convey the qualities of environmental conditions most likely to have a significant effect on students' satisfaction. Perhaps communicating the nature of overall institutional social climate (its relationship, personal development, system maintenance, and change dimensions), for example, from student, faculty, and staff perspectives, might better serve to inform them about important institutional dynamics. Presentation of an institutional profile from the National Survey of Student Engagement (Kuh, 2000) might offer yet another means for assisting prospective enrollees in making a more informed decision about college choice, as they are exposed to potential sources and patterns of student involvement. Such information could also be prepared and distributed for various institutional subenvironments, such as specific academic departments, classes (Winston, et al, 1994), living-learning centers, and various student clubs and organizations (Winston, et al, 1997). The importance of this type of information is that it offers opportunities for individuals to consider sources of compatibility or incongruence in their selection of campus environments.

Another aspect of maximizing educational information concerns what is done with the data already collected on campus from year to year. Too often we gather information from students through questionnaires and surveys but rarely take the time to feed this information back to them for purposes of discussion and insight as to potential understandings and actions. For instance, how these environmental models might be used to communicate to students their collective perceptions of a particular campus environment, in order to facilitate their initial adjustment to college, can be illustrated in the context of residence life.

A residence director could administer the University Residence Environment Scale (URES) (Form E—expected environment, or Form I—ideal environment) (Moos & Gerst, 1988) to assigned residents prior to their arrival on campus or during the orientation process. This would offer planners an understanding of what students consider to be ideal in terms of their expectations of on-campus living arrangements. Such a report or profile could serve as an important source of information for organizing programming that will meet students' needs or, where necessary, for correcting those expectations that may be unrealistic. Following up that assessment six to eight weeks into the term with the URES (Form R—realistic environment, or simply engaging in a guided group discussion of the URES subscale framework and definitions) might help identify sources of discrepancy between what the students expected (or ideally sought) and what they actually found. This give-and-take of information, which can be organized by floor as well, accomplishes several important learning goals.

First, students learn about the design and dynamic of their environments in terms of a conceptual framework that will continue to prove helpful to them as they make decisions about living environments in the future. Second, students learn how they may differ from or share perspectives with peers on what they perceive to be the desirable aspects of living environments. Third, staff members gain an important source of information for purposes of planning and programming to address any discrepancies students perceive between what they expected and what they found to be the case. For example, a significant discrepancy on the emotional support scale of the URES (a relationship dimension with consequences for inclusion and safety) might warrant some interventions of a team-building, service, or human relations nature. Finally, as student residents learn that staff value their perspectives in the planning and experience of a living-learning environment, they are encouraged to become involved in the processes of community change and goal setting.

Other applications might be explored by faculty in departmental and classroom settings as well. Seeking systematic feedback from students particular to their sense of inclusion, safety, involvement, and community in an academic program or course could prove helpful in maximizing the learning potential of those settings. Perhaps this kind of information, in concert with the usual technical descriptions, can assist students in gaining a broader understanding of environmental impact, again an important lesson for subsequent life choices.

Facilitating and Evaluating Environmental Change

The knowledge base on human environments, Moos (1974) argues, is helpful in facilitating and evaluating the consequences of environmental change on campus, whether that involves changing social climate, for example, or changing architectural and organizational characteristics. Campus change is sometimes unexpected and at other times intentional. It can be both evolutionary and revolutionary. The importance of these environmental models lies in their descriptions of the nature and direction of those changes. In concert with some of the established environmental process models (Aulepp & Delworth, 1976; Huebner, 1979; Western Interstate Commission for Higher Education, 1973) they can serve as powerful tools in facilitating desired changes. For example, the ecosystem design model (Aulepp & Delworth, 1976) "is utilized to identify environmental shaping properties in order to eliminate dysfunctional features and to incorporate features that facilitate student academic and personal growth" (p. ix), either at the macrolevel (involving the entire campus community) or microlevel (involving subenvironments for groups within the campus community).

The design process itself encompasses seven steps that should be viewed as interacting components. Design work may begin with any of the steps, but unless an institution is just being set up or wants to initiate an entirely new environment, it will find entry into the model is most natural at step 5. The seven interdependent steps are:

1. Designers, in conjunction with community members, select educational values.
2. Values are then translated into specific goals.
3. Environments are designed that contain mechanisms to reach the stated goals.
4. Environments are fitted to students.
5. Student perceptions of the environments are measured.
6. Student behavior resulting from environmental perceptions is monitored.
7. Data on the environmental design's successes and failures, as indicated by student perceptions and behavior, are fed back to the designers in order that they may continue to learn about student/environment fit and design better environments. [p. ix]

An illustration of the utility of this model on the macrolevel is found in the series of women's climate studies (Seeger, 1994) conducted at Grand Valley State University in Michigan. This ongoing, campuswide effort was recently recognized by the American Association of University Women with its Progress in Equity Award and has resulted in significant institutional changes ranging from construction of a new Children's Center (a physical environment change) to the formation of a twenty-two-member Grand Valley Women's Commission (an organizational environment change). By focusing first on assessing faculty, staff, and student perceptions of the degree of support for women on campus (step 5 in the above model), various campus constituents have a common basis in the data generated for a discussion of campus values and purposes (inclusion, safety, involvement, and community) and for the planning of any environmental intervention or redesign.

Construction or renovation of campus student unions, residence halls, classroom buildings, and recreation centers is also offering an increasing number of institutions the opportunity to take advantage of these concepts and practices at the microlevel, as values and goals of campus community building are pursued with current innovations in aesthetics and design. The Olentangy Project (Rodgers, 1990a) at Ohio State University, a residential-based student development intervention, is one case of how holistic principles of campus ecology can serve to improve a specific campus subenvironment.

Again, the environmental theories and models reviewed in this volume can sensitize campus planners and renovators to questions about various design components, their impact, and their intended purposes. An integrated environmental perspective suggests that each of these questions must be considered if whole change is to be brought about in the functioning of a setting. Changing one element without altering others may diminish the intended impact of the planned design. Many a campus, at one time or another for example, has attempted to alter the environment of a particularly troublesome residence hall unit on campus (the proverbial "zoo") with a housecleaning of new paint, carpet, and furniture. While such cosmetic changes may freshen up the general atmosphere of the facility, rarely is any significant change in student behavior observed until the influences of the human aggregate (such as all male residents) and organizational features (such as few involvement structures) are also taken into consideration. In addition to physical improvements, hall composition can be changed to include females (an aggregate change strategy) and residents can be invited to participate in models of self-governance or territorial design (organizational change strategies). Such changes may more effectively and positively influence the overall social climate of the hall, while attracting, satisfying, and sustaining new aggregates of students who create, over time, an organizational culture supportive of student involvement and community.

Implementing Educational Consultation

As educators we are often called upon to consult with others concerning the functioning of various institutional environments, at both the macrolevel of an entire institution or the microlevel of a particular campus subenvironment, such as a student organization or administrative work group. Understanding the design components, potential impact, and purposes of an environment can help shape the assessment and feedback steps of these consultations. Upcraft and Schuh (1996) referenced a number of process models used in the environmental assessment steps of a typical consultation, including the ecosystem model (Aulepp & Delworth, 1976) already discussed, ecomapping (Heubner & Corrazini, 1975–1976) involving the integration of questionnaire, interview, and observational data, and the culture audit (Whitt, 1993), focusing on artifacts of institutional culture as constructed by various campus constituents. These process models usually offer a step-by-step framework for action, but they do not necessarily indicate what needs to be assessed or for what purpose. Again, this environmental knowledge base can serve to guide such efforts. As suggested in the above theoretical synthesis, for example, gathering information specific to the sense of inclusion or safety of a particular campus group (such as gay, lesbian, bisexual, or transgendered students) may be an important prelude to understanding why a campus environment fails to encourage involvement or the experience of community for some.

The inventory of design components contained in this knowledge base may also suggest strategies that could be applied to the particular problem for which consultation was sought. For example, from a work environment–social climate profile generated in the context of a staff development initiative it is clear by examining the ideal-real discrepancies on the subscales measured that issues of lack of supervisor support, too much work pressure, too little innovation, and limitations of physical comfort abound (see Figure 9.2).

This provides a targeted source of information for purposes of environmental intervention and redesign. For example, the need to address more specifically (perhaps through interviews) issues of physical layout, space usage, and amenities is obvious, since physical comfort is the largest source of discrepancy in the profile. In addition, the lack of innovation perceived in the work setting

**Figure 9.2. Real (Form R) versus Ideal (Form I)
Work Environment Scale Profile**

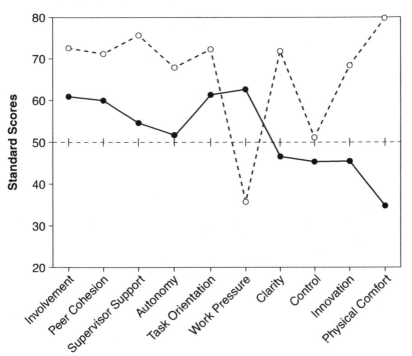

Source: Adapted from Moos, 1994b.

immediately invokes the organizational conceptual framework of
Hage and Aiken (1970) suggesting that an emphasis on quantity of
production in an environment will diminish the dynamics required
for innovation. In this case, the staff members' desire to reduce work
pressure serves as a proxy for this organizational parameter, indi-
cating that more emphasis on quality (rather than quantity) of work
is warranted. Finally, issues of supervisor support also suggest some
changes in the organizational dimensions of the work environment.
Two possible leads implicated in the assessment may be related to
the high degrees of centralization and stratification perceived by
participants, either of which can discourage innovation. In the

**Exhibit 9.2. Work Environment Scale (WES)
Dimensions and Subscales**

RELATIONSHIP DIMENSIONS

Involvement Extent to which employees are concerned about and committed to their jobs.

Coworker cohesion How much employees are friendly and supportive of one another.

Supervisor support Extent to which management is supportive of employees and encourages employees to be supportive of one another.

PERSONAL GROWTH DIMENSIONS

Autonomy How much employees are encouraged to be self-sufficient and to make their own decisions.

Task orientation Emphasis on good planning, efficiency, and getting the job done.

Work pressure Degree to which high work demands and time pressure dominate the job milieu.

SYSTEM MAINTENANCE
AND CHANGE DIMENSIONS

Clarity Whether employees know what to expect in their daily routine and how explicitly rules and policies are communicated.

Control How much management uses rules and pressures to keep employees under control.

Innovation Emphasis on variety, change, and new approaches.

Physical Comfort Extent to which the physical surroundings contribute to a pleasant work environment.

Source: Moos, 1994b. Used by permission.

event that this turns out to be the case, interventions in the form of staff team building, decision making, and supervisory relationships may also improve the dynamic of this work setting. The template of social climate, with its identification of relationship, personal growth, and system maintenance dimensions as important aspects of the environment, serves to guide the analysis as well as the solution (see Exhibit 9.2).

Formulating Ecologically Relevant Case Descriptions

Students, regardless of their circumstances, arrive on campus from an intact life ecology, bringing with them interacting systems of family, peers, culture, and hometown. To that is joined the existing ecology of the campus which, in many cases, may include a residence hall environment, various classroom environments, a social or task group environment, and very often a work environment. These environmental theories and models offer a framework for advisors and counselors to understand the nature of each student's ecology.

For students experiencing transitional adjustment concerns the various social climate dimensions listed in Exhibit 4.6, for example, catalog specific concerns and issues relevant to personal functioning in any of these environments. Combined with dynamics identified in Exhibit 9.1, addressing the nature of the environment's impact, an ecological inventory emerges in the form of an integrated social climate picture relevant to that student's life. Is the presenting issue primarily a relationship dimension concern? Which subenvironment(s) is (are) involved? Family? Which aspects of family relationships are involved? Cohesiveness? Expressiveness? Is the concern one of active stress (a powerful negative influence) requiring immediate relief, or a matter of normal anxiety and frustration in the context of developmental challenge (a powerful positive influence)? In concert with the environmental purposes (inclusion, safety, involvement, community) addressed in this volume, information about each of these social climate dimensions comprising the student's ecology might also serve as a guide for enhancing its overall learning potential, either by adjusting the design of a current environment, or seeking out new ones. Such probes and strategies can help advisors and counselors build a more complete and relevant picture of how individual students are adapting to and coping with various institutional environments.

Enhancing Environmental Competence

In this final application Moos (1979) recommends teaching students how to create, select, and transcend environments, how to maximize person-environment congruence when support is the goal, or how to seek an appropriate amount of incongruence and challenge when the goal is personal growth. The overall intent is to help students understand more fully the impact of the environment on their lives.

Enhancing environmental competence is a goal that encompasses the basic purposes and outcomes of higher education. From a developmental perspective, it can be argued that a person who possesses a simplistic, authority-bound, and categorical view of the world (Perry's dualist or King and Kitchener's prereflective thinker), typical of many entering students, lacks both the motivation and skill for self-directed learning and is ineffective in a world where little is certain and change is constant. Through general education core courses, students are challenged to examine the world environment in all its contexts (historical, cultural, physical, and interpersonal) and to develop the basic tools of inquiry and communication to be able to examine further a select part of that environment through completion of an academic major. The college outcome research consistently supports the finding that students who persist in this process emerge with a more complex view of the world, more appreciative of its subtleties, and more capable of sorting through the maze of opinions, facts, and interpretations necessary for making good judgments about life and the environment surrounding them.

Sensitizing students to the key components, design characteristics, dynamics, and purposes of human environments, through campus experiences and academic coursework, will likely enhance their capacity for making wise choices about environments as they progress through life. Creating a better world begins with understanding more clearly what works well (or not so well) in their current world. Environmental competence is an important tool in shaping such an understanding.

James Garfield once described the ideal college as a student on one end of a log, opposite Mark Hopkins, the renowned educator who taught philosophy and rhetoric for fifty-seven years at Williams College and served as its president from 1836 to 1872. Obviously, much has changed in American higher education since Garfield evoked this image of a powerful educational environment. The simple log has grown to an enormous academic edifice of stone, brick, mortar, steel, concrete, electronic sites, and web pages, reflecting a gallery of real and virtual designs, functions, and purposes. From the log's one end the consummate gentleman scholar, in the person of Professor Hopkins, has given way to a catalog of faculty roles in support of the multifaceted missions of teaching, research, and service. From the log's other end the singular, receptive student sitting in awe of Professor Hopkin's wisdom is now a chorus of active learners voicing an ever rich variety of liberal, technical, and vocational educational interests and goals (Strange, 1996). Higher education in America has indeed changed significantly and dramatically in a relatively short period of time.

The effects of such changes have been especially evident over the past fifty years, as many institutions have witnessed a profound revolution in scale, purpose, and clientele. Once a relatively homogeneous system serving the few who could afford it for purposes of developing character, good moral habits, and social status, American higher education is now a multiplex of institutional types serving a vast number of students for as many different reasons. For every college student enrolled in 1940 there are now eight in nearly twice the number of institutions (Bonner, 1986). The mixture and variety of students have changed as well. Those Cross (1971) called "new students," many underprepared, continue to bring a greater range of expectations of what colleges and universities can and should do for them. Returning adult learners look for assistance in responding to changing life goals and circumstances (Cross, 1981; Schlossberg, Lynch, & Chickering 1989). Previously disenfranchised racial and ethnic groups seek channels of opportunity and access to social change, and students everywhere expect marketable skills, a career-oriented curriculum, and a secure position upon completion of a degree program or certificate.

This revolution in American higher learning has given rise to a maze of state, private, and community-based institutions that is as difficult to comprehend for students who must choose between them as it is challenging for faculty and administrators who work within them. What is the best college to attend? A conveniently located community college? A small private institution ensuring more personalized attention? A large multiversity promising the excitement of cutting edge research and a diversity of student types? What about the choices once within an institution? Should one commute to campus or live in a residence hall? Is a single-sex arrangement best or a coed living-learning center? What are the consequences of not committing immediately to a major?

From the viewpoints of faculty and administrators the task may be equally daunting. What sort of institutional images will attract the types of students who will do well? What can make an institution more attractive and fulfilling to students of differing cultural and ethnic backgrounds? What can be done to increase the student retention rate, especially during the first year? Will teaching strategies for traditional students be as effective with new and different students? What is the potential for creating exciting learning environments in classrooms that hold 200 and more students? What will assist students in making better decisions about the many campus resources and opportunities available to them?

An essential challenge facing postsecondary educators today is the creation and maintenance of campus environments (both proximate and distant) that attract, satisfy, and sustain students in the achievement of their educational goals. That responsibility lies in the hands of all institutional constituents: campus enrollment managers and orientation directors who recruit and acclimate new students to the college environment; residence hall directors who assist them in accommodating the challenges of communal living and learning; faculty in foundational courses who introduce students to the concepts and methods of the disciplines; directors of adult and commuter students who enhance the sense of mattering (Schlossberg, 1989) and belonging among them; coordinators of multicultural affairs and directors of international student advising who create and shape welcoming environments for those whose racial, ethnic, or national heritage differs from the dominant constituent; student activity and organization advisers who engage students in opportunities for campus involvement and leadership; personal counselors who aid students in understanding the adjustments required of life transitions; and academic, career, and vocational advisers who assist students in choosing a personally fulfilling academic and occupational goal. What is needed to guide these functions and practices is a comprehensive model of the college environment that describes its various features and assists campus participants in understanding how such factors can either encourage or inhibit student learning, growth, and development (Strange, 1983b; Strange & King, 1990). We trust that the conceptual framework offered here will prove to be a helpful start in that direction.

References

Adler, R., & Towne, N. (1987). *Looking out-looking in*. Austin, TX: Holt, Rinehart and Winston.

Alexander, C. (1977). *The timeless way of building*. New York: Oxford University Press.

American Council on Education. (1985). *Achieving reasonable campus security. Self-regulation initiatives: Resource Documents for Colleges and Universities*, No. 2: Washington, DC: American Council on Education.

Anderson, C. (1996). Community in cyberspace: Virtual sex on the Internet. *NASPA Forum, 18*(3), 11.

Anderson, P. (1971). The school as an organic teaching aid. In R. McClure (Ed.), *National Society for the Study of Education yearbook, Part 1. The curriculum: Retrospect and prospect*. Chicago: University of Chicago Press.

Arthur, P., & Passini, R. (1992). *Wayfinding*. New York: McGraw-Hill.

Aslanian, C. B., & Brickell, H. M. (1980). *Americans in transition: Life changes as reasons for adult learning*. New York: College Entrance Examination Board.

Astin, A. W. (1968). *The college environment*. Washington, DC: American Council on Education.

Astin, A. W. (1985). *Achieving educational excellence: A critical assessment of priorities and practices in higher education*. San Francisco: Jossey-Bass.

Astin, A. W. (1993). An empirical typology of college students. *Journal of College Student Development, 34*, 36–46.

Astin, A. W., & Holland, J. L. (1961). The environmental assessment technique: A way to measure college environments. *Journal of Educational Psychology, 52*, 308–316.

Astin, A. W., & Panos, R. J. (1966). A national research databank for higher education. *Educational Record, 47*, 5–17.

Aulepp, L., & Delworth, U. (1976). *Training manual for an ecosystem model: Assessing and designing campus environments*. Boulder, CO: Western Interstate Commission for Higher Education.

Baird, L. L. (1988). The college environment revisited: A review of research and theory. In J. C. Smart (Ed.), *Higher education: Vol. 4. Handbook of theory and research* (pp. 1–52). New York: Agathon Press.

Baird, L., & Hartnett, R. T. (1980). *Understanding student and faculty life*. San Francisco: Jossey-Bass.

Banning, J. H. (Ed.). (1978). *Campus ecology: A perspective for student affairs*. Cincinnati, OH: NASPA Monograph.

Banning, J. H. (1989). Impact of college environments on freshman students. In M. L. Upcraft, J. N. Gardner, & Associates (Eds.), *The freshman year experience* (pp. 53–62). San Francisco: Jossey-Bass.

Banning, J. H. (1992). Visual anthropology: Viewing the campus ecology for messages of sexism. *The Campus Ecologist, 10* (1), 1–4.

Banning, J. H. (1993). The pedestrian's visual experience on campus: Informal learning of cultural messages. *The Campus Ecologist, 11* (1), 1–4.

Banning, J. H. (1995) Campus images: Homoprejudice. *The Campus Ecologist, 13* (3), 3.

Banning, J. H. (1997). Designing for community: Thinking "out of the box" with porches. *The Journal of College and University Housing, 26*(2), 3–7.

Banning, J. H., & Bartels, S. (1993). A taxonomy for physical artifacts: Understanding campus multiculturalism. *The Campus Ecologist, 11*(3), 2–3.

Banning, J. H., & Cunard, M. (1986). The physical environment supports student development. *The Campus Ecologist, 4*(1), 1–3.

Banning, J. H., & Kaiser, L. (1974). An ecological perspective and model for campus design. *Personnel and Guidance Journal, 52*(6), 370–375.

Banning, J. H., & Luna, F. (1992). Viewing the campus ecology for messages about Hispanic/Latino culture. *The Campus Ecologist, 10*(4), 1–4.

Banning, J. H., McGuire, F. D., & Stegman, J. (1996). Housing that makes a difference. *College Services Administration, 19*(1), 53–58.

Barker, R. (1968). *Ecological psychology*. Palo Alto, CA: Stanford University Press.

Barker, R., & Wright, H. (1951). *One boy's day*. New York: HarperCollins.

Baum, A., & Valins, S. (1977). *Architecture and social behavior: Psychological studies of social density*. Hillsdale, NJ: Erlbaum.

Bechtel, R. B. (1997). *Environment and behavior: An introduction*. Thousand Oaks, CA: Sage.

Bechtel, R. B., & Zeisel, J. (1987). Observation: The world under a glass. In R. Bechtel, R. Marans, & W. Michelson (Eds.), *Methods in environmental and behavioral research* (pp. 11–40). New York: Van Nostrand Reinhold.

Beeler, K., Bellandese, S., & Wiggins, C. (1991). *Campus safety: A survey of administrative perceptions and strategies* (Report No. HE 024 821). Washington, DC: National Association of Student Personnel Administrators. (ERIC Document Reproduction Service No 336 001).

Bell, P. A., Fisher, J. D., Baum, A., & Greene, T. G. (1990). *Environmental psychology*. Austin, TX: Holt, Rinehart, and Winston.

Bell, P. A., Greene, T. G., Fisher, J. D., & Baum, A. (1996). *Environmental psychology* (4th ed.). Orlando, FL: Harcourt Brace.

Bellah, R. N., Madsen, R., Sullivan, W. M., Swidler, A., & Tipton, S. M. (1985). *Habits of the heart*. New York: HarperCollins.

Berge, Z., & Collins, M. (1995). Overview and perspectives. In Z. L. Berge & M. P. Collins (Eds.), *Computer-mediated communication and the online classroom, Vol. 1* (pp. 1–27). Cresskill, NJ: Hampton Press.

Bickman, L., Teger, A., Gabriele, T., McLaughlin, C., Berger, M., & Sunadry, E. (1973). Dormitory density and helping behavior. *Environment and Behavior, 5*, 465–490.

Birdwhistell, R. (1970). *Kinesics and context*. Philadelphia: University of Pennsylvania Press.

Blau, P. M. (1973). *The organization of academic work*. New York: Wiley.

Blimling, G. S. (1988). The influence of college residence halls on students: A meta-analysis of the empirical research, 1966–1985. Unpublished doctoral dissertation, Ohio State University, Columbus.

Bonner, T. N. (1986, September/October). The unintended revolution in America's colleges since 1940. *Change, 18*, 44–51.

Boyer, E. (1987). *College: The undergraduate experience in America*. New York: HarperCollins.

Brower, A. M., & Dettinger, K. M. (1998, November/December). What is a learning community? *About Campus, 3*(5), 15–21.

Carnegie Foundation for the Advancement of Teaching. (1990). *Campus life: In search of community*. Princeton, NJ: The Carnegie Foundation for the Advancement of Teaching.

Chaffee, E. E., & Tierney, W. G. (1988). *Collegiate culture and leadership strategies*. New York: American Council on Education and Macmillan.

Chickering, A. W. (1969). *Education and identity*. San Francisco: Jossey-Bass.

Chickering, A. W., & Reisser, L. (1993). *Education and identity* (2nd ed.). San Francisco: Jossey-Bass.

Clark, B., & Trow, M. (1966). The organizational context. In T. Newcomb & E. Wilson (Eds.), *College peer groups: Problems and prospects for research* (pp. 17–70). Chicago: Aldine.

Computer brings students, courses together. (1997, October 6). *National On-Campus Reports, 25*(19), 6.

Conyne, R. K., & Clack, R. J. (1981). *Environmental assessment and design: A new tool for the applied behavioral scientist.* New York: Praeger.

Cottrell, L. S., Jr. (1983). The competent community. In R. L. Warren & L. Lyon (Eds.), *New perspectives on the American community* (pp. 401–411). Homewood, IL: The Dorsey Press.

Council of Ontario Universities. (1991). *Women's campus safety audit guide.* Toronto, Canada: Ontario Ministry of Colleges and Universities. (ERIC Document Reproduction Service no. ED 338 129).

Crookston, B. B. (1974). A design for an intentional democratic community. In D. A. DeCoster & P. Mable (Eds.), *Student development and education in college residence halls* (pp. 55–67). Washington, DC: American College Personnel Association.

Cross, K. P. (1971). *Beyond the open door: New students to higher education.* San Francisco: Jossey-Bass.

Cross, K. P. (1981). *Adults as learners.* San Francisco: Jossey-Bass.

D'Augelli, A. R. (1989). Lesbians' and gay men's experience of discrimination and harassment in a university community. *American Journal of Community Psychology, 17,* 317–321.

December, J. (1997, February). Communities exist in cyberspace. *CMC Magazine* [On-line]. Available: http://209.100.136.26/cmc/mag/1997/feb/last.html

Dewey, J. (1916). *Democracy and education.* New York: The Free Press.

Dewey, J. (1933). *How we think: A restatement of the relation of reflective thinking to the educative process.* New York: D. C. Heath.

Dietz-Uhler, B., & Murrell, A. (1992). College student's perceptions of sexual harassment: Are gender differences decreasing? *Journal of College Student Development, 33*(6), 540–546.

Dober, R. (1992). *Campus design.* New York: Wiley.

Doheny-Farina, S. (1994, December). The virtualization of local life: A tale of two teachers. *CMC Magazine* [On-line]. Available: http://209.100.136.26/cmc/mag/

Dunlop, C., & Kling, R. (1991a) The dreams of technological Utopianism. In C. Dunlop & R. Kling (Eds.), *Computerization and controversy: Value conflicts and social change* (pp. 14–30). Boston: Academic Press.

Dunlop, C., & Kling, R. (1991b). Social relationships in electronic communities. In C. Dunlop & R. Kling (Eds.), *Computerization and controversy: Value conflicts and social change* (pp. 322–329). Boston: Academic Press.

Dunne, J. (1986). Sense of community in l'Arche and in the writings of Jean Vanier. *Journal of Community Psychology, 14*, 41–54.

Dyer, W. G., Jr. (1986). The cycle of cultural evolution in organizations. In R. Kilman, M. Saxton, R. Serpa, & Associates (Eds.), *Gaining control of the corporate culture* (pp. 200–229). San Francisco: Jossey-Bass.

Dziech, B. W., & Weiner, L. (1984). *The lecherous professor: Sexual harassment on campus*. Boston: Beacon Press.

Eckman, P. (1985). *Telling lies: Clues to deceit in marketplace, politics, and marriage*. New York: Norton.

Ellen, R. (1982). *Environment, subsistence and system*. Cambridge University Press.

Ellsworth, J. (1995). Using computer-mediated communication in teaching university courses. In Z. L. Berge & M. P. Collins (Eds.), *Computer-mediated communication and the online classroom: Vol. 1.* (pp. 29–36). Cresskill, NJ. Hampton Press.

Engstrom, C., & Kruger, K. (Eds.). (1997). *Using technology to promote student learning: Opportunities for today and tomorrow*. New Directions for Student Services, No 78. San Francisco: Jossey-Bass.

Etzioni, A. (1964). *Modern organizations*. Englewood Cliffs, NJ: Prentice-Hall.

Etzioni, A. (1993). *The spirit of community: Rights, responsibilities and the communitarian agenda*. New York: Crown.

Evans, N. J., Forney, D. S., & Guido-DiBrito, F. (1998). *Student development in college: Theory, research and practice*. San Francisco: Jossey-Bass.

Evans, N. J., & Rankin, S. (1998). Heterosexism and campus violence: Assessment and intervention strategies. In A. M. Hoffman, J. H. Schuh, & R. H. Fenske (Eds.), *Violence on campus: Defining the problems, strategies for action* (pp. 169–186). Gaithersburg, MD: Aspen

Evans, N. J., & Wall, V. A. (Eds.). (1991). *Beyond tolerance: Gays, lesbians, and bisexuals on campus*. Alexandria, VA: American College Personnel Association Media Publication.

Feldman, K. A., & Newcomb, T.M. (1969). *The impact of college on students*. San Francisco: Jossey-Bass.

Finley, C., & Corty, E. (1993). Rape on campus: The prevalence of sexual assaults while enrolled in college. *Journal of College Student Development, 34*(2), 113–117.

Fisher, B., & Nasar, J. L. (1992). Fear of crime in relation to three exterior site features: Prospect, refuge, and escape. *Environment and Behavior, 24*(1), 35–65.

Forrest, L., Hotelling, K., & Kuk, L. (1986). *The elimination of sexism in the university environment.* Pingree Park, CO: Student Development Through Campus Ecology, Second Annual Symposium. (ERIC Document Reproduction Service # ED 267 348).

Friedman, M. (1983). *The confirmation of otherness.* New York: The Pilgrim Press.

Fry, T. (Ed.). (1981). *RB 1980: The rule of St. Benedict.* Collegeville, MN: The Liturgical Press.

Gabriel, T. (1996, November 11). Computers can unify campuses, but also drive students apart. *New York Times,* pp. A1, C10.

Garbarino, J. (1978). *The human ecology of school crime.* Hackensack, NJ: National Council on Crime and Delinquency.

Gardner, J. W. (1990). *On leadership.* New York: The Free Press.

Gehring, D. D. (1993). Understanding legal constraints on practice. In M. J. Barr (Ed.), *The handbook of student affairs administration* (pp. 274–299). San Francisco: Jossey-Bass.

Gilligan, C. (1982). *In a different voice: Psychological theory and women's development.* Cambridge, MA: Harvard University Press.

Goldman, N. (1961). Socio-psychological study of school vandalism. *Crime and Delinquency, 7,* 221–230.

Goldstein, A. P. (1994). *The ecology of aggression.* New York: Plenum.

Goldstein, A. P. (1996). *The psychology of vandalism.* New York: Plenum.

Goodman, D. (1994). *Living at light speed.* New York: Random House.

Gozdz, K. (Ed.). (1995). *Community building: Renewing spirit and learning in business.* San Francisco: New Leaders Press.

Griffith, J. C. (1994). Open space preservation: An imperative for quality campus environments. *Journal of Higher Education, 65,* 645–669.

Guernsey, L. (1998, July 17). College-bound students use the web, but value printed information more. *The Chronicle of Higher Education,* p. A12.

Gunnings, B. B. (1982). Stress and minority student on a predominantly white campus. *Journal of Non-White Concerns in Personnel and Guidance, 11,* 11–16.

Hage, J. (1980). *Theories of organizations: Forms, process, and transformation.* New York: Wiley.

Hage, J., & Aiken, M. (1970). *Social change in complex organizations.* New York: Random House.

Hall, E. T. (1976). *Beyond culture.* New York: Doubleday.

Hall, E. T. (1996). *The hidden dimension.* New York: Anchor Books.

Hall, R. M., & Sandler, B. R. (1982). *The campus climate: A chilly one for women. Report of the project on the status and education of women.* Washington, DC: Association of American Colleges.

Hall, R. M., & Sandler, B. R. (1984). *Out of the classroom: A chilly campus climate for women. Report of the project on the status and education of women.* Washington, DC: Association of American Colleges.

Hancock, E. (1990). Zoos, tunes, and gweeps: A dictionary of campus slang. *Journal of Higher Education, 61,* 98–106.

Hand, C. (1994, September). Meet me in cyperspace. *CMC Magazine* [On line]. Available: http//: 209.100.136.26/cmc/mag/1994/sep/meetme.html.

Hansen, W. B., & Altman, I. (1976). Decorating personal places: A descriptive analysis. *Environment and Behavior, 8,* 491–505.

Harvey, O. J., Hunt, D. E., & Schroder, H. M. (1961). *Conceptual systems and personality organization.* New York: Wiley.

Hawkins, B. C. (1989). Students on predominantly white campuses: The need for a new commitment. *NASPA Journal, 26*(3), 175–179.

Heilweill, M. (1973). The influence of dormitory architecture on resident behavior. *Environment and Behavior, 5,* 337–412.

Hiss, T. (1990). *The experience of place.* New York: Knopf.

Holland, J. L. (1966). *The psychology of vocational choice: A theory of personality types and model environments.* Waltham, MA: Blaisdell.

Holland, J. L. (1973). *Making vocational choices: A theory of careers.* Englewood Cliffs, NJ: Prentice Hall.

Hopkins, R. D. (1994). The mythical ivory tower: Student perceptions of safety in residence halls. Unpublished master's thesis, Colorado State University, Fort Collins.

Horowitz, H. L. (1984). *Alma mater: Design and experience in women's colleges from their nineteenth century beginnings to the 1930s.* New York: Knopf.

Horowitz, H. L. (1987). *Campus life: Undergraduate cultures from the end of the eighteenth century to the present.* New York: Knopf.

Hostettler, J. A. (1993). *Amish society* (4th ed.). Baltimore, MD: The Johns Hopkins University Press.

Hudson, D. (1997). *Rewired: A brief (and opinionated) net history.* Indianapolis, IN: Macmillan Technical Publishing.

Huebner, L. A. (Ed.) (1979). *Redesigning campus environments*. New Directions for Student Services, No. 8. San Francisco: Jossey-Bass.

Huebner, L. A., & Corazzini, J. (1975–1976). Eco-mapping: A dynamic model for intentional campus design. Colorado State University: *Student Development Staff Papers*, Vol. VI, No. 2.

Huebner, L. A., & Lawson, J. M. (1990). Understanding and assessing college environments. In D. G. Creamer & Associates (Eds.), *College student development: Theory and practice for the 1990s* (pp. 127–151). Alexandria, VA: American College Personnel Association.

Hunt, M. (1984). Environmental learning without being there. *Environment and Behavior, 16*, 307–334.

Hunt, M. (1997, December). A different voice in the digital revolution. CMC *Magazine* [On-line]. Available: http://209.100.136.26/cmc/mag/1997/dec/hunt.html.

Jackson, G. S., & Schroeder, C. C. (1977). Behavioral zoning for stimulation seekers. *Journal of College and University Student Housing, 7*(1), 7–10.

Jackson, J. (1984). *Discovering the vernacular landscape*. New Haven, CT: Yale University Press.

Jeffrey, C. R. (1977). *Crime prevention through environmental design*. Newbury Park, CA: Sage.

Johnson-Lenz, P., & Johnson-Lenz, T. (1995). Groupware and the great turning. In K. Gozdz (Ed.), *Community building: Renewing spirit and learning in business* (pp. 243–257). San Francisco: New Leaders Press.

Jones, S. R. (1996). Toward inclusive theory: Disability as social construction. *NASPA Journal, 33*(4), 347–354.

Jung, C. G. (1971). *The collected works of C. G. Jung: vol. 6, Psychological types* Princeton, NJ: Princeton University Press. (Original work published 1923).

Kaiser, L. R. (1975). Designing campus environments. *NASPA Journal, 13*, 33–39.

Kanter, R. M. (1972). *Commitment and community: Communes and utopias in sociological perspective*. Cambridge, MA: Harvard University Press.

Kaplan, S., & Kaplan R. (Eds.). (1978). *Humanscape: Environments for people*. Scituate, MA: Duxbury.

Kelly, T. (1998, September). Peeling the cyber-onion. CMC *Magazine* [On-line]. Available: http://209.100.136.26/cmc/mag/draft/kelly.html.

Kiernan, V. (1998, May 29). Some scholars question research methods of expert on internet abuse. *Chronicle of Higher Education*, pp. A25–A27.

Kiesler, S. (1987). The hidden messages in computer networks. *Harvard Business Review*, 64(1), 46–60.

Kiesler, S., Siegel, J., & McGuire, T. (1991). Social psychological aspects of computer-mediated communication. In C. Dunlop & R. Kling (Eds.), *Computerization and controversy: Value conflicts and social change* (pp. 330–349). Boston: Academic Press.

Kilmartin, C. T. (1996). The white ribbon campaign: Men working to end men's violence against women. *Journal of College Student Development, 37*, 347–348.

King, P. M., & Kitchener, K. S. (1994). *Developing reflective judgement*. San Francisco: Jossey-Bass.

Kling, R. (1991). When organizations are perpetrators: Assumptions about computer abuse and computer crime. In C. Dunlop & R. Kling (Eds.), *Computerization and controversy: Value conflicts and social change* (pp. 676–692). Boston: Academic Press.

Kolb, D. (1983). *Experiential learning: Experience as the source of learning and development*. Englewood Cliffs, NJ: Prentice Hall.

Koss, M. P., Gidycz, C. A., & Wisniewski, N. (1987). The scope of rape: Incidence and prevalence of sexual aggression and victimization in a national survey of higher education students. *Journal of Consulting and Clinical Psychology, 55*(2), 162–170.

Krehbiel, L. E., & Strange, C. C. (1991). Checking of the truth: The case of Earlham College? In G. D. Kuh & J. H. Schuh (Eds.), *The role and contribution of student affairs in involving colleges* (pp. 148–167). Washington, DC: National Association of Student Personnel Administrators.

Kuh, G. D. (Ed.). (1993). *Cultural perspectives in student affairs work*. Washington, DC: American College Personnel Association.

Kuh, G. D. (1996). Organizational theory. In S. R. Komives, D. B. Woodard, & Associates (Eds.), *Student services: A handbook for the profession* (pp. 269–294). San Francisco: Jossey-Bass.

Kuh, G.D. (1999). *The college student report*. National Survey of Student Engagement, Center for Postsecondary Research and Planning. Bloomington: Indiana University.

Kuh, G.D. (2000). *The national survey of student engagement: Conceptual framework and overview of psychometric properties*. Bloomington, IN: Center for Postsecondary Research and Planning, Indiana University School of Education.

Kuh, G. D., & Hall, J. E. (1993). Using cultural perspectives in student affairs. In G. D. Kuh (Ed.), *Cultural perspectives in student affairs work* (pp. 1–20). Lanham, MD: American College Personnel Association.

Kuh, G. D., Schuh, J. H., Whitt, E. J., Andreas, R. E., Lyons, J. W., Strange, C. C., Krehbiel, L. E., & MacKay, K. A. (1991). *Involving colleges: Encouraging student learning and personal development through out-of-class experiences.* San Francisco: Jossey-Bass.

Kuh, G. D., & Whitt, E. J. (1988). *The invisible tapestry: Cultures in American colleges and universities.* ASHE-ERIC Higher Education Report Series, No. 1. Washington, DC: Association for the Study of Higher Education.

Ladd, J. (1991). Computers and moral responsibility: A framework for an ethical analysis. In C. Dunlop & R. Kling (Eds.), *Computerization and controversy: Value conflicts and social change* (pp. 664–675). Boston: Academic Press.

Langham, D. (1994, August). Preserving democracy in cyberspace: The need for a new literacy. CMC *Magazine* [On-line]. Available: http://209.100.136.26/cmc/mag/1994/aug/literacy.html.

Lanham, R. (1993). *The electronic word: Democracy, technology, and the arts.* Chicago: University of Chicago Press.

Levinson, D. J. (1978). *The seasons of a man's life.* New York: Ballantine.

Levinson, D. J., & Levinson, J. D. (1996). *The seasons of a woman's life.* New York: Knopf.

Lewin, K. (1936). *Principles of topological psychology.* New York: McGraw-Hill.

Livingood, J. (1995, April). Revenge of the introverts. CMC *Magazine* [On- line] Available: http://209.100.136.26/cmc/mag/1995/apr/livingood.html.

Love, P. G., & Guthrie, V. L. (Eds.). (1999). *Understanding and applying cognitive development theory.* New Directions for Student Services, no. 88. San Francisco: Jossey-Bass.

Lundberg, C. C. (1985). On the feasibility of cultural intervention in organizations. In P. J. Frost, L. F. Moore, M. R. Louis, C. C. Lundberg, & J. Martin (Eds.), *Organizational culture* (pp. 169–186). Thousand Oaks, CA: Sage.

Lynch, K. (1960). *The image of the city.* Cambridge, MA: Massachusetts Institute of Technology Press.

Lyons, J. (1993). The importance of institutional mission. In M. J. Barr (Ed.), *The handbook of student affairs administration* (p. 315). San Francisco: Jossey-Bass.

Mandell, J. I. (1981). The psychological sense of community and the small college campus: A community psychology perspective on the role of deans of students. Unpublished doctoral dissertation. University of Massachusetts, Amherst.

Martin, P. Y., & O'Connor, G. G. (1989). *The social environment: Open systems application.* New York: Longman.

Masland, A. T. (1985). Organizational culture in the study of higher education. *Review of Higher Education, 8*, 157–168.

Maslow, A. H. (1968). *Toward a psychology of being*. New York: Van Nostrand.

Maslow, A. H., & Mintz, N. (1956). Effects of those aesthetic surroundings: Initial effects of those aesthetic surroundings upon perceiving "energy" and "well-being" in faces. *Journal of Psychology, 41*, 247–254.

Matthews, A. (1997). *Bright college years: Inside the American campus today*. New York: Simon & Schuster.

McAdams, M. (1996, March). Gender without bodies. *CMC Magazine* [On-line] Available: http://209.100.136.26/cmc/mag/1996/mar/mcada3.html.

McMillan, D. W., & Chavis, D. M. (1986). Sense of community: A definition and theory. *Journal of Community Psychology, 14*, 6–23.

Mehrabian, A. (1981). *Silent messages* (2nd ed.). Belmont, CA: Wadsworth.

Mehrabian, A., & Wiener, M. (1967). Decoding of inconsistent communications. *Journal of Personality and Social Psychology, 6*, 109–114.

Michalski, J. (1995) The role of technology. In K. Gozdz (Ed.), *Community building: Renewing spirit and learning in business* (pp. 259–269). San Francisco: New Leaders Press.

Michelson, W. (1970). *Man and his urban environment: A sociological approach*. Reading, MA: Addison-Wesley.

Miller, M., & Banning, J. (1992). Campus design: Guidance from voices of the past. *The Campus Ecologist, 10*(2), 1–4.

Moffatt, M. (1989). *Coming of age in New Jersey: College and American culture*. New Brunswick, NJ: Rutgers University Press.

Moos, R. H. (1974). *Family environment scale-Form R*. Palo Alto, CA: Consulting Psychologists Press.

Moos, R. H. (1979). *Evaluating educational environments*. San Francisco: Jossey-Bass.

Moos, R. H. (1986). *The human context: Environmental determinants of behavior*. Malabar, FL: Krieger.

Moos, R. H. (1994a). *The social climate scales: A user's guide*. Palo Alto, CA: Consulting Psychologists Press.

Moos, R. H. (1994b). *The work environment scale manual*. Palo Alto, CA: Consulting Psychologists Press.

Moos, R. H., & Gerst, M. (1988). *The university residence environment scale manual* (2nd ed.). Palo Alto, CA: Consulting Psychologists Press.

Mugerauer, R. (1993). Toward an architectural vocabulary: The porch as a between. In D. Seamon (Ed.), *Dwelling, seeing, and designing: Toward a phenomenological ecology* (pp. 103–128). Albany, NY: State University of New York Press.

Murray, H. (1938). *Exploration in personality*. New York: Oxford University Press.

Myers, I. B. (1980). *Gifts differing*. Palo Alto, CA: Consulting Psychologists Press.

Myers, I. B., & McCaulley, M. H. (1985). *Manual: A guide to the development and use of the Myers-Briggs Type Indicator*. Palo Alto, CA: Consulting Psychologists Press.

Nadler, A., Bar Tal, D., & Drukman, O. (1982). Density does not help: Help-giving, help-seeking, and help-reciprocating of residents of high and low student dormitories. *Population and Environment, 5*(1), 26–42.

Nasar, J. L., & Fisher, B. (1992). Design for vulnerability: Uses and reactions to fear of crime. *Social and Social Research, 76*(2), 48–58.

National Institute of Education. (1984). *Involvement in learning*. Washington, DC: National Institute of Education.

Newbrough, J. R, & Chavis, D. M. (1986). Psychological sense of community. *Journal of Community Psychology, 14*, 3–4.

Newman, O. (1972). *Defensible space: Crime prevention through urban design*. New York: Collier Books.

Nock, A. J. (1943). *Memories of a superfluous man*. New York: HarperCollins

Oldenburg, R. (1989). *The great good place*. New York: Paragon House.

Pablant, P., & Baxter, J. C. (1975). Environmental correlates of school vandalism. *Journal of the American Institute of Planners, 41*, 270–279.

Pace, C. R. (1969). *College and university environment scales*. Princeton, NJ: Institutional Research Program for Higher Education, Educational Testing Service.

Pace, C. R. (1984). *Measuring the quality of college student experience*. Los Angeles, CA: Higher Education Research Institute, The University of California.

Pace, C. R. (1990). *The undergraduates: A report of their activities and progress in college in the 1980s*. Los Angeles, CA: Center for the Study of Evaluation, University of California.

Pace, C. R., & Baird, L. (1966). Attainment patterns in the environmental press of college subcultures. In T. M. Newcomb & E. K. Wilson (eds.), *College peer groups*. Chicago: Aldine.

Pace, C. R., & Kuh, G. D. (1998). *College student experience questionnaire* (4th ed.). Center for Postsecondary Research and Planning. Bloomington: Indiana University.

Pace, C. R., & Stern, G. G. (1958). An approach to the measurement of psychological characteristics of college environments. *Journal of Educational Psychology, 49*, 269–277.

Palmer, C. J. (1996). Violence and other forms of victimization in residence halls: Perspectives of resident assistants. *Journal of College Student Development, 37*(3), 268–277.

Palmer, P. J. (1977). *A place called community.* Wallingford, PA: Pendle Hill.

Palmer, P. J. (1987, September/October). Community, conflict, and ways of knowing. *Change, 19*(5), 20–25.

Palmer, P. J. (1998). *The courage to teach: Exploring the inner landscape of a teacher's life.* San Francisco: Jossey-Bass.

Palloff, R. M., & Pratt, K. (1999). *Building learning communities in cyberspace: Effective strategies for the on-line classroom.* San Francisco: Jossey-Bass.

Paludi, M. A., & Barickman, R. B. (1991). *Academic and workplace sexual harassment: A resource manual.* Albany, NY: State University of New York Press.

Parsons, T. (1960). *Structure and process in modern societies.* New York: The Free Press.

Pascarella, E. T. (1985). College environmental influences on learning and cognitive development: A critical review and synthesis. In J. C. Smart (Ed.), *Higher education: Vol. 1. Handbook of theory and research* (pp. 1–61). New York: Agathon Press.

Pascarella, E. T., & Terenzini, P. T. (1991). *How college affects students.* San Francisco: Jossey-Bass.

Paulsen, M. (1995). An overview of CMC and the online classroom in distance education. In Z. L. Berge & M. P. Collins (Eds.), *Computer-mediated communication and the online classroom: Vol. 1* (pp. 31–57). Cresskill, NJ: Hampton Press.

Peck, M. S. (1987). *The different drum.* New York: Simon & Schuster.

Perry, W. G. (1970). *Forms of intellectual and ethical development in the college years: A scheme.* Austin, TX: Holt, Rinehart and Winston.

Phelps, L. A. (1990). High-rise residence halls: A response to the uniqueness of these buildings. Unpublished master's thesis, Colorado State University, Fort Collins.

Phillips, G. H. (1982). *Rural vandalism.* Washington, DC: National Institute of Justice Vandalism Prevention Workshop.

Polin, L. (1993) Global village as virtual community. *Writing notebook: Visions for Learning, 11*(2), 14–16, 47.

Popcorn, F. (1991). *The Popcorn report.* New York: Doubleday.

Por, G. (1995). The quest for collective intelligence. In K. Gozdz (Ed.), *Community building: Renewing spirit and learning in business* (pp. 271–279). San Francisco: New Leaders Press.

Porteus, J. (1977). *Environment and behavior.* Reading, MA: Addison-Wesley.

Provost, J. A., & Anchors, S. (1987). *Applications of the Myers-Briggs type indicator in higher education*. Palo Alto, CA: Consulting Psychologists Press.

Pushkarev, B., & Zupan, J. (1975). *Urban space for pedestrians*. Cambridge, MA: The MIT Press.

Rapaport, A. (1982). *The meaning of the built environment*. Thousand Oaks, CA: Sage.

Rawlins, G. (1996). *Moths to the flame: The seductions of computer technology*. Cambridge, MA: The MIT Press.

Rendon, L. I. (1994). Validating culturally diverse students: Towards a new model of learning and student development. *Innovative Higher Education, 19*, 33-51.

Rheingold, H. (1993). *The virtual community: Homesteading on the electronic frontier*. Reading, MA: Addison-Wesley.

Rodgers, R. F. (1980). Theories underlying student development. In D. G. Creamer (Ed.), *Student development in higher education: Theories, practices and future*. (ACPA Media Publications, No. 27). Alexandria, VA: ACPA Media.

Rodgers, R. F. (1990a). An integration of campus ecology and student development: The Olentangy project. In D. G. Creamer & Associates (Eds.), *College student development: Theory and practice for the 1990s* (pp. 155–180). Alexandria, VA: American College Personnel Association.

Rodgers, R. F. (1990b). Recent theory and research underlying student development. In D. G. Creamer & Associates (Eds.), *College student development: Theory and practice for the 1990s* (pp. 27–29). Alexandria, VA: American College Personnel Association.

Rodgers, R. F. (1991). Using theory in practice in student affairs. In T. K. Miller, R. B. Winston, Jr., & Associates (Eds.), *Administration and leadership in student affairs: Actualizing student development in higher education* (pp. 203–251). Muncie, IN: Accelerated Development.

Rosenberg, M., & McCullough, B. C. (1981). Mattering: Inferred significance to parents and mental health among adolescents. In R. Simons (Ed.), *Research in community and mental health*. (Vol. 2, pp. 163–182). Greenwich, CT: JAI Press.

Rush, S. C., & Johnson, S. (1989). *The decaying American campus: A ticking time bomb*. Alexandria, VA: Joint Report of the Association of Physical Plant Administrators of Universities and Colleges and the National Association of College and University Business Officers.

Sandeen, A., & Rhatigan, J. J. (1990). New pressures for social responsiveness and accountability. In M. J. Barr & M. L. Upcraft (Eds.), *New futures for student affairs* (pp. 98–113). San Francisco: Jossey-Bass.

Sanford, N. (1966). *Self and society: Social change and individual development*. New York: Atherton Press.

Santoro, G. (1995). What is computer-mediated communication? In Z. L. Berge & M. P. Collins (Eds.), *Computer-mediated communication and the online classroom, Vol. 1*. (pp. 11–27). Cresskill, NJ: Hampton Press.

Saunders, D. R. (1969). A factor analytic study of the AI and CCI. *Multivariate Behavioral Research, 4*, 329–346.

Schein, E. H. (1985). *Organizational culture and leadership*. San Francisco: Jossey-Bass.

Schein, E. H. (1992). *Organizational culture and leadership* (2nd ed.). San Francisco: Jossey-Bass.

Schlossberg, N. K. (1989). Marginality and mattering: Key issues in building community. In D.C. Roberts (Ed.), *Designing Campus Activities to Foster a Sense of Community*, New Directions for Student Services, no. 48. (pp. 5–15). San Francisco: Jossey-Bass.

Schlossberg, N. K., Lynch, A., & Chickering, A. W. (1989). *Improving higher education environments for adults*. San Francisco: Jossey-Bass.

Schroeder, C. C. (1978–1979). Territoriality: Conceptual and methodological issues for residence educators. *Journal of College and University Student Housing, 8*, 9–15.

Schroeder, C. C. (1993). Creating residence life programs with student development goals. In R. B. Winston, Jr., S. Anchors, & Associates (Eds.), *Student housing and residential life* (pp. 517–534). San Francisco: Jossey-Bass.

Schroeder, C. C. (1994). Developing learning communities. In C. C. Schroeder, P. Mable, & Associates (Eds.). *Realizing the educational potential of residence halls* (pp. 165–189). San Francisco: Jossey-Bass.

Schuh, J. H. (1980). Housing. In W. H. Morrill, J. C. Hurst, & E. R. Oetting (Eds.), *Dimensions for intervention for student development* (pp. 189–205). New York: Wiley.

Schuh, J. H. (1991). Making a large university feel small: The Iowa State University story. In G. D. Kuh & J. H. Schuh (Eds.), *The role and contribution of student affairs in involving colleges* (pp. 30–41). Washington, DC: National Association of Student Personnel Administrators.

Schuh, J. H. (1993). Fiscal pressures on higher education and student affairs. In M. J. Barr (Ed.), *The handbook of student affairs administration* (pp. 49–68). San Francisco: Jossey-Bass.

Schuh, J. H., Andreas, R. E., & Strange, C. C. (1991). Students at metropolitan universities: Viewing involvement through different lenses. *Metropolitan University, 2*(3), 64–74.

Seeger, M. A. (1994). *Women's climate study: A report to the Grand Valley campus community*. Allendale, Michigan: Grand Valley State University, Academic Resources and Special Programs.

Selznick, P. (1992). *The moral commonwealth: Social theory and the promise of community*. Berkeley, CA: University of California Press.

Sherill, J. M., & Siegel, D. G. (Eds.) *Responding to violence on campus*. New Directions for Student Services, no. 47. San Francisco: Jossey-Bass.

Siegel, D. (1994). *Campuses respond to violent tragedy*. Phoenix: The American Council on Education and Oryx Press.

Smart, J. C., Feldman, K. A., & Ethington, C. A. (2000). *Academic disciplines: Holland's theory and the study of college students and faculty*. Nashville, TN: Vanderbilt University Press.

Smith, M. C. (1988). *Coping with crime on campus*. New York: American Council on Education and Macmillian.

Smith, M. C., & Fossey, R. (1995). *Crime on campus: Legal issues and campus administration*. Phoenix: The American Council on Education and the Oryx Press.

Smith, S. (1987). *Planning and implementing pedestrian facilities in suburban and developing rural areas*. National Cooperative Highway Research Program Report 294A and 294B. Washington, DC: Transportation Research Board.

Sommer, R. (1978). *Personal Space: The behavioral basis of design*. Englewood Cliffs: NJ: Prentice Hall.

Spitzberg, I. J., Jr., & Thorndike, V. V. (1992). *Creating community on college campuses*. Albany, NY: State University of New York Press.

Stern, G. G. (1970). *People in context: Measuring person-environment congruence in education and industry*. New York: Wiley.

Stern, R. A. (1986). *Pride of place: Building the American dream*. New York: Houghton Mifflin.

Strange, C. C. (1981). Organizational barriers to student development: Strategies for institutional change. *NASPA Journal, 19*, 12–20.

Strange, C. C. (1983a). Traditional perspectives on student affairs organizations. In G. D. Kuh (Ed.), *Understanding student affairs organizations*. New Directions for Student Services, no. 23. San Francisco: Jossey-Bass.

Strange, C. C. (1983b). Human development theory and administrative practice in student affairs: Ships passing in the daylight? *NASPA Journal, 21*, 2–8.

Strange, C. C. (1991). Managing college environments: Theory and practice. In T. K. Miller, R. B. Winston, Jr., & Associates. *Administration and leadership in student affairs: Actualizing student development in student affairs* (2nd ed.) (pp. 159–199). Muncie, ID: Accelerated Development.

Strange, C. C. (1993). Theories and concepts of campus living environments. In R. B. Winston, Jr., S. Anchors, & Associates (Eds.), *Student housing and residential life: A handbook for the professional committed to student development goals* (pp. 134–166). San Francisco: Jossey-Bass.

Strange, C. C. (1994). Student development: The evolution and status of an essential idea. *Journal of College Student Development, 35,* 399–412.

Strange, C. C. (1996). Dynamics of campus environments. In S. R. Komives, D. B. Woodard, & Associates, *Student services: A handbook for the profession* (3rd ed.) (pp. 244–268). San Francisco: Jossey-Bass.

Strange, C. C., & Hagan, H. (1998). Benedictine values and building campus community. *The Cresset: A review of literature, arts and public affairs, Special Lilly Issue,* 5–12.

Strange, C. C., & Hannah, D. (1994, March). The learning university: A model for the twenty-first century. Paper presented at the meeting of the American College Personnel Association, Indianapolis, IN.

Strange, C. C., & King, P. M. (1990). The professional practice of student development. In D. Creamer & Associates (Eds.), *College student development: Theory and practice for the 1990s* (pp. 9–24) Alexandria, VA: American College Personnel Association.

Strangelove, M. (1994, September). The internet, electric gaia, and the rise of the uncensored self. *CMC Magazine* [On-line]. Available: http//: 209.100.136.26/cmc/mag/1994/sep/self.html.

Sturner, W. F. (1973). The college environment. In D. W. Vermilye (Ed.), *The future in the making* (pp. 71–86). San Francisco: Jossey-Bass.

Sugerman, D., & Hotaling, G. (1989). Dating violence: Prevalence, context and risk markers. In M. Pirog-Good & J. Stets (Eds.), *Violence in dating relationships: Emerging social issues* (pp. 3–32). New York: Praeger.

Taming Campus Vandals. (1980). *American School and University, 53*(2), pp. 44–45, 48.

Territo, L. (1983). Campus rape: Determining liability. *Trial,19,* 100–103.

Thayer-Bacon, B. J., & Bacon, C. S. (1998). *Philosophy applied to education: Nurturing a democratic community in the classroom.* Upper Saddle River, NJ: Merrill.

Thelin, J. R., & Yankovich, J. (1987). Bricks and mortar: Architecture and the study of higher education. In J. C. Smart (Ed.), *Higher education: Handbook of theory and research,* Vol. 3 (pp. 57–83). New York: Agathon Press.

Tierney, W. G. (1993). *Building communities of difference: Higher education in the twenty-first century.* Westport, CT: Bergin & Garvey.

Tribe, C. (1982). *Profile of three theories: Erikson, Maslow, Piaget*. Dubuque, IA: Kendall/Hunt.

Trickett, E. J., & Moos, R. H. (1995). *Classroom environment scale manual*. Palo Alto, CA: Consulting Psychologists Press.

Turner, P. V. (1995). *Campus: An American planning tradition*. Cambridge, MA: The MIT Press.

Ulrich, R. (1983). Aesthetic and affective responses to natural environments. In I. Altman & J. Wohllwill (Eds.), *Human behavior and the natural environment: Volume 6, Behavior and environment* (pp. 85–125). New York: Plenum.

Untermann, R. (1984). *Accommodating the pedestrian*. New York: Van Nostrand Reinhold.

Upcraft, M. L., & Schuh, J. H. (1996). *Assessment in student affairs: A guide for practitioners*. San Francisco: Jossey-Bass.

Walsh, W. B. (1973). *Theories of person-environment interaction: Implications for the college student*. Iowa City, IA: American College Testing Program.

Walther, J. (1992). Interpersonal effects in computer-mediated interaction: A relational perspective. *Communication Research, 19*(1), 52–90.

Warren, R. L., & Lyon, L. (Eds.). (1983). *New perspectives on the American community*. Homewood, IL: The Dorsey Press.

Warshaw, R. (1988). *I never called it rape*. New York: HarperCollins.

Weber, M. (1947). *The theory of social and economic organization*. (A. M. Henderson & Talcott Parsons, Trans.). New York: The Free Press.

Weinmayer, V. M. (1969). Vandalism by design: A critique. *Landscape Architecture, 59*, 286.

Weinreich, F. (1997, February). Establishing a point of view toward virtual communities. *CMC Magazine* [On-line]. Available: http://209.100.136/cmc/mag/1997/feb/wein.html.

Wellman, B., Salaff, J., Dimitrova, D., Garton, L., Gulia, M., & Haythornthwaite, C. (1996). Computer networks as social networks: Collaborative work, telework, and virtual community. *Annual Review of Sociology, 22*, 213–238.

Wells, R. L. (1996). Leadership for community: A case study of individuals perceived as creators and maintainers of a psychological sense of community in a university. Unpublished doctoral dissertation. Temple University.

Wensyel, J. W. (1987). *Campus public safety and security*. Springfield, IL: Thomas.

Western Interstate Commission for Higher Education (1973). *The ecosystem model: Designing campus environments*. Boulder, CO: Western Interstate Commission for Higher Education.

Whitaker, L. C., & Pollard, J. W. (Eds.). (1993). *Campus violence: Kinds, causes, and cures.* New York: Haworth Press.

Whitt, E. J. (1993). Making the familiar strange: Discovering culture. In G. D. Kuh (Ed.), *Using cultural perspectives in student affairs* (pp. 81–94). Alexandria, VA: ACPA Media

Whyte, W. (1988). *City: Rediscovering the center.* New York: Doubleday.

Wicker, A. W. (1973). Undermanning theory and research: Implications for the study of psychological and behavioral effects of excess populations. *Representative Research in Social Psychology, 4,* 184–206.

Wicker, A. W. (1984). *An introduction to ecological psychology.* Cambridge University Press.

Widick, C., Knefelkamp, L., & Parker, C. (1975). The counselor as developmental instructor. *Counselor Education and Supervision, 14,* 286–296.

Wilcox, B. L., & Holahan, C. J. (1978). Residential satisfaction and friendship formation in high-rise and low-rise student housing: An interactional analysis. *Journal of Educational Psychology, 70,* 237–341.

Winston, R. B., Jr., Bledsoe, T. Goldstein, A. R., Wisbey, M. E., Street, J. L., Brown, S. R., Goyen, K. D., & Rounds, L. E. (1997). Describing the climate of student organizations: The student organization environment scales. *Journal of College Student Development, 38,* 417-427.

Winston, R. B., Jr., Vahala, M. E., Nichols, E. C., Gillis, M. E., Wintrow, M., & Rome, K. D. (1994). A measure of college classroom climate: The college classroom environment scales. *Journal of College Student Development, 35,* 11–18.

Wissler, C. (1929). *An introduction to social anthropology.* New York: Holt.

Zeisel, J. (1976). Stopping school property damage. *CEFP Journal, 15,* 6–11, 18–21.

Zeisel, J. (1981). *Inquiry by design.* Monterey, CA: Brooks/Cole.

Zimbardo, P. G. (1969). The human choice: Individuation, reason, and order versus deindividuation, impulse, and chaos. In W. J. Arnold & D. Devine (Eds.), *Nebraska Symposium on Education* (pp. 237–307). Lincoln, NE: University of Nebraska Press.

Zimmerman, D., & West, C. (1975). Sex roles, interruptions, and silences in conversations. In B. Thorne & N. Henley (Eds.), *Language and sex: Difference and domination* (pp. 105–130). Rowley, MA: Newbury House.

Name Index

Subject Index

Credits